PANMUNJOM

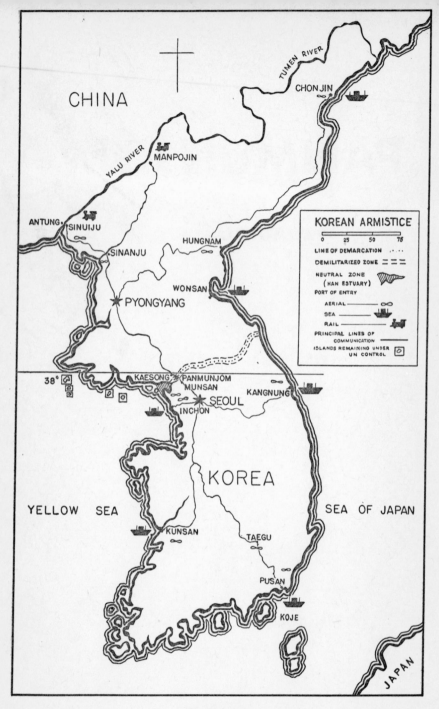

Map of Korea

Prepared by Robert Walker

PANMUNJOM

THE STORY OF THE KOREAN MILITARY ARMISTICE
NEGOTIATIONS

BY

WILLIAM H. VATCHER, JR.

FREDERICK A. PRAEGER, INC., Publishers
New York, N. Y.

BOOKS THAT MATTER

First published in the United States of America in 1958
by Frederick A. Praeger, Inc., 15 West 47 Street, New York 36

Library of Congress Catalog Card Number 58-7887
Printed in the United States of America

TO

Lieutenant General William K. Harrison, Jr., USA, whom I shall always remember as a competent soldier, an able scholar, and a devout Christian.

FOREWORD

Professor William H. Vatcher, Jr., served as Psychological Warfare Adviser to the Senior United Nations Delegate at the Korean armistice conference. Because of his access to official records and his first-hand knowledge of the negotiating methods employed by the Communists and by the delegation of the United Nations Command, he was in an excellent position to write an authoritative account of the Korean armistice conference.

I find Dr. Vatcher's story to be factual, accurate, and objective. It is a well written, well documented, and an extremely interesting chronological account of those trying days when we were negotiating for a cease-fire with our Red enemies. Professor Vatcher has done the free world a real service by writing this straightforward and illuminating account of the conference. I recommend it highly to all Americans who are interested in learning how difficult it is to deal with our ruthless Communist adversaries across the conference table.

CHARLES TURNER JOY
Admiral, United States Navy

PREFACE

Panmunjom has become the symbol of a strug-
gle; conceived in frustration, it was an enigma to many, but in
reality it was a wrestling for control of mankind by the forces
of Communism seeking to force revolutionary dogma on a world
which regards resistance as fundamental to civilized life. Panmunjom represented the battleground between two ideologies—
one dedicated to world revolution, the other to evolution; one
seeking to impose its ideals by force or subversion, the other attempting to protect its ideals. But Panmunjom represented, too,
the climax to the friction which had been growing for more years
than most people liked to recall—a struggle that began in earnest
in 1917 and was interrupted briefly during World War II by
the "ferocious genius" in the personality of Adolf Hitler and his
cohorts, only to return in even greater strength as soon as these
detractors were removed from the scene. Panmunjom, as the
culmination of the Korean conflict, can be considered as a turning point, perhaps *the* turning point, in this world conflict. For
this reason in particular, the Korean entanglement attracted
world attention such as none of the previous "skirmishes" had
done. And for this reason, too, the story of the Korean armistice
negotiations deserves a special place in our repertory of experiences.

Much has been written about Korea. Much of this literature
is about the Korean War in general. Less has been written about
the negotiations that brought that war to its ignominious conclusion. Admiral C. Turner Joy's book. *How Communists Negotiate,* is a provocative reminder of the complexities and lessons
of the negotiations for an armistice. The *Survey of International
Affairs* has presented very ably the Korean negotiations in relation to their world setting. Professor Leland Goodrich in his
writings, *Korea: A Study of United States Policy in the United
Nations* and *Korea: Collective Measures Against Aggression,* has
competently described Korea as a problem of the United Nations.
The United States Department of State and the United Nations
Department of Public Information have issued a number of excellent pamphlets on the negotiations—too many to list here.
The present book is designed to complement these writings. It
would be pointless to repeat what has been done. Shortly before
his untimely death, Admiral Joy wrote to the author: " I certainly
agree with you that the more books that are published on the
subject of the Korean Armistice the better will be the chances
of getting the American public to understand the dangerous nature of our Communist enemies and the difficulty of dealing with
them." The writer has approached the negotiations chronolog-
ically—not so much in the perspective of their world setting,
nor as a problem of the United Nations, nor purely as lessons
to be learned—but as an examination of what actually transpired
inside the truce tent and what lessons can be drawn from these
experiences.

In the preparation of this work the writer drew upon his
first-hand observations as a member of the negotiating team, his
access to the transcripts of the meetings and other documents,
and his conversations with other members of the negotiating
team.

It is to be hoped that the present volume, in conjunction with
other works on the negotiations, will help to complete the picture
of what transpired at the armistice meetings. It is to be hoped,
too, that this story will help to equip those persons who might
be dealing in the future with the Communists with the necessary
knowledge of what to expect from their adversaries, and to guide

them in formulating effective policy. Finally, it is to be hoped that this study will assist individuals toward a clearer understanding of the difficulties involved in dealing with Communists.

No one writes a book completely unassisted. The writer of this volume was no exception. The writer would like to express his appreciation to those who have aided in one way or another in the preparation of this story. For having read the manuscript and having offered valuable suggestions: Mr. Arthur Conrad, President of the Heritage Foundation; the late Admiral C. Turner Joy, United States Navy and Senior Delegate, Korean armistice negotiations; Mr. George Mardikian, author of *Song of America* and restaurateur; Mr. Stuart Ward, Secretary, Commonwealth Club of California; Professor Claude Buss, Department of History, Stanford University; Professor Graham Stuart, Department of Political Science, Stanford University; Mr. Robert Weir, attorney, and his wife, Professor Ruth Weir, Department of Romanic and Germanic Languages, Stanford University; and my mother and father. For having aided immeasurably in shaping the ideas for this book: Colonel Kenneth K. Hansen, United States Army, Chief, Psychological Warfare, Far East Command; Lieutenant General William K. Harrison, Jr., United States Army, Senior Delegate, Korean armistice negotiations; Colonel Donald Nugent, United States Marine Corps, Public Relations Officer, Far East Command; Admiral Arleigh Burke, United States Navy, Delegate, Korean armistice negotiations; Mr. David Lawrence, Editor, *United States News and World Report*; Major General Harlan C. Parks, United States Air Force, Senior Delegate, Korean Military Armistice Commission; Professor Harold H. Fisher, Chairman, Hoover Institute and Library, Stanford University, Lieutenant Kenneth Wu, United States Army, Chinese interpreter, Korean armistice negotiations; Lieutenant Horace Underwood, United States Navy, Korean interpreter, Korean armistice negotiations; and the staff of the Hoover Institute and Library, Stanford University, for their great patience and very loyal assistance.

WILLIAM H. VATCHER, JR.

Palo Alto, California
May, 1957

CONTENTS

LIST OF ILLUSTRATIONS

FIGURES

The United States does not claim to have the key to human wisdom or success. But we do claim the right to be judged on facts and not on fiction.

GENERAL GEORGE C. MARSHALL, USA

1

INTRODUCTION

"There's glory for you!" "I don't know what you mean by 'glory'" Alice said. Humpty-Dumpty smiled contemptuously. "Of course you don't— till I tell you. I meant, 'there's a nice knock-down argument for you!'" "But 'glory' doesn't mean 'a nice knock-down argument,'" Alice objected. "When I use a word," Humpty-Dumpty said in a rather scornful tone, "it means just what I choose it to mean—neither more nor less." "The question is," said Alice, "whether you can make words mean so many different things." "The question is," said Humpty-Dumpty, "which is to be Master—that's all."
LEWIS CARROLL, Through the Looking-Glass

At 1000 hours 27 July 1953, after two years and seventeen days, 575 regular meetings, 18,000,000 words, the Korean Armistice Agreement was signed at Panmunjom. Twelve hours later the guns were silenced along the front lines and the troops began to fall back behind the four-kilometer-wide buffer zone. Thus ended the longest truce talks in world history.

The Korean armistice represented a *modus vivendi*, a temporary solution to a long series of conflicts that had been brewing

1

for many years in Korea. It represented, too, a stalemate in one
area of the global conflict between two antagonistic ideologies.
But for Korea, the truce added little that was new to a history
filled with wars of aggression and of attempts to fulfill the desire
for national independence.

An ancient Korean proverb professes that when whales fight,
small fish are eaten. Unhappily for her, Korea has always been a
weak power sandwiched between great powers. Nature abhors a
vacuum, and Korea has been no exception to domination by
stronger, usually contiguous, powers—a pawn in international
politics. The history of Korea reflects a series of attempts to assert
or maintain independence. Historically, Korea has been the pawn
of China and Japan. Japan feared foreign control of Korea, and
has from time to time sought to control this dagger pointed at its
heart. China, the Middle Kingdom, traditionally considered herself the mistress of the world—for there could be but one Son of
Heaven. Thus Korea, like all the states with whom China had
dealings, was considered nothing more than a tributary.

But Korea has been more than that. It has served as the
highway for the interchange of culture between China and Japan.
And it has acted as a highway over which passed armies of conquest. In the thirteenth century Kublai Khan used Korea as a
means of getting his troops to the closest point in his attempted
conquest of Japan. In the sixteenth century Toyotomi Hideyoshi
tried to humble Korea as a prelude to the conquest of China.
With the coming of the Europeans to the Far East in the sixteenth century, the Korean pawn faced new contenders.

Russia bore down upon Korea by land from the north. The
Spanish, Portuguese, British, French, Dutch, Italians, Americans,
and later Germans pressed upon Korea by sea. By the time that
Chinese territory had been divided up into spheres of influence
among the Japanese, Russians, Germans, British, and French at
the end of the nineteenth century, the serious contenders had
been reduced to a few powers. In 1894–95 Japan fought a war
with China over Korea and eliminated this contender. Russia
alone remained to challenge Japan's ambitions, and Japan took
care of her in the Russo-Japanese War of 1904–05. In 1910,
after a polite delay, Japan annexed Korea. From 1910 until

Japan's collapse in 1945, Korea was administered by Japan for Japan. No one challenged Japan's position until she became an active belligerent with Germany and Italy in World War II.

During the forty years of Japanese occupation the force of Western thinking, especially the idea of self-determination, gradually seeped into Korea, and strong-willed individuals like Syngman Rhee, a student of Woodrow Wilson, dedicated themselves to working for independence. Korea nationalists never hesitated to use force to emphasize their demands. In 1919 they staged a riot in Seoul which coincided with the Paris Peace Conference, then responsible for remaking the map of the world. In 1909 Prince Hirobumi Ito was assassinated by a Korean nationalist. In 1932, at Shanghai, Korean nationalists took the life of the Japanese Army commander, General Yoshinori Shirakawa, the eye of the Third Fleet commander, Admiral Kichisaburo Nomura, later ambassador to the United States, and the leg of the Japanese Minister, Plenipotentiary to China Mamoru Shigemitsu, who later as Japanese Foreign Minister signed the surrender of Japan on the battleship *Missouri*.

After Japan launched its attack against the United States, a fight to the finish was inevitable, and Korean nationalists in America moved about anxiously to ensure the liberation of their country. The Communists were not asleep. Russia had looked upon Korea with acquisitive eyes for well over half a century. Communist Russia was no different from Czarist Russia in her desire to gain Korea and warm-water ports. However, in addition to her desire for control, Communist Russia seeks a political and philosophical revolution of those she conquers. Thus the Communist dogma was superimposed upon the historic extension of territory. For communism and for Russia, the acquisition of Korea would be a step toward winning Japan, the most advanced industrial power in the Far East. Russia had her puppet leaders prepared for the time when Japan would surrender, and she intended to use them.

The submission of the Axis Powers terminated the *raison d'être* of the strange alliance between the Communists and the Western Allies, and at the same time eliminated the buffers that had existed between Russia and the West. Reason would have prophecied a direct struggle now between the Communists, long-time and self-appointed enemies of the Western systems, and the West. Friction was unavoidable. The immediate causes of friction lay along the borders of the East and West blocs, while indirect ones were the subversive efforts of the Communists throughout the world to overthrow from within. Korea, like Germany, Indo-China, and other points of contact, became a battleground for the contending ideologies. Thus the traditional place of Korea as a pawn in power politics remained unchanged. And, as Leland M. Goodrich has observed in his book, *Korea: Collective Measures Against Aggression,* "As world relations between the United States [representing the Western bloc] and the Soviet Union [representing the Eastern bloc] deteriorated, each government became more insistent on a solution of the Korean problem which would prevent the other from bringing the whole territory within its sphere of dominant influence."

Between the ending of the war against the Japanese empire in 1945 and the commencement of open warfare in June 1950, there was a general jockeying for control in Korea. The Russians were prepared at the outset to implement their objectives. The United States, still drunk with the World War II alliance with Communist Russia, believed it possible to carry out the agreements concerning Korea. But as time passed the United States came to recognize the realities of the moment—unhappily—too late. The history of these five years is one of difficulties wrought with enigmas and fraught with dangers. The first official action concerning Korea came at Cairo in 1943. There Roosevelt, Churchill, and Chiang Kai-shek issued a declaration that marked the cornerstone of Korea's future. The three powers proclaimed that "in due course Korea shall become free and independent." In 1944 a provisional government for Korea was set up at Chungking, to be ready for the time when Japan would surrender. At Yalta in 1945 it was decided that Russia would enter the war against Japan after the defeat of Germany, and that Russia would take the surrender of the Japanese in the northern part of Korea while the United States took the surrender in the south. Later, at Potsdam, it was agreed that the 38th Parallel would be the dividing line for the demilitarization of the Japanese.

To the United States this was interpreted as meaning that this
would be a military, not a political, divide. Russia had other
plans. The first order to General Douglas MacArthur as the Supreme Commander for the Allied Powers (SCAP) directed the
implementation of the agreement. As soon as Japan succumbed,
the United States rushed the battle-seasoned troops of Okinawa
fame to Korea to receive the Japanese surrenders and to administer the country under General Douglas MacArthur. Lieutenant General John R. Hodge, USA, acted for MacArthur.
Except for an early implementation of the Cairo Agreement,
which Russia accepted at Potsdam, the United States had done
little in the way of planning for the future of Korea. The Russians,
who had declared war on Japan one week before her surrender,
poured into Manchuria and North Korea well prepared to carry
out their intentions. Newly released Korean Communists who
had spent years of incarceration under the Japanese as political
prisoners, underground Communists who now came to light, and
the Soviet-trained Koreans who entered with the Russian troops
set up People's Committees throughout Korea. These Committees
were utilized by the Russians as the organs of control. The United
States, south of the 38th Parallel, refused to recognize such
bodies. Instead, the United States temporarily continued to use
the existing Japanese administrators. This did little to endear
her to ardent Korean nationalists. The Russians sealed off their
zone with guns and tanks and refused to permit entrance to
American authorities responsible for the occupation, while
Russians were permitted to move about freely in the south.
Such a situation as this had not been anticipated by the United
States, and it took steps to settle the imbroglio at the Moscow
Conference of Foreign Ministers in December 1945. At that
meeting, it was agreed that a Joint Commission would be established, represented by the United States and the USSR, to assist
in setting up a Provisional Government for Korea and to coordinate economic and administrative affairs in both the northern
and southern zones. In establishing a Provisional Government,
the Commission was directed to consult with democratic parties
and social organizations. All decisions of the Joint Commission
were to be approved by the United States, Russia, the United

Kingdom, and Nationalist China. It was also agreed that the Provisional Government would be administered as a trusteeship of the four powers for a period of five years. The trusteeship arrangement did not prove to be popular. The ardent nationalists in the southern zone were free to criticize the arrangement, which they did bitterly. The Koreans in the north were forced to be obedient to the People's Committees and were not permitted to show resentment.

A further point of bitterness related to the land policy of the United States. At the end of the war the Japanese owned three-fourths of the arable land of Korea worked by tenant farmers and laborers. The Communist propagandists to the north boasted that they had stripped the Japanese of their holdings and had turned them over to the people, thus aggravating the situation further. However, the steady stream of refugees that poured into the southern zone, amounting to several million by 1950, tended to counteract the validity of Communist propaganda.

Representatives of the People's Committees met at Pyong-yang in February of 1946 to establish a Democratic People's Republic for all of Korea. This government was headed by Russian-trained and Russian-controlled Kim Il Sung, whose name was assumed from that of the well-known Korean patriot who had terrorized the Japanese by his guerrilla tactics. The Russians ran their zone as a police state through their puppets. They lived off the land. They drafted Koreans into the army they organized. After the Russians had set up their government in the north they were willing to negotiate with the United States. Sensitive to public opinion, the Communists had to create the impression that they were always willing to cooperate, that it was the United States that was uncooperative.

The Joint Commission was doomed to failure from the start. It met for the first time in March 1946. The meetings broke up in May. Dissension arose over the Moscow statement calling for consultation with democratic parties and social organizations. The USSR refused to consult with those groups in the south that had demonstrated against the trusteeship. The United States favored talking with everyone. Communist organizations in the south had been instructed not to demonstrate. Certainly the

Russians would not tolerate opposition in their zone. Thus the only groups that the Russians considered eligible for consultation were those that had not demonstrated. These were all Communists. The Russians refused to even discuss administrative and economic cooperation of the two zones, and continued always to demand that the Provisional Government be made up of democratic parties and social organizations that had not demonstrated their opposition to the Moscow Conference decisions—i.e., Communist. In October 1946, and again in April 1947, there was an exchange of notes. Secretary of State George Marshall pressed for a resumption of the meetings at Seoul during his meeting with Soviet Foreign Minister Molotov in Moscow in March 1947. General Hodge quite logically wanted some clarification of the words "democratic elements" and "social organizations," the different interpretations of which had led to protracted negotiations and an impasse.

The Joint Commission resumed meetings in May 1947 and as usual accomplished nothing. The meetings were recessed on 12 August. The Russians had offered to accept a Provisional Assembly made up of an equal number of members from the northern zone, with only one-third of the country's population, and the southern zone, with two-thirds. They remained adamant in their refusal to permit participation of any opposition groups in the Provisional Government.

Meanwhile the United States had turned the responsibilities of government over to the Koreans in its zone in November 1946. Americans remained as advisors. In December a Provisional Legislative Assembly met at Seoul to prepare for an independent South Korean government. After the failure of the meetings of the Joint Commission in 1947, it became clear to the United States that the establishment of an independent government composed of representative groups was impossible. In desperation it handed the whole matter over to the General Assembly of the United Nations in November 1947. The General Assembly set up a Temporary Commission on Korea. This Commission (UNTCOK) went to Korea to supervise the establishment of an Assembly, which was to draw up a constitution.

Russia refused to have anything to do with the Commission

and especially to permit its members to enter the northern zone. The Assembly met without representation from the north and drew up a constitution. This was adopted in July 1948, and the following month elections for the National Assembly were held. Even though the North Koreans refused to participate in the elections, seats were reserved for them in the event they should later change their minds. Syngman Rhee, who had been flown to Korea shortly after Japan had surrendered, was chosen by the National Assembly to be the first President of the Republic of Korea (ROK). The United States transferred authority to this new government, and on 1 January 1949 accorded it full recognition. In December the United Nations established a new Commission on Korea (UNCOK) to explore further avenues for unification, recognized the ROK government as the only lawful government of Korea, and recommended that foreign troops be withdrawn as soon as possible.

The Russians responded to the establishment of the Republic of Korea by holding elections in their area for a Supreme People's Assembly. This Assembly drew up a constitution, amazingly similar to that of the USSR. The government that was set up, the Democratic People's Republic, proclaimed authority over all of Korea. Kim Il Sung was named the prime minister. Russia and all of her satellites recognized this government as the only legitimate government of Korea. Russia signed pacts of economic aid and cultural exchange with the new government, but not a pact of mutual aid and friendship, as she had with China after the Communists had gained full control over all China with the exception of the island of Formosa.

Thus with the establishment of two diametrically opposed governments each asserting authority over all of Korea, the noose was tightened around the neck of Korean unification.

Early in 1949 the Russians, assured of continued control, announced they had withdrawn their troops from North Korea and by 29 June of the same year the United States had withdrawn all its forces with the exception of a small military advisory group to assist the training of the ROK army. In contrast to full Russian assistance to the government in North Korea, the United States supplied only a small amount of equipment to the

ROK—not enough for an offensive action against North Korea, which the South Koreans had threatened to launch.

During the five years, 1945–1950, Russia had tightened the Iron Curtain along the 38th Parallel, which had been selected purely as a military expedient to disarm the Japanese, and she had subjected the Koreans to a well-prepared program of propaganda. The Russians taught that the United States had prevented the unification of Korea because she wanted to maintain military bases in the south. The Russians had organized a dependable government with an army of several hundred thousand men, well-trained and highly indoctrinated, who believed that when they marched they would be marching to unify their country. The Russians had never intended that a settlement should be made. They knew that a representative government would not be representative of them. They had a hold on North Korea and were interested only in extending that control.

This was the situation in Korea in June 1950, when the Communists opened full-scale operations against the Republic of Korea. Why did the Communists decide to launch their attack against the Republic of Korea? To understand the reasoning behind such a course of action, one must first of all recognize Communist motives. Communism envisages the eventual submission of all peoples through force of violence or subversion, to its own ideology. The realization of such an objective demands singleness of purpose, complete determination to succeed, vigorous pursuit, and absolute dedication to the cause. This is achieved best through a small, violently resolute, monolithic structure that obeys without hesitation and question the decisions of the party. The objective of world communism is dynamic. It is energized by the force of its forward motion. Once it stops, it faces stagnation and decay. To progress toward its goal, communism pushes every advantage. It seeks out and exploits existing or latent vulnerabilities, no matter how trivial. It feeds on doubt, fear, insecurity, poverty, prejudice, despair, pride, ambition. It masks its intentions in seductive phraseology. It moves about calculatingly and stealthily, striking quick, cobra-like blows, but it is careful never to jeopardize the gains that it has made.

The Communists marked Korea as an area ripe for exploitation with little risk. Without doubt the Communists interpreted official United States statements concerning the Far East as having written off Korea. Certainly the attitude of the high brass in Tokyo was no secret. They considered Korea a strategic liability unworthy of defense.

Furthermore, the Republic of Korea had only a small army equipped by the United States with only light weapons. In contrast, the North Korean army was well equipped, well manned, well trained, well indoctrinated. Some of its leaders had served in the Russian army; others had fought with the Chinese Communist guerrillas against the Japanese.

The Communists believed that Korea was the best calculated risk at the moment. The risk would be reduced by the fact that Russia herself, America's greatest adversary, would not be involved directly. Russia would create the illusion that she was the great defender against "American imperialism," that she was a "peace-loving state" untainted by any "wars of aggression," that she was a "refuge of peace" in a world of "warmongers." If she could convey such an attitude, even though no material gains were made, communism would gain by that much. Russia would thus hide behind the shield of innocence, while her underlings would take the risks. Out of sight, she would manipulate the strings of her puppet forces. She would supply the necessary war equipment: planes, tanks, guns, ammunition. She would direct the operations through "advisors." [1] And the Communists certainly reasoned that even if the United States should decide to intervene, she would be restricted by commitments in Europe. And if the United States threatened their Korean marionettes with defeat, they could induce their Communist cohorts in China to introduce "volunteers," which, while keeping China's hands officially clean of aggression, would prevent a complete debacle. Certainly they reasoned correctly that the Sino-Russian Treaty of Friendship and Mutual Assistance of 1950 would deter American action against China proper. In this the Communists exploited Western respect for treaties. Trea-

[1] During the fighting in Korea, Russia had more than ten thousand of such "advisors" on hand to oversee operations.

ties in themselves mean little to Communists, who apply the principle of employing any means to achieve their ends. But they knew all too well the Western acceptance of the rule of law, and they knew the West would expect the Communists to uphold the 1950 treaty. This treaty would act as the Damoclean sword to discourage reprisals against China.

In December 1949 and January 1950, Mao Tse-tung was in Moscow conferring with Stalin on what was reputedly his first visit outside China. Apparently, the decision to attack the Republic of Korea was made at that time. And it was during that visit that the Sino-Russian Treaty was signed. The size of the planned operation against the Republic of Korea was such that it required at least six months of careful preparation. The army, the guns, the people—all were carefully prepared for the "peaceful unification" of Korea. As someone has quipped: "Communists don't conquer. They liberate!" By 25 June 1950 all was in readines. Clausewitz once remarked that war is a continuation of politics by other means. The Communists had not accomplished their objective of uniting all of Korea under their control. The situation appeared practical for employing a different tactic, and as Clausewitz also observed, "War therefore is an act of violence intended to compel our opponent to fulfill our will." Thus at daybreak 25 June 1950 (Korean time) North Korean tank columns and infantry crossed the 38th Parallel in force, intent upon compelling the Republic of Korea to fulfill their will. They captured Kaesong, three miles below the border, and within two days were at the gates of Seoul. The United Nations Commission on Korea was on hand to proclaim the action "aggression" in execution of a carefully prepared plan. The following day the United States requested an emergency session of the UN Security Council. The absence of the USSR from the Security Council, in protest against the UN's refusal to admit Red China, permitted that body to act quickly in declaring the attack "a breach of the peace," calling for an immediate cessation of hostilities and the withdrawal of North Korean forces to the 38th Parallel, asking the UN Commission on Korea to observe the withdrawal and keep the Security Council informed, and asking UN members to "render every assistance to the United Nations in the execution of this resolution and refrain from giving assistance to the North Korean authorities." In accordance with this resolution, President Truman authorized the United States Far East commander, General Douglas MacArthur, to furnish the Republic of Korea with military supplies and to employ air and sea forces "to give the Korean Government troops cover and support." He also ordered the Seventh Fleet to prevent belligerent actions between Formosa and the Chinese mainland. A cable from UNCOK revealed how real the crisis was: "Danger is that critical operations now in progress may end in matter of days and question of cease-fire and withdrawal of North Korean forces suggested Council resolution may prove academic."

On 27 June (New York time) the Security Council adopted another resolution requesting member states to assist the ROK. Fifty-three states approved the United States sponsored resolution and thus gave their moral support. Sixteen states eventually offered armed forces.[2] Others gave supplies and services. Another resolution of 7 July, sponsored jointly by France and the United Kingdom, provided for the establishment of a unified command under the flag of the United Nations. The United States was asked to designate a commander and to make periodic reports on the course of action taken by the command. General MacArthur was named as the Supreme United Nations Commander. United Nations Command (UNC) became the official title of the force.

The Russian attitude over the UN's actions was expressed in a reply to a United States note to Russia asking that she use her influence to stop the invasion. The Russians insisted that the United Nations action in Korea was illegal. They based their contention on the fact that the Russian representative had been absent during the Security Council debates, that the Chinese member on the Security Council represented the wrong power, and that the Korean situation was an internal affair and therefore outside the competence of the United Nations.

It was clear that the Communists were in no mood to exchange initial successes for the ignominy of a withdrawal. Suc-

[2] States contributing armed forces were Australia, Belgium, Canada, Colombia, Ethiopia, France, Greece, Luxembourg, Netherlands, New Zealand, Philippines, Thailand, Turkey, Union of South Africa, United Kingdom, and the United States.

cess is its own best argument. It was not until both sides realized that continued efforts were achieving little that it was agreed to negotiate a settlement. But that time came only after the belligerents had chased each other back and forth across the Korean peninsula in football-like fashion four times, with a heavy toll in supplies and, more precious, millions of lives.

At first the UN forces were frustrated by their weakness. The Republic of Korea army was routed, and the United Nations Command was forced into a tiny pocket around Pusan in the south before it was able to stave off further advances. Had China entered the war at that time, the UN forces could not have held. But determination, increased supplies, and further troops, along with a rejuvenated ROK army, stemmed the tide.

A brilliant end-run landing at Inchon on 15 September caught the Communists by surprise. The UNC now had the initiative, and it moved north toward the 38th Parallel. Should the UNC cross the line? A General Assembly resolution of 7 October implied the answer. The resolution reaffirmed its objectives of unifying the country and holding elections in Korea in order to set up a "unified, independent, and democratic government." The resolution pledged that the "United Nations forces should not remain in any part of Korea otherwise than so far as necessary for achieving the objectives specified."

The UNC crossed the 38th Parallel and drove north to capture the North Korean capital of Pyongyang and reach the Yalu River by 26 October. The North Korean army was decimated, but a new threat now loomed at the horizon. The Chinese Communists had already stated that they would intervene if foreign troops came near their borders. MacArthur maintained a different view. During his meeting with President Truman at Wake Island in October, he expressed doubts that either the Chinese or the Russians would enter the fracas. Later, during a visit to Korea, and even after the Chinese secretly penetrated deep into Korean territory, General MacArthur consoled his troops with the belief that the war would be over by Thanksgiving and that they could expect to be home by Christmas. On 24 November MacArthur launched his ill-fated offensive, an "end-the-war-by-Christmas" drive. Two days later the Chinese Communists launched their

attack with thirty divisions of "volunteers" and compelled the
UNC to retreat to a position well below the 38th Parallel. The
withdrawal was orderly but bitter. Few who were on that retreat,
who suffered the siege of the Chosin Reservoir, will forget the
cold anxiety of that long, hard road to the sea and the evacuation
—only to be thrown back into the front lines again in the south,
to help stem the onward tide of the Chinese hordes. General Mac-
Arthur used the Chinese invasion to drive home his thesis that
the enemy must be hit where it hurts the most, that an army
cannot fight with its hands tied behind its back. He insisted upon
intensifying the economic blockade against Red China, imposing
a naval blockade, initiating air reconnaissance of Chinese
coastal areas and Manchuria, and removing the restrictions on
Formosa.

The death of Lieutenant General Walton Walker in a jeep
accident on 23 December led to the establishment of a single
command for Korea under Lieutenant General Matthew B. Ridgway, USA, of World War II paratrooper fame. The division of the
UNC into two separate commands had robbed the defenders of
complete coordination. It is probable that had there previously
been one command, the Chinese invasion would have been discovered earlier. General Ridgway's tactics paid off, and the
Chinese advance was halted. The Chinese paid a terrible price
for their efforts. Hopes again mounted that the war might be
ended. MacArthur, however, was quick to stress the advantage
the Communists possessed through their "inviolate sanctuary"
in Manchuria.

At the United Nations in New York City, a representative
of the People's Republic of China was invited to appear before
the Security Council. Mr. Wu Hsin-chuan attacked the United
States as having bombed Chinese territory ninety times and
as having endangered China's security by advancing to the Man-
churian border. He argued that Formosa was not a question
within the competence of the United Nations, since it had been
recognized as an integral part of China at Cairo and Teheran;
that the United States must withdraw from Formosa and, along
with other states, from North and South Korea as well, in order

to permit the Koreans to settle their own problems. Needless to say his complaints were not accepted by the United Nations.

The United Nations continued to explore avenues for a solution to the Korean problem. In December a group of Middle Eastern and Asiatic nations explored the possibilities of a cease-fire. The Communists approved, on their own conditions: removal of all "foreign forces" from Korea, United States withdrawal of protection to Formosa, admittance of Red China to the UN. On 14 December the General Assembly, undisturbed by Communist reactions, set up a three-man Cease-fire Group to explore a satisfactory cease-fire in Korea. By January the committee reported its complete inability to inveigle the Communists into even discussing the matter. Another cease-fire effort was tried 13 January; again rejected. Meanwhile the United States was pushing for a resolution branding the Chinese Communists as aggressors. On 1 February the General Assembly approved a modified version of such a resolution: "By giving aid and assistance to those who were already committing aggression in Korea, and by engaging in hostilities with the United Nations forces there, [the People's Republic of China] has itself engaged in aggression." The resolution also set up a three-man "good offices" committee (Committee on Additional Measures) to work for a peaceful solution to the Korean War. Sanctions against China were not approved but the resolution did constitute a victory for the United States; for Communist China, like North Korea, was now labeled an aggressor.

By February the question was again being raised as to the desirability of recrossing the 38th Parallel. Mr. Truman declared that the 7 October resolution of the UN General Assembly still held good, and that it was up to the Supreme UN Commander to decide whether the 38th Parallel should again be crossed. Yet the feeling was beginning to permeate official Washington that a truce line at the 38th Parallel might be practical. Such a consideration was repugnant in the extreme to MacArthur and Syngman Rhee. MacArthur wanted to completely disable the aggressors. His views were expressed in a telegram to the president of the United Press in March 1951. He stated that conditions in Korea did not favor a truce at any particular line across the peninsula. A force large enough to hold the 38th Parallel would be large enough to drive the enemy out of Korea.

The UNC continued to push the Chinese, now comprising about 95 per cent of the enemy forces, back up the peninsula. On 14 March Seoul was retaken for the last time, and the UNC was approaching the 38th Parallel. On 24 March MacArthur, learning in advance that Washington was about to make serious overtures for a settlement, jumped the gun by declaring in a press interview: "I am ready at any time to confer in the field with the commander-in-chief of the enemy forces in an earnest effort to settle the war without further bloodshed." He concluded with words interpreted by the Communists as a veiled threat: "The enemy must by now be painfully aware that a decision of the United Nations to depart from its tolerant effort to contain the war in the area of Korea, through an expansion of our military operations to his coastal areas and interior bases, would doom China to the risk of imminent military collapse." The Communists were defiant in their declination, and Washington sizzled at MacArthur's seemingly insubordinate attitude.

By April the tides of battle were beginning to stabilize. The UNC was gradually forcing the aggressor back up the peninsula, and it appeared that, barring full-scale Russian intervention, the balance of forces now favored the UNC to a slight degree. However, being unable to strike the enemy in his inner sanctum of Manchuria made a conclusive settlement—i.e., the unification of Korea—an impossibility. The United States could not convince its allies in Europe of the primary importance of a "calculated risk" in the Far East—of embroiling them in an all-out war. General Omar Bradley later declared that such action "would involve us in the wrong war, at the wrong place, at the wrong time, and with the wrong enemy." The UNC therefore was forced to localize the war. The Supreme UNC Commander, attempting to carry out the assignment that had been given to him, found his mission increasingly ambiguous and increasingly difficult to accomplish. In MacArthur's judgment there was no substitute for victory and the restrictions of Korea did not lend themselves to such prospects. He was convinced that, in sound military logic, victory demanded hitting the enemy where he was most vulnerable and where it would do the most good—not in Korea, but in China and Manchuria. He also believed in employing the optimum strength available—likewise sound military logic. In this regard he made no secret of his desire to bring the forces of Chiang Kai-shek on Formosa into the fray. Frustrated by his inability to convince his superiors in Washington of the feasibility of his views, he sought out friends in Washington.

MacArthur's views were expressed in a reply to a letter from House Republican leader Joseph Martin, in which the latter had suggested the use of Nationalist Chinese troops. General MacArthur believed that the suggestion followed the traditional American pattern of "meeting force with the maximum counterforces as we have never failed to do in the past." He felt that the Communists had chosen Asia as their battleground for their intended conquest of the world. If Asia were lost to the Communists, the fall of Europe would be only a matter of time. "Here we fight Europe's battle with arms while the diplomats there still fight it with words."

The opinions of the General were not in harmony with those of the President, the Secretary of Defense, nor the Joint Chiefs of Staff. No one, of course, questioned his right to an opinion. Criticism arose over the fact that he was exciting political opposition to the policy of those to whom he was responsible. MacArthur's letter to Representative Martin climaxed the friction that had been brewing for many months and resulted in an unhappy ending to the otherwise brilliant career of one of history's outstanding military figures. On 11 April 1951 General of the Army Douglas MacArthur was relieved of his duties and replaced by General Matthew B. Ridgway. This action provoked a bitter debate in the United States between the supporters of MacArthur and those of the President, and led in June to a series of Congressional investigations, which had the effect of exposing America's "dirty laundry" to the world.

The excitement caused by MacArthur's removal did not stop the fighting in Korea. The war raged on. On 17 May Senator

Edwin C. Johnston introduced a resolution asking the United
Nations to urge the belligerents in Korea to declare an armistice
by 25 June, the first anniversary of the war, along the 38th Pa-
allel; to agree to the exchange of all war prisoners; and to
withdraw all foreign troops by the end of the year. The sense
of the resolution was not out of line with the Communist demands, and they quickly snatched it up, while the United States
Senate just as quickly tabled it. The resolution was given wide
publicity throughout Russia, which action was interpreted as a
desire on the part of the Communists to bring the combatants to
the conference table. The sleeping giant, peace, was beginning to
stir, and rumors of peace were everywhere—all denied in official
quarters.

On 26 May Mr. Lester Pearson, President of the UN General Assembly, declared that the complete surrender of the aggressors might not be necessary, that it would be sufficient to
achieve the objective of stopping the aggression. On 1 June the
UN Secretary General, Mr. Trygve Lie, expressed the belief that
the time was right to attempt to stop the fighting in Korea. He
noted that the UNC had forced the invaders back beyond the
38th Parallel. He opined that if a cease-fire could be arranged
with the 38th Parallel as the approximate line of demarcation,
the resolutions of the Security Council of 25 and 26 June and
7 July would be fulfilled, with the proviso that full peace and
security be restored to the area. On 2 June Mr. Dean Acheson,
United States Secretary of State, expounded similar ideas. He
drew a distinction between long-term political problems and immediate military problems. He said that the political goals for
Korea, the establishment of a free, independent, and democratic
state, had not changed. The troops that had been sent to Korea
in 1950 had been sent to deal with the military aggression. He
observed that, to solve the military problem, the aggression must
end and the United Nations must have reliable assurances against
the recurrence of such aggression. In that event foreign troops
might be removed. On 7 June Secretary Acheson told the Senate
investigators that the United Nations forces in Korea would
agree to a reliable armistice on the 38th Parallel.

By the time the Russians recommended a cease-fire in Korea on 23 June 1951, circumstances indicated the general desirability of transferring what amounted to a military impasse to the conference table—not with the thought of beating swords into ploughshares, but because both sides recognized that further fighting was adding nothing toward the realization of their respective goals.

2

FIGHT FOR THE AGENDA

The fight to stop aggression in Korea is a fight to prevent it everywhere else in the world. The aim is not to settle political issues by force, but to prevent the aggressor from imposing a settlement by force. The aim is not conflict without limit, but peace without appeasement. That is the victory we seek.

AMBASSADOR WARREN AUSTIN

The strictest loyalty to the ideas of Communism must be combined with the ability to make all the necessary compromises, to "tack," to make agreements, zigzags, retreats, and so on, in order to accelerate the coming into power of the Communists.

LENIN

The first concrete indication that the Communist forces would welcome a chance to talk peace came on the eve of the first anniversary of the Korean War. On 23 June 1951, one year after the Communists had launched their assault against the United Nations–sponsored government of the Republic of Korea, the Russian delegate to the United Nations, Mr. Yakov A. Malik, proposed that "the problem of the armed conflict in

20

Korea could . . . be settled." In a dramatic broadcast obviously directed to the American people and designed to create the impression that the Russians were simply intervening as interested observers, Mr. Malik suggested that "as the first step, discussions should be started between the belligerents for a cease-fire and an armistice providing for mutual withdrawal of forces from the 38th parallel." He concluded with the prophetic remark: "I think [that such a step can be taken] provided there is a sincere desire to put an end to the bloody fighting in Korea." [1]

Malik's address was in reality a series of concessions to the demands that had been made by the United Nations Command: 1) a cease-fire; 2) a demilitarized zone following the 38th Parallel; and 3) supervision of Korea during the armistice.

Up to that time the Communist demands had been: 1) withdrawal of all foreign forces; 2) Korean affairs to be settled by Koreans; 3) United States withdrawal of protection to Formosa; and 4) admission of Communist China to the United Nations.

Within hours after Malik's suggestion that "belligerents on both sides" take part in discussing an armistice, the United States issued a challenge to the Soviets to make the proposal an official one and not merely a propaganda move.

Two day following Yakov Malik's statement President Truman said that the United States "is ready to join in a peaceful settlement in Korea now as we have always been," but he added "it must be a real settlement which fully ends aggression and restores peace and security to the area and to the gallant Korean people. . . . We must build up our strength but we must always keep the door open to a peaceful settlement of differences."

For its part, the United Nations Command realized by this time that it could not hope to win a victory in Korea or attain the objective of uniting all of that country unless it was able to carry the fighting into China and cut off the sources of supply and reinforcements entering North Korea. The spectacular recall of General Douglas MacArthur in April 1951 had made quite plain the UNC's decision not to broaden the scope of the war.

---

[1] For the complete text of Mr. Malik's proposal see Appendix III.

So the UNC welcomed the chance to settle this problem on what it believed might be honorable terms.

For their part, the Communists had failed to achieve their objective of driving out all non-Communist elements south of the 38th Parallel, and the exigencies of the moment indicated a worsening position. General James Van Fleet, the Eighth Army commander in Korea, has stated that at the time Malik made his proposal, UNC forces were on the offensive and pushing the opponent back. A limited victory was not inconceivable. The North Korean forces had been decimated. The Chinese had suffered untold destruction. Under these circumstances it was wise policy for the Communists to seek peace before other gains were lost.

Further, the Communists had not been unattentive to the MacArthur hearings in Washington, which had come to an eight-week end on 25 June 1951. These hearings had exposed the inner fabric of United States policy and had permitted foreign states to draw valuable conclusions. During the 7 June hearing Secretary of State Dean Acheson declared that the United Nations forces in Korea would agree to a reliable armistice on the 38th Parallel—a point of which the Communists made much in subsequent propaganda when the UNC made known its refusal to accept this line as an armistice demarcation division.

Inasmuch as UNC forces were advancing and had already made significant gains above the 38th Parallel on the eastern segment of the peninsula, the Communists would gain a tactical victory by a return to this imaginary line.

Certainly the Communists eyed the forthcoming Japanese Peace Conference at San Francisco with great interest. They knew all too well that they could not expect to forge any diplomatic gains at that time unless Korean peace was re-established.

Finally, the Communists were aware of the dissidence of the Republic of Korea's President, Dr. Syngman Rhee, who had made known his refusal to accept less than complete unification of Korea under his hegemony. To suggest peace would thus cause a split in the UNC ranks and embarrass the free world. Fishing is good in troubled waters.

Mr. ACHESON, YOUR STRIPED PANTS ARE DOWN!

Here's What You Said in June:

WASHINGTON, June 7 (AP) —Secretary of State Acheson repeated at the Senate's MacArthur inquiry Thursday that UN forces in Korea would agree to a reliable armistice on the 38th parallel.

Here's What You Say in August:

38°

WASHINGTON, Aug. 1 (USIS)—The U.S. cannot accept the Communist proposal that a demilitarized zone in Korea be set up along the 38th parallel, according to Secretary of State Acheson.

Now you and your pals are stalling the peacetalks, refusing to agree to the 38th parallel.

You think you're a smart diplomat.

But American boys are paying for your smartness with their lives.

BUDDIES, BE ON GUARD FOR PEACE — FIGHT FOR PEACE! THE POLITICIANS IN WASHINTON WILL DOUBLE-CROSS PEACE IF THEY CAN

— AN AMERICAN SOLDIER —

（一個美國兵所寫又布道傳號和談的傳單）

Fig. 1. Communist leaflet disseminated among United Nations troops in Korea in 1951, which capitalized on the U.S. Secretary of State's declarations.

The rift came only a matter of days following Mr. Malik's statement and the UNC's eager interest. On 30 June Dr. Rhee listed the conditions for acceptance of an armistice. These included: 1) the Chinese Communist forces must withdraw north of the Yalu river without further hostilities or damage to property; 2) complete disarmament of all North Korean Communists; 3) United Nations guarantees that no third power would assist the North Korean Communists either militarily or financially; 4) the Republic of Korea to have full participation in any international conference considering not only the cease-fire but "any phase of the Korean problem"; and 5) a refusal to accept any situation that "conflicts with national sovereignty or territorial integrity of the Republic of Korea." And again on 4 July, just a few days before the armistice conference was to commence, Dr. Rhee made it quite clear that a cease-fire at the 38th Parallel would not be acceptable. He added his demands for a continuation of the war and the realization of complete unification of Korea.

Following diplomatic feelers, the United Nations Command moved to propose a conference to discuss an armistice. On 30 June 1951, the UNC Commander-in-Chief, General Matthew B. Ridgway, USA, radioed the Commander-in-Chief of the Communist Forces in Korea:

I am informed that you may wish a meeting to discuss an armistice providing for the cessation of hostilities and all acts of armed forces in Korea, with adequate guarantees for the maintenance of such armistice.

General Ridgway proposed the Danish hospital ship *Jutlandia*, stationed at Wonsan Harbor, as the site of the meetings. On the following day, Kim Il Sung, Supreme Commander of the North Korean Forces, and Peng Teh-huai,[2] Commander of the Chinese Volunteers, ignoring this latter recommendation of the UNC Commander, agreed to such a meeting "in the area of Kaesong on the 38th Parallel."[3]

---

[2] This reply revealed for the first time the identity of the leader of the Chinese Volunteers.

[3] One periodical termed this counterproposal a "face-saving" device, in

"In the interest of expediting the end of bloodshed and to demonstrate the good faith under which the United Nations Command was proceeding," the UNC accepted the Communists' demand to meet at Kaesong. This acceptance later proved of conspicuous disadvantage to the UNC.

The United Nations Command set up its truce headquarters, known as Base Camp, in an apple orchard on the outskirts of Munsan, a small village fourteen miles east of Panmunjom and on the east side of the Imjin river. In the Apple Orchard tents were erected to house the delegation and its staff. By the time the negotiations came to an end, Base Camp had assumed an air of permanency with an elaborate arrangement. There were volley ball courts, baseball diamonds, horseshoe pits, even a skeet range. There was a large tent for the showing of motion pictures, a social club and mess tents for the enlisted personnel, one for the junior officers, and still another for the senior officers. There was a conference tent in which preparatory meetings were held. There was a heliocopter strip where the delegates departed for and returned from the meetings. All the correspondents assigned to the negotiations were billeted in the "Press Train," which had been placed on a siding at Munsan station, one mile west of Base Camp.

The Communist delegation lived at Kaesong, less than ten miles to the west of Panmunjom, ninety air miles and nearly twice that many road miles below their capital at Pyongyang. Kaesong, three miles below the 38th Parallel, was at first about twenty miles within the Communist lines. The Communists continued to make their headquarters at Kaesong throughout the period of the negotiations.

On 8 July the United Nations Command and Communist liaison officers met at Kaesong to discuss preparation for the meetings. Colonel James C. Murray, USMC, one of the three UNC

---

that the *Jutlandia* was technically United Nations territory, from which organization the Chinese and North Koreans had been excluded. "It would have been really surprising if [the Reds] had accepted the proposal."—*New Republic*, 9 July 1951, p. 6. Admiral Joy noted that "Communist reluctance to do business in an alien atmosphere of a neutral ship was understandable." He added that Kaesong was considered to be in no-man's land; its location would not seriously interfere with the fighting; it was readily accessible. This observation was made before the commencement of negotiations. (*Collier's*, 16 August 1952, p. 38.)

liaison officers attending the first meeting, recalls that meeting
with the Communists:

Through an exchange of radio broadcasts a meeting of liaison
officers was arranged. Along with Air Force Colonel Jack Kinney
and Republic of Korea Army Colonel Lee Soo Young, I represented
the Commander-in-Chief United Nations Command at this meeting.
At an agreed time, 0900 hours, 8 July 1951, we crossed the Imjin
River at Munsan by heliocopter and set a course for enemy-held
Kaesong. Arriving there some minutes later, we circled about searching the ruins of the bombed-out city for signs of the expected Red
envoys. At first we found no life except a jeep driven crazily along
the cratered streets. Had the enemy envoys been delayed? Had
there been some misunderstanding as to the time and place of the
meeting?

Circling once more, a white aircraft marking panel laid on a field
at the north edge of the town came into view. We descended there.
The landing field was ringed with Red soldiers who watched the
descent with fascination. We dismounted from the helicopter and
waited. As the sound of its motors died out, an ominous silence
fell with the Reds eyeing us and vice versa. After a short interval
an escort officer and two interpreters—one a girl—moved out from
the encircling soldiers and approached us apprehensively. They
were to take us to the meeting place—a former tea house which
subsequently became the site of the armistice negotiations. Transportation was by jeep—battered American jeeps captured during the
preceding winter.

As we entered the tea house the enemy group rose. Following identification both groups resumed seats. The formality of a cigarette
completed, Colonel Chang led the way to an adjacent room where
the now familiar green cloth table had been laid out. We began
negotiations.

The conversations during that first meeting revealed a great
deal about Communist, and, it might be added, Oriental, logic.

Colonel Kinney: Is your delegation agreeable to meeting
on July 10?

Colonel Chang: The time of meeting has been arranged by
the commanders.

Kinney: No, the commanders have agreed that the delegation should meet between the tenth and fifteenth of July.
They have not set the exact date.

Chang: The date of meeting of the delegations shall be as the commanders have agreed.

Kinney: But when? Shall it be the tenth, eleventh, twelfth. What date?

Chang: This matter has been arranged by the commanders and is not for negotiation by liaison officers.

Colonel Murray suggested to Colonel Kinney that he set the date unilaterally, since it appeared the Communist officer did not have authority to agree to a date.

Kinney: The United Nations Command delegation will arrive in Kaesong at 1100 hours on July 10.

Chang: The commanders have agreed and it shall be so.

While these officials carried on negotiations for the proposed armistice talks, the seventeen Allied nations with forces in Korea met and agreed on the following terms to be presented to the Communists:

1. Enforcement of a cease-fire throughout Korea under conditions that would guarantee the security of both commands for the period of the armistice.

2. Establishment of an approximate twenty-mile buffer zone, with the southern extremity of the zone running from just south of the 38th Parallel on the west coast of the peninsula to a point about fifteen miles north of the Parallel on the east coast.

3. Both sides to stay on their side of the demilitarized zone and to go no nearer than three miles offshore of the other's territory.

4. A halt of shipments of war matériel, troops, and replacements to Korea or increases in the number of troops in Korea.

5. Establishment of an international commission—not necessarily under the United Nations—with unrestricted access to all Korea to supervise the truce.

6. Exchange of prisoners.

7. Provision of security of troops and refugees and other problems.

General Ridgway, who was responsible to the Joint Chiefs of Staff—which was in turn acting for the United States government, the body selected by the United Nations to carry out the Korean operations—had received explicit instructions not to discuss any political or territorial questions during the armistice negotiations. He was not authorized to discuss the Chinese Communist claims to Formosa and a seat in the UN, nor was he authorized to enter into any permanent political division of Korea into zones. His mission was to propose a purely temporary dividing line between the two forces, for the purpose of keeping those forces on either side of the demilitarized zone close to the 38th Parallel. He was not to agree to the 38th Parallel, however, as a political line. The sole purpose of the armistice negotiations at Kaesong was to put an end to the killing and to create machinery to ensure that the armistice was carried out. Once this was accomplished and assured, entirely separate conversations were to consider such questions as the political and territorial settlement of Korea, the unification and security of the country, and provisions for elections.

Neither the United States nor the United Nations had ever recognized the right of the Communists to establish political control over North Korea at any time, and they did not propose to recognize such a political division during the armistice negotiations or subsequently.

General Ridgway as the Supreme UNC Commander recognized certain responsibilities inherent in his position. He recognized that in an armistice, as in a war, he had to provide for the security of his own forces. He would demand a demarcation line that would permit the establishment of a defensible position.

From the outset of their occupation of North Korea in 1945, the Communists had sealed off their zone from all United States and UN observation. Had North Korea been open to observation, it is conceivable that the assault would never have been launched. To ensure the security of his command General Ridgway had decided to insist upon certain tangible arrangements being established for the freedom of movement throughout Korea—the right of aerial reconnaissance, the right of the UN observations, mixed UN–Communist Commission to police armistice arrangements.

It was against this backdrop of events, heavily saturated with the Communist propaganda line that the United Nations forces had been the original aggressor in Korea, that the UNC delegation departed from Munsan on 10 July 1951 at 1000 hours, to attempt to work out a compromise with the Communists to bring the war in Korea to a peaceful conclusion. The Senior UNC Delegate, Vice Admiral C. Turner Joy, USN, symbolized the hopes of a war-tired world as he climbed aboard the helicopter at Base Camp in preparation for leaving for the first meetings:

We, the delegates from the United Nations Command, are leaving for Kaesong fully conscious of the importance of these meetings to the entire world. We are proceeding in good faith prepared to do our part to bring about an honorable armistice, under terms that are satisfactory to the United Nations Command.

The importance of the occasion was marked by conspicuous optimism throughout the free world, which Washington sought to restrain.[4]

As Admiral Joy's helicopter was approaching Kaesong, the first sign of Communist perfidy was being demonstrated. It had been agreed in the preparatory meetings that the United Nations delegations and staff would carry the white flag on their vehicles as a symbol of their mission. As the UNC staff approached Kaesong by car, their white flags were clearly visible. The Communist photographers made capital of this event by explaining in their propaganda that the UNC was coming to Kaesong to surrender. This offered sufficient evidence from the outset of the impracticability of meeting at Kaesong.

To emphasize that they were the hosts, the Communist delegation planned and expected that the UNC would remain at

---

[4] A front-page article in the *New York Times*, 8 July 1951, was boldly captioned: "Fighting for Several Weeks Is Foreseen by Washington."

the conference city. They had prepared a building for the
UNC delegation and staff as living quarters. The beds were even
made. The Communists offered the UNC food. Being adept at
propaganda, they recognized the old maxim that one does not
bite the hand that feeds him. Admiral Joy rightfully declined
their offer. The UNC camp had already been established at
Munsan—about twenty miles southeast of Kaesong—in the now
famous Apple Orchard.

At 1100 hours, 10 July 1951, the respective delegations
commenced what was to become a seemingly interminable series
of "merry-go-round talkathons," in the vernacular of the front-
line GI. The Communist delegates were five in number: General
Nam Il, North Korea Senior Delegate; Major General Lee Sang
Cho, North Korea; Major General Chang Pyong San, North
Korea; Lieutenant General Tung Hua, Chinese; and Major Gen-
eral Hsieh Fang, Chinese.[5] The UNC delegation comprised Vice
Admiral Charles Turner Joy, USN, Senior Delegate; Major Gen-
eral Laurence C. Craigie, USAF; Major General Henry I. Hodes,
USA; Rear Admiral Arleigh Albert Burke, USN; and Major
General Paik Sun Yup, Republic of Korea Army.[6]

The backgrounds of the respective delegates offered further
evidence of the existing inequalities. For the most part the Communist delegates had devoted considerable time to propaganda
work. They were not "fighting men." They were comparatively
young. For example, their Senior Delegate, General Nam Il, was
thirty-seven years of age. He was Chief of Staff of the North
Korean Supreme Headquarters. He graduated from a university
in Manchuria and in 1942 went to Russia as a teacher. He was

[5] It was significant that the Communist delegation contained three North
Koreans and two Chinese, even though the Chinese had 95 per cent of the
front-line troops. This was obviously a propaganda move.
[6] No account of the armistice talks would be complete without some acknowl-
edgment of the work of the UNC interpreters, Lieutenant Horace Underwood,
USN, and his brother, Lieutenant Richard Underwood, AUS, who had spent
a good portion of their lives in Korea. Their parents and grandparents had
been missionaries in Korea, which afforded them the opportunity to learn the
Korean language and to intimately know the people. Their services to the
UNC delegates were incalculable. Lieutenant Kenneth Wu, AUS, attended every
meeting from the beginning on 8 July 1951 to 27 July 1953 as Chinese interpreter. All the interpreters contributed a great deal to the progress of the
meetings and final consummation of the Armistice.

returned to North Korea in 1945 when the Russians occupied the area. From 1945 until the outbreak of the Korean War he held a succession of governmental education posts. Major General Hsieh Fang had graduated from a Moscow university and was later Chief of Propaganda, Political Department, in Manchuria. It is believed that he was one of the individuals involved in the kidnapping of Chiang Kai-shek at Sian in 1936. As the meetings progressed, the dominance of Hsieh Fang became increasingly noticeable, which tended to confirm suspicions relative to North Korean–Chinese relations. Lieutenant General Tung Hua had since 1948 been the Commanding General of the Fifteenth Army Group, Fourth Field Army. He had also served in a number of political posts. Major General Lee Sang Cho was Chief of Staff, North Korean Army Front Headquarters. Colonel Andrew J. Kinney has lucidly described General Lee: "Four black flies were very much at home crawling over North Korean General Lee Sang Cho's face. The tough Communist negotiator made no move to flick them off.

"I watched, fascinated. Not a facial muscle twitched as one fly wandered over a bushy eyebrow and another paced down the bridge of his nose. He remained perfectly motionless, his face expressionless.

"I wondered: 'What's he trying to prove? That flies don't bother him? That American DDT, used to spray the Korean Armistice tent, is worthless? Is he entertaining us with Oriental muscle control? . . .'"[7]

Major General Chang Pyong San was Chief of Staff of the North Korean First Corps.

The UNC delegation could only boast of glittering careers as combat veterans.

That the Communist delegation had been well indoctrinated in Communist logic became immediately apparent. After the exchange of credentials there were opening allusions to pious hopes for peaceful settlement, about which neither side disagreed. Admiral Joy noted:

---

[7] Colonel Andrew J. Kinney, USAF: "Secrets from the Truce Tent," *This Week*, 31 August 1952, p. 7.

Success or failure of the negotiations begun here today depends
directly upon the good faith of the delegations here present. With
good faith on both sides there can be created an atmosphere of
mutual confidence. In such an atmosphere there is every reason
to hope for success. Such an atmosphere can exist where truth
prevails.

Admiral Joy then sat down, and General Nam Il and Tung
Hua spoke. Nam Il produced what was to become his pet phrase,
"all peace-loving people of the world." [8] This, of course, implied
that North Korea was on the side of the "peaceloving peoples."
General Tung Hua, speaking for the Chinese volunteers, remarked that "peoples of all countries bitterly hate war and desire
peace ardently."

As Nam Il sat down, Admiral Joy observed suddenly that
he was seated in a chair which was considerably closer to the
floor than was that of his adversary. Nam Il appeared as though
he were looking down on Joy. The latter immediately demanded
rectification of this inequality. For the Communists, apparently
nothing was too insignificant to be overlooked.

The Senior UNC Delegate then observed that "the first item
to be settled is the limitation of these discussions to military
matters only." He also noted that the meetings should be restricted to matters dealing with Korea. He proposed that such
an agreement be signed at the outset. To this Nam Il replied:

[8] Colonel Kinney comments on General Nam:
"Take General Nam at the first plenary session at Kaesong on 10 July 1951.
He was nervous and uneasy. He repeatedly forgot to permit his interpreter to
translate his remarks from Korean into Chinese.
"At one point he vainly attempted to light one of his Russian cigarettes
with Chinese matches. None fired, although he struck perhaps a dozen.
"Embarrassed and desperate, he brought out an American cigarette lighter.
It clicked and flared brightly. He took one deep drag and then, apparently
feeling that somehow he had been disloyal to things Communistic, he tossed
the American lighter out the window behind him!
"Another time General Nam was nervously chain-smoking while North
Korean Major To Yu Ho put his earlier remarks into English.
" 'Our side is unfair, unjust, and unreasonable,' " Major To said loudly
and positively.
"There was frantic whispering among the English-speaking Communists.
General Nam became agitated. Obviously displeased and looking frightened,
he flagged Major To to a halt.
" 'I mean your side is,' Major To blurted out." *Loc. cit.*, p. 6.

This meeting was to begin arrangements to stop the fighting in Korea and I would like to know the reason for any such statement as this and the necessity for signing such a statement and those are the major premises under which we came to the meeting to begin with, limited to the military forces and I would like to know the opinion of the other party might be here.[9]

This refusal to sign indicated that the scope of the talks was intended to cover more than mere military matters. General Nam Il submitted his proposals for an armistice. These included:

1. The establishment of the 38th Parallel as the military demarcation line between both sides and the establishment of a demilitarized zone, as basic conditions for the cessation of hostilities in Korea.

2. Withdrawal of all armed forces of foreign countries from Korea.

3. Concrete arrangements for the realization of a cease-fire and armistice in Korea.

4. Arrangements relating to prisoners of war following the armistice.

The United Nations Command offering its recommendations noted that the first order of business was to decide upon an agenda which would include topics of a general and not conclusive nature; as opposed to the Reds' proposals that an agenda was simply a list of topics that both sides agreed to discuss. The proposed UNC agenda included nine points:

1. Adoption of Agenda.

2. Location of, and authority for International Red Cross Representatives to visit, prisoner of war camps.

3. Limitations of discussions at this and all subsequent meetings to purely military matters related to Korea only.

[9] The quotations used throughout are taken directly from the official transcripts of the meetings. The statements of the Communists were translated into English by their own interpreters and recorded by the stenographers. The author has not changed these in any way. A set of the transcripts is on file at the Hoover Institute, Stanford University.

4. Cessation of hostilities and of acts of armed force in Korea under conditions that would assure against resumption of hostilities and acts of armed force in Korea.

5. Agreement on a demilitarized zone across Korea.

6. Composition, authority and functions of Military Armistice Commission.

7. Agreement on principle of inspection within Korea by Military Observer Teams, functioning under Military Armistice Commission.

8. Composition and functions of these teams.

9. Arrangements pertaining to prisoners of war.

Following submission of this agenda, Admiral Joy handed Nam Il a copy for his consideration and requested a copy of his. The Communists then requested a three hour and thirty-five minute recess, ostensibly to prepare a copy, but presumably to study the UNC agenda and seek advice from their superiors relative to their own agenda.

During the recess the Communists placed the flag of North Korea on the conference table close to the United Nations flag, which had been placed on the table by the UNC prior to the opening—it being assumed the Communists would do likewise. The North Korean flag was several inches taller than the UNC flag, which difference was supposed to symbolize defeat. Upon resumption of the meetings, and as Nam Il was submitting his written agenda, a group of Communist photographers, beckoned aside during the opening session undoubtedly because of the absence of their flag, now rushed into the conference room to take pictures. Admiral Joy immediately protested their actions as something that required previous mutual agreement. Admiral Joy then presented the proposal that twenty selected newsmen be permitted to move to and from the conference area as a part of the UNC delegation. He emphasized that they would not be admitted to the conference room, but only to the area of the conference. General Nam Il at first was forced to accept, since his newsmen were in the area, but later he reversed this decision on the grounds that he would have to receive confirmation first from his superior commander. He said that until he received the answer he would postpone the matter. Inasmuch as the matter remained unsettled by the second meeting on 11 July, Admiral Joy read a note from General Ridgway, which stressed the importance of permitting newsmen to accompany the delegation. Admiral Joy concluded, "If by tomorrow morning the newsmen are still unacceptable at the site of the conference, it is requested that we be informed by 0730 hours tomorrow on what date it will be possible to resume the conference with newsmen present at the conference site."

The day before the commencement of the talks General Ridgway visited the correspondents' billets in Seoul to assuage their fears over arrangements for news coverage. He was aware of the importance of a free press and asked Admiral Joy to strongly insist upon permission for twenty newsmen at the conference site.[10]

The following morning the convoy started on the road to Kaesong with the twenty newsmen. It was refused passage beyond Communist control posts and so returned to Munsan. Admiral Joy immediately dispatched a note to Nam Il stating that he would return to the conference and continue the discussions "upon notification from you that my convoy, bearing personnel of my choosing, including such press representation as I consider necessary, will be cleared to the conference site."

The Communists replied that they did not stop the delegates, only the newsmen, and that they believed the problem of the newsmen should be delayed "since the conference at the present stage is still strictly a military one and even the agenda has not been agreed upon."

General Ridgway thereupon directed a firm message to the Communists pointing out the many difficulties that had arisen from holding the meeting in Communist territory. Had the meetings instead been held on the Danish hospital ship "it would

---

[10] *Time* speculated that Joy's position on the reporter issue was made to counter the impression disseminated by the Reds that the UNC came begging for peace, humbly and unarmed. It also noted that the Communist papers carried photos showing the delegation under the white flag, unarmed. (*Time*, 23 July 1951.)

have provided a completely neutral atmosphere, free of the
menacing presence of armed troops of either side." General
Ridgway was careful to observe:

Since the first meeting at Kaesong, your delegation has placed restrictions upon the movements of our delegation. It has subjected
our personnel to the close proximity of your armed guards. It has
delayed and blocked passage of our couriers. It has withheld its
cooperation in establishment of two-way communications with our
base, even though it agreed to do so immediately. It has refused
admittance to the conference area of certain personnel in our convoy.

General Ridgway then reiterated the assurances he required.
He suggested:

the establishment of an agreed conference area of suitable extent,
completely free of armed personnel of either side, each delegation
must have complete reciprocity of treatment to include complete and
equal freedom of movement to, from and within the agreed conference area, and complete and equal freedom at all times in selection
of the personnel in its delegation party to include representatives of
the press.

General Ridgway concluded that "should you continue to
insist that restrictions are necessary for our personal safety, or
for any other reason, I propose that the conference site be
moved to a locality which will afford the few simple assurances
I have specified."

On 14 July Kim Il Sung and Peng Teh-huai agreed "to
make Kaesong the neutral zone as you have proposed. . . . We
accept your proposal to send twenty reporters with your delegation and have already issued the necessary instructions to that
effect." Thus the suggestion of pressure removed the continuance
of delay.

Following three days of interruption, the negotiations again
convened. Admiral Joy expressed regrets for being nine minutes
late but stated that it was the result of action by Communist
sentries delaying the convoy. The senior member of the UNC
delegation then elaborated on certain details of General Ridgway's proposals for neutralizing Kaesong.

1. The road leading to the conference site (Kaesong) should be open to unrestricted use by vehicles of the United Nations Command delegation. No notice should be required for such movements.

2. The neutral area, five miles in radius, with the traffic circle in Kaesong as its center, would contain no armed personnel except the minimum needed for military police purposes. Such personnel could be armed with small arms.

3. Any personnel required for security at the conference site would be unarmed. The conference site would be defined as an area having a radius of one-half mile centered on the conference house.

Admiral Joy suggested further that the personnel of each delegation's party should not exceed 150. The composition of each delegation would be the sole responsibility of each side, but those who entered the conference chamber would do so by mutual agreement.

General Nam Il agreed with the recommendations and suggested that final details be worked out by the liaison officers.

The conference again got down to the business at hand—the problem of what should be discussed. General Nam Il, in what was to prove a typical response, stated that "you regard our proposed agenda as incorrect and cannot consider our proposed agenda as appropriate." He dogmatically added that "we consider your agenda as inappropriate."

Admiral Joy pointed out that the "proper order of business is to first establish the general topics which both sides agree to discuss, then subsequently to determine the specific agreement, the details on which agreement can be reached." He directed his statement to the particular item on the Communist agenda which established the 38th Parallel as the military demarcation line.

The Communist delegation offered a particular demarcation line and a particular demilitarization zone as an agenda item. The delegation of the United Nations Command believes that first it should

be agreed that discussions of some demarcation line and some
demilitarization zone is desired by and agreeable to both parties.
Once this general topic is agreed on, later meetings can approach
the question as to which particular line and zone can be agreed upon.

Pertaining to the withdrawal of all foreign forces from
Korea, Admiral Joy observed that this was a matter outside
the purview of the conference and that he was not empowered
to discuss political matters.

Admiral Joy's allusion to "Communist" brought sharp and
immediate rebuttal: "The term 'Communists' is not proper here
because you are not handling with the Communists but with
the Korean People's Army and the Chinese Volunteers." It
might be noted here that, from that time to the signing of the
Armistice Agreement, the UNC referred to the Communists by
the title they preferred. In contrast, the Communist delegation
on no occasion employed the correct title in referring to the
government of the Republic of Korea or to that of the Republic
of China (Formosa). Instead they used highly derogatory ad-
jectives such as "the murderer Rhee" and "your puppet on
Formosa."

The Communists remained adamant in insisting upon retaining their item pertaining to the 38th Parallel and the withdrawal of all foreign troops. Further, "without ceasing hostilities
in Korea and without carrying out cease-fire in Korea we cannot
discuss the armistice."

Admiral Joy requested that they repeat this statement.

Without agreeing upon item two we cannot discuss the armistice
in Korea. Without agreeing upon Item Two we cannot discuss—
without agreeing upon Item Two we cannot discuss the Armistice.
We cannot discuss other questions without agreeing upon Item
Two. Without having Item Two and Item Three agreed upon, we
cannot discuss further items. Is that clear? Without having Items
Two and Three agreed upon it is difficult to discuss further items.

Nam Il doggedly held to his demands.

We cannot consider the 38th Parallel line as an imaginary line.
The 38th Parallel line had existed and the war broke out right on
that line. Therefore, it is the principle that the question of the

cease-fire must be concluded also on the 38th Parallel line. There-fore, this must be on the agenda.

The UNC's demands for Red Cross visits to the prisoner-of-war camps evoked a particularly anxious response from the North Korean General. "Which would be better for the prisoners of war, to be comforted by delegates of the Red Cross or to be released and go back home and be with their families as soon as possible? Which would be better for them?" As subsequent in-vestigations by the UNC proved, it would have been very em-barrassing for the Communists to have their prisoner-of-war camps visited.

Admiral Joy made clear to General Nam Il that "on 13 July 1950 the Government of North Korea sent a telegram to the Secretary General of the United Nations in which it expressly stated its intentions of adhering to the principles of the Geneva Convention. One of these principles is to permit the Red Cross to visit prisoner of war camps." He cryptically queried: "It is difficult for the United Nations Command delegation to under-stand why the delegate of the North Korean Army can take a stand contrary to that expressed by his government, and in op-position to the humanitarian purposes of the Geneva Conven-tion." However, the UNC delegate concluded that "while we continue to maintain that this question is a military matter of high urgency, we are prepared to accept your representations and discuss this problem under the general topic of 'Prisoners of war' as a later item on the agenda." This was a significant concession.

This UNC concession laid the ground for a Communist equivalent. On the following day Nam Il, after reviewing his demands for the inclusion of the 38th Parallel on the agenda concluded that "in order to reach an agreement, we are not going to have this concrete military demarcation line in the agenda, and we agree to have the general military demarcation line on the agenda as you propose." But he reaffirmed his de-termination that "we will insist on definitely having the 38th Parallel as the military demarcation line between both sides when we come to discuss the agenda." He continued to insist upon the withdrawal of all foreign forces. This indicated the importance the Communists attached to this item.

Recognizing that an armistice is merely a suspension of hostilities prior to the convocation of a peace conference and that certain military guarantees must be obtained to ensure against a rupture in the peace conference and a return to fighting, the UNC was insisting upon the establishment of a Military Armistice Commission to supervise the conduct of the armistice and an inspection team to visit the areas behind both lines to see that both sides abide by the terms of the agreement.

A Military Armistice Commission supervises the inspection of the activities of both belligerent forces during the duration of the military armistice. It reports violations of the terms of the armistice to the commanders of the belligerent forces. The membership of the Military Armistice Commission would be subject to agreement by commanders of the belligerent forces.

The Military Observer Teams are the eyes and ears of the Military Armistice Commission. The Communists recommended that Item Four of the agenda read: "Concrete arrangements for the realization of cease-fire and armistice in Korea, including the composition, authority, and functions of a supervising organ for carrying out the terms of cease-fire and armistice." This the UNC accepted, as it had also their Item Two: "Fixing a military demarcation line between both sides so as to establish a demilitarized zone as a basic condition for the cessation of hostilities in Korea," and Item Five: "Arrangements relating to prisoners of war."

The Communists maintained their "unshakable determination" not to concede on the withdrawal of foreign forces.

If the question of withdrawal of all foreign forces from Korea is not settled in this conference a premise will be lacking for the forthcoming peace conference.

In propagandistic phrases Nam Il noted:

It is the unanimous demand of the peoples of the whole world that all armed forces of foreign countries be withdrawn from Korea to

insure completely against the breakout anew of war in Korea. . . .
We deem that it is because foreign armed forces have been drawn
into the Korean war, thus preventing the Korean people from
settling their own affairs, that it has not been possible to restore
peace in Korea. . . . Do you mean to have hostilities suspended so
that the foreign armed forces might stay and go about sight-seeing
in Korea? This is inadmissible. . . . The withdrawal of all foreign
armed forces from Korea is the basic condition for making the
resumption of war in Korea impossible. . . . It is our unshakable
stand. . . .

In reply to the Communist contention that the withdrawal
of foreign troops was the basic and principal guarantee against
resumption of hostilities in Korea, Admiral Joy observed causti-
cally:

There were no foreign forces in Korea in June of 1950, when the
hostilities began. Thus, history demonstrates clearly that hostilities
did occur in Korea in the absence of foreign forces. How, then,
could absence of foreign forces be a guarantee against hostilities
resuming in Korea? You assert that the absence of foreign forces
will insure against the repetition of violent events which in fact
occurred in the absence of foreign forces. This is total confusion
as to cause and effect. This is upside-down reasoning. Furthermore,
we recall that for a period of time after the end of World War II,
foreign troops were in Korea. No war occurred as a result of the
presence of those troops; rather, their presence was an aspect of the
ending of a war. . . . You have stated that the presence of foreign
troops prevents the Korean people from settling their problems
themselves. By what means was the settlement of these problems
progressing in June of 1950, before the appearance of foreign
forces in Korea?

Without alluding to Russia, Admiral Joy answered:

By guns, tanks, aircraft—by war, as all the world knows. By immediately withdrawing foreign forces from Korea, we would restore
the conditions as to presence of troops in Korea that was the case
in June of 1950. Would we have a guarantee against resumption
of hostilities?

With his strange brand of logic, Nam Il replied:

Judging from the surface, there were indeed no foreign forces in Korea on 25 June 1950, but the occurrence of the incident of 25 June and subsequent developments were inseparable from the fact that large numbers of foreign armed forces arrived in Korea on 27 June which prevented the peaceful settlement of the internal problem of Korea for which we have consistently stood, and converted the war into one involving many countries. It was only when the foreign troops participated and one side had penetrated deep into the interior of the Democratic People's Republic of Korea and directly threatened the security of the People's Republic of China, that the Chinese people were compelled to send volunteer units to assist the Korean people to fight against intervention by foreign armed forces. . . .

Finally, after a three-day recess asked for by the Communists, the conferees reconvened on 25 July. After Nam Il viewed his determined stand not to concede on the withdrawal of foreign forces, he concluded:

In order that an agreement may be reached on an armistice at an early date so that the primary wishes of the peace-loving people of the world may be realized, we agree to your view that the question of the withdrawal of all foreign armed forces be left to another conference for settlement. . . . In view of the deep-rooted relations between the question of withdrawal of all foreign armed forces from Korea and the cease-fire and armistice we seek to achieve, and the eagerness of the soldiers of the various foreign countries participating in the fighting to go back home for a peaceful life after the armistice . . . we propose to add a fifth item to the four items on the agenda already agreed upon: "Recommendations to the governments of the countries concerned on both sides . . . that within a definite time limit after the armistice agreement becomes effective a conference of their representatives of a higher level be convened to negotiate on the question of withdrawal, by stages, of all foreign armed forces from Korea."

Nam Il concluded with a statement quite prophetic when viewed in terms of subsequent events: "When these four items are agreed upon, has the other party good faith to consider item five then? And to have good result?" Obviously what was meant here was that all foreign forces would be withdrawn from Korea. Admiral Joy replied: "The United Nations Command delegation wishes to assure you that we will discuss this item fully and in good faith in an endeavor to reach a mutually satisfactory agreement."

With this Nam Il asseverated that "we think that you agree on the whole agenda."

The agenda as agreed upon included five items:

1. Adoption of agenda.

2. Fixing of military demarcation line between both sides so as to establish a demilitarized zone as a basic condition for the cessation of hostilities in Korea.

3. Concrete arrangements for the realization of cease-fire and armistice in Korea, including the composition, authority, and functions of a supervisory organ for carrying out the terms of cease-fire and armistice.

4. Arrangements relating to prisoners of war.

5. Recommendation to governments of countries concerned on both sides.

On 26 July, sixteen days following the convocation of the first meeting at Kaesong, the agenda was agreed to by both parties—an agenda approaching the recommendations of Malik as subsequently clarified by Gromyko, viz., a cease-fire and limitation of the talks to strictly military questions.

The anticipations of the war-weary world had been dampened by the delays in reaching an agreement on the items to be discussed. The impediments the Communists had injected into the meetings prophesied further and more serious troubles during the negotiations on the agreed agenda items. The Communists had already exposed their reluctance to accept any line other than the 38th Parallel as the demarcation line; they had voiced concerned opposition to the admission of the International Red Cross representatives; they had made it quite plain that a cease-fire should precede the final signing of the armistice; they had expressed grave doubts as to the feasibility of employing observation teams as a means of ensuring that both parties abide faithfully by the final agreement.

Certainly any optimism that had existed at the outset over an early settlement now lacked substance. But, as Admiral Joy opined, "Unless you come prepared to spend time you only short-change yourself and cheat those who depend on you. . . . Time is the price you pay for progress."

3

CHARGE, COUNTERCHARGE

"I can't believe that!" cried Alice. "Can't you?"
the Queen said in a pitying tone. "Try again;
draw a long breath, and shut your eyes." Alice
laughed. "There's no use trying," she said, "one
can't believe impossible things." "I dare say you
haven't had much practice," said the Queen.
"When I was your age, I always did it for half-
an-hour a day. Why, sometimes I believed as
many as six impossible things before breakfast."

LEWIS CARROLL, Alice in Wonderland

Foreign politics demand scarcely any of those
qualities which a democracy possesses; and they
require, on the contrary, the perfect use of almost
all those faculties in which it is deficient.

ALEXIS DE TOCQUEVILLE,
Democracy in America

General Nam Il's assertion, "We will insist on
definitely having the 38th Parallel as the military demarcation
line between both sides when we come to discuss the agenda,"

still resounded in the conference room at Kaesong as the delegates began work on details for a military cease-fire line and demilitarized zone.

The Communists opened the discussions on Item Two by repeating their previously stated position:

We hold firmly that the 38th Parallel should be made the military demarcation line between both sides and that both sides withdraw ten kilometers from the 38th Parallel in order to establish a demilitarized zone.

Nam Il supported his demands with the argument that the 38th Parallel "is consistent with the historical fact recognized by the whole world." He rationalized that the Korean War broke out

. . . because one of the belligerents violated first the demarcation line of the 38th Parallel. The reason why the war could not be stopped later is again that one of the belligerents ignored the position of the Korean people and of the Chinese people and violated once again the 38th Parallel.

Finally, he added that the line of contact on the ground could not be considered as the military demarcation line because "no stable battle lines exist before an armistice is agreed upon and implemented."

In reply Admiral Joy noted the logic of Nam Il's statement that the war began on the 38th Parallel. "This fact by itself constitutes no basis whatever for the contention that this line should be selected as the military demarcation line under current conditions." He opined that had an armistice been concluded a year previously, when the United Nations Command forces had withdrawn to the Naktong River where the military situation stabilized, "it is difficult to believe that you would have agreed to a military demarcation line along the 38th Parallel." He concluded that a military demarcation line, or line to limit the advance of opposing forces during an armistice, bears no relation to past history.

The 38th Parallel had been established in 1945 purely for purposes of demilitarizing the Japanese forces—Russia to the north and the United States to the south. The 38th Parallel was never intended as a political subdivision of Korea. However, it did in effect become one when the Russians refused to permit the United Nations to hold free elections in their zone as a means of establishing a government, but instead set up a government of their own with its capital at Pyongyang.

The UNC was aware of the Communist demand and recognized that for bargaining purposes, to attain a line which would be defendable for both parties, it would necessarily have to propose a line exceeding its requirements. The UNC further realized that an armistice was only a temporary suspension of hostilities pending a political settlement, and that it must secure a demarcation line that could be defended. It knew all too well that consummation of an armistice was no guarantee of attaining a political settlement.

The United Nations Command could not condone acceptance of the 38th Parallel, for it would compel the UNC to give up its defensible positions on the east, to occupy indefensible positions on the west, and to double the length of its lines. In simpler terms, the total effect would upset the balance of power in favor of the Communists. The very fact that the belligerents had crossed the 38th Parallel four times was good indication of the indefensibility of the line.

The UNC suggested that the demarcation line should represent "certain military realities." It recommended a line that was commensurate with comparative military capabilities. It pointed out that the UNC maintained air superiority over all of Korea, controlled the entire sea area around Korea, and controlled on the ground everything south of a line running from just below the 38th Parallel on the west coast to a point considerably above the 38th on the east coast. On this basis the Supreme United Nations Commander, General Ridgway, believed that the line should be somewhere between the Yalu and Tumen rivers on the north and the line of contact on the ground. Admiral Joy contended:

Considering only ground forces, a cease-fire arrangement with all forces remaining in place would appear reasonable. This, however, would stop only a part of the hostile action. Our Navy would still be free to blockade and bombard along both coasts of North Korea. Our Air Force would still be able to reconnoiter and inflict military damage over all of North Korea. If, then, we are to agree on a military armistice whereby our ground, air, and naval forces cease operations against your forces, we contend that the location of the demilitarized zone, in all fairness, must be appropriately influenced by all of these factors.

Then Admiral Joy formally proposed:

1. Cessation of all ground action, and the establishment of a demilitarized zone from which all military forces would be withdrawn.

2. Cessation of our air effort in the area extending southward from the Yalu and Tumen Rivers to the southern boundary of the demilitarized ground zone to be agreed upon.

3. Cessation of our naval bombardment and blockade along the coasts of Korea from the mouth of the Yalu on the west coast and the mouth of the Tumen River on the east coast, southward to the southern boundary of the demilitarized ground zone to be agreed upon.

Communist employment of invective and vilification is clearly illustrated by Nam Il's retort:

I heard with surprise your incredible statement and had a glance at that map of yours on which were three lines which anybody with red, blue, and black pencils could have drawn. One of the three lines was apparently advocated by you to be fixed as the military demarcation line. At the time I already felt that such lines drawn at random were not worthy of attention, and when I had heard the arguments you raised in support of these lines, I was even more convinced that they were not worthy of attention, because your arguments were naive and illogical. . . .

Has it occurred to you that according to your logic, should our army, acknowledged as mighty and superior by the whole world, stop fighting so that your troops will escape the fate of annihilation, are we not entitled to an even greater compensation and to propose a demarcation line and demilitarized zone to the neighborhood of the Naktong River?

Nam Il alluded to "any military manual worthy of its name" in stating that "your battle lines on the ground are the concentrated expression of the military effectiveness of your land, air, and sea forces." He added that "such logic of yours can only deceive those who are neurotic or muddle-headed." However, in typical jargon, he asserted, "Our proposal is also one which is recognized by the whole world and one which is just, reasonable, realistic, and practicable."

What are the characteristics of the battlefront at the present stage? Since this year, the situation of the battlefront has been changing all the time. In January, the troops of our side advanced to the . . . south of the 38th Parallel, and since then, the battle line of contact between both sides has been shifting south and north of the 38th Parallel all the time. . . .

What is more worthy of notice—during the last seven months our troops stayed nearly five months south of the 38th Parallel and the period during which your troops twice stayed north of the 38th Parallel amounted to a little more than two months. The positions held by you at present are only less than two months old. How then can it be called stable? When our troops advanced south of the 38th Parallel the first time this year and reached the Han river area, they stayed there three and one-half months. That is nearly double the length of time your troops have stayed at the present positions.

Seeing that you made such a completely absurd and arrogant statement, for what actually have you come here? Have you come here to negotiate for peace, or just to look for an excuse for extending the war?

Admiral Joy replied:

In your discourtesy, you have resorted to bluster directed at this delegation. All here are presumed to be military men. Those peoples whose military organizations are respected throughout the world are proud of the reputation for courtesy and for objective mental attitudes toward serious questions unfailingly demonstrated by the personnel of their armed services. Military men are expected to be sufficiently mature to realize that bluster and bombast phrased in intemperate language do not and cannot affect the facts of any military situation. No amount of such vituperation as was indulged in by you this morning . . . will sway the concentration of the UNC delegation on the serious problems before this conference. No amount of discourtesy will tempt the UNC delegation to utilize similar tactics.

To this Nam Il replied:

The courtesy of the army men which you are talking about must start from your side, and it does not apply to us. We expect that you have more earnestness and fair attitude and statement for a smooth procedure of proceedings of the armistice talks. . . .

Your answer to my question that I had no good faith to the armistice conference—that is not appropriate. I clearly explained time and again and especially yesterday, that you have no good faith to the armistice conference. I explained it time and again and especially yesterday that you have no good faith to the armistice conference. Time and again I have explained in detail that you have not good faith to the armistice conference. I am not going to repeat it again. . . .

Finally, he declared:

In your statement . . . you stated that I stated that in your statement you tried to intimidate us. I never made any such statement and your statement can never intimidate us. I only said that your statement could intimidate a neurotic person.

Admiral Joy added force to his argument that naval and air strength must be considered in addition to ground forces. He observed that in the war against the Japanese it was largely the Navy and Air Force that determined its success. To this Nam Il replied:

You said that in the last war Japan was defeated as a result of blows inflicted by your naval and air forces. You have forgotten that it was the Korean people's liberation struggle and as a result of the Chinese people's war of eight years, war and resistance by the Soviet Union, in addition to the operations of the other wartime allies, which defeated the forces of Japanese imperialism and that the decisive role was played by operations conducted mainly by the ground forces of China and the Soviet Union. Your naval and

air forces fought Japan for nearly three years without being able
to defeat them. It was only participation by the Soviet Army that
a crushing blow was dealt that Japan was finally defeated. Can
these historical facts be negated lightly? Your own action to refute
your own theory.

Completely and apparently intentionally misinterpreting
Admiral Joy's statement, Nam Il noted:

You put forth the talk that a cease-fire on the ground without
cease-fire in the air and on the sea would appear reasonable, and
today you have virtually repeated it again. Thus there can be no
other explanation than that you are preparing an excuse for extending the war and one cannot but question your sincerity for peace.

To this Admiral Joy protested:

Let this be quite clear. The United Nations' delegation has not, does
not, and will not propose a cease-fire on the ground without a
cease-fire on the sea and in the air.

In rebutting the UNC position that UNC naval and air
strength was uncontended in Korea, Nam Il replied:

You mentioned . . . the effect of your naval and air forces in ground
operations. We have pointed out that your naval and air forces have
no other might than that of wanton bombing and bombardment,
killing peaceful civilians and destroying peaceful towns and villages.
This is clearly demonstrated by facts. If you are so powerful as
you claim, why did you retreat all the way to the south of the Han
River? Even during our negotiations we still hear continuously the
frantic roaring of your guns, but such bombardment has no other
effect than killing peaceful civilians and destroying peaceful
villages. . . .

If you have the desire and good faith to stop the war in Korea,
you should refrain from repeating such fallacious statements as
you have presented, and consider seriously and accept our correct
proposal.

Admiral Joy clarified the UNC stand by stating:

Our position on the principles that must be considered in establishing
a demilitarized zone have been clearly and logically stated. Briefly
these principles are:

1. The zone must be located geographically in relation to the existing over-all military situation.

2. The zone must be outlined by easily recognized terrain features.

3. Suitable defensive positions must be available on both sides and in close proximity to the zone.

The advantages you gain in case of a cease-fire are not those that necessarily reflect in the current situation. They are simply the military advantages which incur to you as a result of an armistice and which are in turn distinct losses to the UN forces.

Your superiority is in numbers of ground forces. Our superiority is in the air and at sea.

The benefit that your ground forces gain in cease-fire is represented primarily in the logistic fields. You can repair at liberty the damage to your transportation and if through some unfortunate incident the war should be resumed it would take many weeks for our air and naval forces to again place you in a logistic situation such as presently faces your commanders and staff.

You will be able to repair, unmolested, your railroads, your roads, and your bridges. You will be free to utilize these for the transportation of supplies essential to the health and well being of your troops. Your power lines, industries, ports, and shipping would operate again. The loss of expensive and valuable equipment will be ended. An armistice would bring about from its inception an end to the destruction of your facilities and create opportunities for restoration and rehabilitation. By virtue of these factors you would be in a greatly improved position militarily should unfortunate events lead to a resumption of hostilities. No corresponding improvement could accrue to us since our communications and facilities are not now subject to attack.

Admiral Joy concluded:

The line and zone you have proposed fulfills none of the requirements we believe essential. Its only significance is a political one dating back to 1945 but violated in 1950. If it is discussed again at any time in the future it should not be by military commanders . . . but by heads of state. Furthermore, there are no reasonably sound defensible positions near the 38th Parallel and there is no reason why there should be due to the nature of the line. . . . The UNC is in a defensible position at present. It does not intend to jeopardize the security of its forces by relinquishing such a position. . . . It would be practically impossible to draw any degree of latitude across Korea which would even generally coincide with a defensible ground position.

Nam Il retorted, "We cannot accept the line you propose as the demarcation line at all. . . . Our stand is absolutely immovable."

On 30 July 1951 Nam Il contended:

As to the continuation of the hostilities during the negotiations, you say that I held that the hostilities should cease during the negotiations. That is an absolutely incorrect statement. I thought that the hostilities would continue during the negotiations and I will think so. Until the signing of the agreement on the armistice, the hostilities will continue on both sides.

This statement refuted Nam Il's statement of 11 July in which he said, "Without ceasing hostilities in Korea and without carrying out cease-fire in Korea we cannot discuss the armistice."

The Communist delegation on all occasions exhibited particular sensitiveness to any reference to aggressions against the 38th Parallel on 25 June 1950. At one point in the discussions General Nam Il queried:

In your statement as a reason for your opposition against our stand—our fair and reasonable stand that the 38th Parallel should be made the military demarcation line, you said that we said we want to go back to the 38th Parallel where the aggressive war was broken out. What is meant by the "aggressive war" which you say, and whom do you mean is the aggressor? Whom do you mean? Who has provoked the aggressive war?

However, the UNC delegation at all times generalized "aggressor" so as to avoid further irrelevant discussions which the Communists continually injected into the meetings.

After many grueling sessions which resulted in no progress, the Communists reasoned:

You are still insisting on your proposal. For this we can only conclude that what you are seeking by your proposal is not the military objective of cessation of hostilities on the basis of the present battle

line and military realities, but some other ulterior objective. It is
well known that the original purpose of your waging the war is to
conquer the Democratic People's Republic of Korea. On this the
United Nations, under the domination of the United States of
America, in fact passed a resolution on 7 November last year
[1950], but your improper attempt has failed.

Completely ignoring realities, Nam Il continued:

On 27 June 1950 a large number of foreign armed forces came to
Korea attempting to accomplish the objective of dominating Korea
and menacing China through direct intervention of armed forces.
The fighting in Korea became thereby a war against foreign aggression. But the courageous resistance of the Korean people and the
Chinese people has shattered long ago your objective of dominating
the whole of Korea.

Nam Il attempted to detract attention from Communist
objectives by accusing the United Nations Command of "an
attempt to achieve under the cover of your absurd so-called
military logic, military theory, and military realities, the political
objective which you could not gain by armed force."
Ten fruitless sessions on Agenda Item Two caused Admiral
Joy to conjecture: "How do you propose this deadlock be
broken?" [1]

We continue to make no progress. So far you have failed to offer
any proposal for the location of a demilitarized zone based solely
on current military realities. We are left no recourse but to believe
that your objective is only a face-saving one. You wish only to
return to the condition of 25 June 1950.

[1] On 10 August, following a five-day recess, the conference underwent a
new experience—a prolonged period of silence. The United Nations Senior
Delegate opened the meeting with a lengthy statement supporting United
Nations contentions in connection with Item Two. After the statement was
concluded the Communist Senior Delegate, in complete disagreement, remained silent. For two hours and eleven minutes neither side spoke a word.
During the hiatus Major General Lee Sang Cho passed a note to his chief,
General Nam Il, written in bold Korean characters. The message, conspicu-
ously visible to the United Nations delegation, read: "The Imperialist errand
boys are lower than dogs in a morgue."
At length Admiral Joy suggested, as a means of ending the stalemate, that
the conversations leave Item Two temporarily and move to Item Three. This
suggestion was curtly declined by the Communists. However, it did end the
silence.

We have proposed to you the general location of a reasonable demilitarized zone. It has been arrived at after long and careful study. It is in the general area of the battle line. It is based on a fair assessment of the current over-all military situation.

Your attitude is inflexible and unreasonable. We have offered to discuss adjustments to this demilitarized zone. We continue to remain flexible to reasonable, logical, and pertinent discussion within the military field but on no other grounds.

We are always willing to discuss a demarcation line and a demilitarized zone based on the battle line and current military realities. For the second time I trust this is clear. We will not discuss further the 38th Parallel as a military demarcation line. It appears that we are temporarily deadlocked on Item Two.

Nam Il proposed that "the solution of the deadlock . . . is to have the 38th Parallel as the military demarcation line. . . . I shall continue to state our views in connection with this fair, reasonable, and just proposal of ours."

Finally, after five more abortive conferences, Admiral Joy on 15 August observed that "we show no prospect of progress along present lines of procedure." He therefore recommended a new effort to break this deadlock.

One of our prime difficulties is the formality of each delegation regarding the points at issue. This is necessary in order to preserve order in these meetings involving ten delegates and their various assistants. Nevertheless, our present manner of exchanging views is tedious and somewhat stilted.

We suggest that each delegation appoint one delegate to membership in a joint subcommittee of the delegations. We suggest that these two delegates meet informally, to exchange views on Item Two of our agenda. We suggest that the two delegations jointly charge this subcommittee to make recommendations to the two delegations as to ways and means of emerging from the present deadlock.

We suggest two assistants, including interpreters, be appointed for each side.

It is our thought that neither delegation be bound by implication or contract to honor the recommendations of the joint subcommittee. Such recommendations would of course require ratification by the delegations. It is our thought that this subcommittee meet around, rather than across the table, and seek objectively to work out a solution to our present problem.

On the following day Nam Il replied in a fashion typical of Communist procedure. He spent sixty minutes denouncing in the strongest possible language the UNC stand and praising in contrast the Communist position while Major General Lee Sang Cho, sitting to his left, prompted the English interpreter to use more emphasis in his translations. At length, after forcing his opponent to endure his verbosity, he concluded: "I agree . . . to your proposal of forming a subcommittee to discuss the second item on the agenda." He did propose several minor amendments—that the subcommittee be composed of two delegates and two assistants, the number of assistants being subject to change upon mutual agreement, and that the plenary session should recess during the subcommittee meetings. The UNC accepted these amendments.

On 17 August 1951 the first session of the Sub-Committee on Agenda Item Two met. After six meetings the sessions were abruptly terminated by the Communists on the premeditated charges that the UNC had bombed the Kaesong neutral zone. However, at the last meeting, 22 August, some progress was made. Both sides accepted the principle that their demands were "adjustable." This led Major General Lee Sang Cho to conclude the meeting with the declaration, "I think we have reached a point where both sides have come much nearer."

When the subdelegation commenced talks, Admiral Joy returned to Tokyo to confer with General Ridgway. En route he stopped in Seoul to confer with Eighth Army General James Van Fleet. The latter informed Admiral Joy he would favor a demarcation along the line of contact, with slight withdrawal by each side to create a buffer zone. Van Fleet also suggested the proposal be timed with the limited offensive planned for September, designed to straighten the line of contact. In Tokyo Admiral Joy recommended to General Ridgway presentation of a final proposal to the Communists in line with the ideas discussed in Seoul. However, Ridgway, eyeing the forthcoming Japanese Peace Conference in San Francisco, deferred. Action was therefore left to the Communists.

The inequities of the conference site were accented at the

outset of the negotiations by the many well-armed Communist soldiers patrolling the area, ostensibly for the "protection" of UNC personnel.[2] This fact was even more significant inasmuch as UNC personnel were entirely unarmed. It had become obvious that the unneutralness of Kaesong would have a marked effect upon the procedure and progress of the negotiations. On 4 August, during the lunch recess, a company of heavily armed Chinese Communist soldiers passed within a few hundred yards of the staff house used by the UNC. The UNC delegation made immediate representations over this "violation of the Kaesong neutral zone." General Ridgway subsequently canceled the talks until "explanation of this violation and assurances of nonrecurrence are received."

Meanwhile the Communists commenced presentation of their tedious series of complaints to the United Nations Command—allegations which in all but three instances proved to concern either absolute fabrications or the work of irregular groups with absolutely no overt or covert connection with the UNC. This latter possibility was exposed when on one occasion the North Korean Liaison Officer revealed to the UNC Liaison Officer that personnel within the neutral zone had distributed handbills opposing the armistice conferences, and might even be laying mines in roads within the neutral zone. He further admitted that his delegation personnel wished to keep personal arms with them at their residence within the neutral zone for their own protection. This clearly indicated the cause for concern that partisan activities presented within the neutral zone. Before the resumption of meetings on 25 October 1951 the Communists alleged thirteen major violations had been committed by the UNC, in addition to many more minor ones. In each case the UNC faithfully fulfilled its duties by making a careful investigation of the charges. Such allegations as these impeded immeasurably the progress of the conferences and did much to confirm UNC suspicions as to the Communists' real intentions.

---

[2] As Major General Lee Sang Cho explained it: "The . . . military police are especially for your safety. They are severely guarding against those who wish to break the conference or attack you. They have been carrying their duties since the start of the conference."

During the two years of negotiations, scarcely a day passed without some charge being lodged by the Communists. These were without doubt designed to reveal UNC infidelity and thus give the impression, in contrast, of Communist righteousness and eagerness to accomplish an armistice "desired by the peoples of the whole world." The Communists rarely admitted an error, and eagerly accepted UNC confirmation of errors as support of all their other contentions.

The charges of 4 August in which the United Nations Command protested the company of armed Chinese soldiers parading past its headquarters in the Kaesong neutral zone were accepted by the Communists as an infraction of the 14 July agreement. This acceptance was obviously a result of the variety of photographs which were taken of the event by the newsmen at the scene.

On 9 August General Nam Il protested UNC strafing of "a supply truck of our delegation, with white cloth over its hood and carrying a white flag in conformity with agreement . . . in the preparatory meeting of the liaison officers of both sides on July 8 . . . while on its way from Kaesong to Pyongyang . . ."

Admiral Joy immediately replied, noting that the 8 July agreement provided that the Communists would first communicate such movements to the United Nations Commander-in-Chief. This information was not furnished the UNC. As a result, "Your complaint is completely without validity." It had been substantiated that on numerous occasions the Communists took advantage of this agreement to move war supplies to the front down the highway from Pyongyang, disguising their vehicles with these markings that would make them immune from attack. Because of this, the UNC had to be especially alert to such trickery.

Admiral Joy quoted from the information sheet handed the Communists on 8 July:

A Communist convoy marked with white crosses will not be attacked by United Nations forces to and from Kaesong, at such time and over such routes as is communicated to Commander-in-Chief, United Nations.

The Communists sought to ignore knowledge of any agreement on 8 July. However, on 9 July they did furnish the UNC notification of the time and route of transit of their convoy proceeding to Kaesong, which indicated their understanding of the requirements for notification. Again on 21 July the UNC informed the Communists that prior notification of the time and route of travel of their vehicles between Pyongyang and Kaesong was a necessary prerequisite to exemption from attack. Again the Communists indicated an understanding. Admiral Joy could only question the sincerity of the Communists.

I note that the location of the attack you allege is considerably east of the main road between Pyongyang and Kaesong. This fact raises the question in mind whether your forces are abusing the use of white markings for the purpose other than serving your delegation.

Joy concluded that "your complaint is completely without validity."

The Communists continued these bombardments of complaints against aerial attacks against their "clearly marked" vehicles moving between Kaesong and Pyongyang until the conference site was transferred to Panmunjom.

For its part, the UNC could not grant blanket clearance to all vehicular traffic that was distinctly marked moving along the main supply route leading to the enemy front. There would have been no assurance that the use of markings would not be abused.

Despite all UNC efforts, the Communists persisted in ignoring the necessity to submit prior notification of movement of its delegation vehicles, choosing instead to issue complaints to the UNC and to the world press and demanding that the violators be punished.

The Communist accusation of 19 August, proved groundless by the UNC, was unique. They charged that "thirty plus" UNC personnel entered the Kaesong conference site and killed one of their platoon leaders. In rendering the charge, Major General Lee Sang Cho stated:

[Yao] is the first victim of the efforts for peace, the first to die by faithfully living up to the peaceful agreement. The people of Kaesong are spontaneously holding a memorial service at 1100 this morning. The organizers of this meeting have asked to let you come. I think comrade Yao was a real partisan for peace, who died for peace, who lived up to the agreement. No one could refuse to show honor to and sorrow for him. I hope you will go to the service with us.

It was somewhat difficult for the UNC members of the Sub-Committee on Item Two to decline the invitation. It would have been even more awkward had they accepted.

After continual barrages of complaints against the United Nation Command the Communists on the night of 22-23 August staged their most insidious charge. It exemplifies well the method and technique of Communist treachery and perfidy.

At 2330, 22 August 1951, a radiotelephone message was received at UNC Base Camp at Munsan from the Communists asserting that at 2320 the armistice conference site at Kaesong had been bombed and strafed by a UNC aircraft. They demanded immediate investigation.

Colonels Kinney and Murray, UNC liaison officers, and two interpreters, upon instructions from Admiral Joy, set out in jeeps at approximately 0030, 23 August, for Kaesong. Since the Imjin River bridge was out, it was necessary to cross the river by boat. Due to the low tide the party was forced to disembark approximately fifty yards from shore and wade the remainder of the distance. Other jeeps were obtained on the north bank of the Imjin, and the party proceeded without incident to the conference house in Kaesong. They arrived at 0145.

Colonels Chang and Tsai, North Korean and Chinese liaison officers, and the Communist press corps of reporters and photographers, were waiting on the porch of the conference house when the UNC group arrived.

Chang: At 2320 your aircraft bombed our area here. Right after, we heard the sound of bombing. The witnesses include our Senior Delegate himself. Everyone living here saw it.

Kinney: Please tell us your story. Who saw this alleged bombing?

Chang: Everyone in this vicinity heard the aircraft. They heard the sound of the aircraft circling very low. The bomb was dropped within the boundary of the conference site.

Kinney: The bomb? Is that singular or plural?

Chang: Well, at present I do not know as to how many there were. As to our men who made the investigation, you can ask them later.

Kinney: Colonel Chang and Colonel Tsai heard it?

Chang: Not only two of us but all of us who live in this vicinity. Then your aircraft made another circling and dropped "napalm" on the way to the United Nations' house. We'll find out when we go look.

Kinney: Was "aircraft" singular or plural?

Chang: As we were not notified prior to the attack we did not know how many. In other words, if we were notified in advance we would have watched. But inasmuch as we were surprised, we didn't know.

Kinney: Is there anyone here who could hear how many planes there were?

Chang: We believe that we can find how many when we go to make the investigation. [Showing pieces of broken metal]. This was found on our car serving our delegation.

Kinney: What is the evidence of bombing?

Chang: You will find out later.

The entire group then proceeded to the road leading to the UNC delegation house. On this road, approximately one hundred yards from the UNC house, was a rumpled piece of metal resembling, and about the size of, an aircraft oil tank. There was no crater under this piece of metal and no scorched earth. About ten feet away was a small depression perhaps thirty inches in diameter and ten inches deep at the center. A hole of this type might be made by a partially buried explosive of a force equivalent to a grenade. There was no evidence of burning to be seen. Nonetheless Colonel Chang declared these two items proved a napalm bomb was dropped.

The group then proceeded to a site northwest of the residence of the Communist delegates, where four holes similar to that seen at the first site but of lesser size, and pieces of duraluminum metal averaging six inches by ten inches, were pointed out. Several of these pieces of metal contained flush riveting. They appeared to be pieces of an aircraft fuselage or engine nacelle. Near one of the holes there was a tail fin of a rocket, although there was no physical evidence of a rocket impact. No damage to any structure, person, or crop was claimed by the Communists nor observed by the UNC investigators. There were no bomb craters to be seen, no scorched earth, no rocket furrows, and no pieces of metal remotely resembling a bomb casing.

Kinney: I'm getting very impatient with this nonsense.

Chang: This is what we found here tonight.

Kinney: Anyone here who has seen a bomb dropped?

Chang: We can ask the witnesses later.

Kinney: I've seen all I want to see. That object is not a bomb and has no connection whatsoever with a bomb. As anyone who has seen a bomb will know. I've seen nothing here indicating a bombing. However, we are here to investigate. So please say what you have to say.

Chang: If you're a military man and a man of conscience, you can't deny what you saw. I point out the grave implications tonight. According to my Senior Delegate's instructions I make a most serious protest verbally for the time being. I notify hereby that we will call off the meeting which is scheduled for tomorrow, and I reserve the right to make a further protest to you. We're instructed by our Senior Delegate to tell you that . . .

Kinney: Do you mean the Sub-Delegation meeting or the liaison officers' meeting is canceled?

Chang : All meetings from this time.

The UNC liaison team then departed Kaesong for Munsan. When the group was about halfway to Panmunjom, it was overtaken by the Chinese liaison officers in a jeep. Colonel Tsai urged

Colonel Kinney to return to Kaesong to "complete the joint investigation" of this incident. Colonel Chang arrived shortly.

> Communists: You should return and complete this joint investigation, get all the facts, and reach the obviously clear solution.
>
> UNC: We have seen enough of this ridiculous "evidence" and see no reason to return now, in the dark and rain. We will return when it is light and everything is clearly visible. Meanwhile there is no reason to return to view such trivia. If you had something worth seeing . . .
>
> Communists: We have a very significant piece of evidence which you must come and see. It is your responsibility to examine all evidence, and you are in the wrong to avoid your responsibility in this manner.
>
> UNC: You yourself terminated the investigation when you arrived at your own conclusion and announced that the meetings were suspended.

With Colonel Chang's assurance that the new evidence was of great significance, with the understanding that it was to be an investigation and not a press show, and with the agreement that all press personnel would be barred, the UNC group returned to Kaesong, where they were led to a sandstone ridge. Here two more holes were seen, about two feet in diameter and one foot deep. These holes, according to the report, "might have been formed by the impact of a falling object of small size." Near both holes were pieces of aircraft metal showing flush riveting. At the first hole there was a mild odor of gasoline, and adjacent to the hole, about four superficially burned areas three to five inches in diameter. In the vicinity of the second hole there was about seventy square inches of a substance which might have been a poor mixture of napalm. This had not been ignited. In the course of this investigation a Chinese Communist soldier gave a supposed eyewitness account. He stated immediately and without hesitation that the attack came at 2320—the exact minute previously given by Chang. He stated further: "Plane was seen at 2320 to circle around with two bright lights shining ahead [gesturing indicated beams of landing lights]. It dropped several bombs in this area." Colonel Kinney inquired: "Were lights on before or after bombing?" Soldier answered: "All the time." At this point a European Communist newsman intervened, accusing Kinney of "distortion" and "tricking a simple soldier." Colonel Kinney told him he was quite out of order and to keep out of the investigation. He remonstrated. Colonel Kinney stopped, called Colonel Chang, and stated that the understanding was that no newsmen were to be present. Therefore, until the situation was made equal by removal of Communist press or else the arrival of UN press, he would suspend the investigation. After some argument the newsmen were ordered to leave, and the investigation continued.

Colonel Kinney requested Colonel Chang to agree to continue the investigation in the morning, so as to permit daylight examination of the evidence. Colonel Chang stated that so far as he was concerned the investigation was completed. This was at 0430. Colonel Chang demanded Colonel Kinney accept full responsibility for the bombing. Kinney refused. Colonel Chang replied: "The evidence is clear. There is only one possible conclusion." Colonel Kinney asked that all evidence be allowed to remain untouched so that it might be viewed in daylight. Colonel Chang stated all evidence would be collected "for analysis." Colonel Chang stated the evidence was clear and no further investigation was necessary. Colonel Kinney vehemently disagreed. The investigation ended in a deadlock. Meanwhile all meetings of all agencies of the delegations were summarily canceled by the Communists.

Subsequently the matter was referred to the Fifth Air Force to determine the possibility of a UNC airplane's presence in the area. Investigation proved that none had been, but that the Fifth Air Force's radar screen had picked up an unidentified aircraft proceeding from the west directly toward Kaesong. This aircraft was approximately two minutes from Kaesong at 2318 on 22 August, at which time it faded from the radar screen. The Air Force reasoned that the fade probably was due to the aircraft's descending behind the hill masses between Kimpo airfield near Seoul and Kaesong below radar coverage.

The UNC liaison team concluded:

The incident was 100 per cent staged by the Communists; such staging including use of one of their own aircraft, which burned landing lights to attract attention. It is probable that only a small number of the Communists at Kaesong, including the delegates, liaison officers, and a few other selected personnel, knew beforehand of the fraudulent nature of the incident.

The following day Kim Il Sung and Peng Teh-huai addressed a protest to Matthew Ridgway:

Before the blood of our brave fighter, Platoon Commander Yao Ching-hsiang sacrificed under the unlawful murder of your armed personnel could dry, aircraft of your side further unlawfully intruded into the air above the conference site area in the Kaesong neutral zone . . .

It should be clear to you that all the dealings between our side and your side so far are based on the principle of equality and reciprocity. If your side does not show with deeds that you respect this principle, but on the contrary brazenly assumes the air of a victor and wantonly violates all the agreements based on the principle, including the Kaesong neutral zone agreement, the responsibility resulting therefrom and all the consequences rest entirely with your side. . . .

The Communists, in an effort to raise doubts in the world's minds as to the UNC's denials, added:

With regard to this provocative incident of bombing the Kaesong neutral zone by your armed forces . . . with the intention of murdering our delegation, we hereby raise a strong protest before all the just people of the world, and await a satisfactory reply from your side.

The following day General Ridgway replied:

This most recent addition to alleged incidents by elements of the United Nations Command, so utterly false, so preposterous, and so obviously manufactured for your own questionable purposes, does not, in its own right, merit a reply. Nor do the other incidents you have cited as intentional violations by the United Nations Command of the neutral zone at Kaesong. When not fabricated by you for your own propaganda needs, these incidents have proven to be the actions of irregular groups without the slightest connection overtly or covertly with any forces or agencies under my control.

General Ridgway concluded his letter by declaring:

. . . when you are prepared to terminate the suspension of armistice negotiations . . . I will direct my representatives to meet with yours with a view to seeking a reasonable armistice agreement.

The Communists then shifted the blame for terminating the negotiations to the UNC and denied having made any statement that the meetings were off.

"As far as our side is concerned, we did not . . . . reject your making a reinvestigation. . . . And we are still waiting for your side to do so."

To ensure the widest dissemination of this fantastic fabrication, the Communists challenged General Ridgway to release "in full" the texts of all communications "in order to enable people throughout the world to understand the full and true picture of the incident."

It was this incident which finally convinced General Ridgway that further meetings at Kaesong should not be held. Meeting under such adverse conditions had contributed little to the mission of obtaining an armistice. A more neutral area must be found.

Various reasons were suggested as to why the Communists selected that time to call off the meetings. One theory held that inasmuch as the Communists had been unsuccessful at the conference table in compelling the United Nations Command to accept its proposals regarding the 38th Parallel as the demarcation line, it would force the UNC on the field of battle. Another theory explained that the Communists had been disappointed at not having Red China invited to the Japanese Peace Conference in San Francisco. Admiral Joy maintained that the Communists believed that, given time, the UNC would eventually capitulate to their demands for the 38th Parallel. When he suggested the subdelegation proposal, the Communists greedily accepted on the assumption the UNC was ready to give in. However, their assumptions were soon thwarted, and they needed time to determine their next move. Recalling the 4 August incident in which a company of Chinese Communist soldiers marched through the neutral zone, and the subsequent five-day recess, they decided to stage the 22 August incident to stall for time. Had the United Nations Command accepted responsibility for the incident, the Communists would have had no excuse for delaying the talks. They knew the UNC would not. The many incidents that followed this one and the admission of error by the UNC on three occasions —which the Communists played up as UNC admission for all incidents—presented the Communists with further excuses for stalling and for discrediting the UNC.

The United Nations Command had learned its lesson during the meetings at Kaesong. It learned that the basic premises of the delegations for wanting a conference differed. To the Communists, negotiation is a technique in their broad strategy. What they cannot accomplish by one method, they attempt by another. Having been unsuccessful in attaining their objectives on the Korean field of battle, they turned to the conference table as a means of achieving their ends. Their use of the conference table was obvious indeed: to gain precious time while they rebuilt and strengthened their forces, to obtain every possible benefit from the UNC, and to serve as a sounding board for their propaganda. This they attempted to achieve by haggling over the agenda, demanding the UNC withdraw to the 38th Parallel, manufacturing incidents and pointing to the UNC as instigator, maliciously injecting propaganda into the substance of the meetings in order to create a false impression of UNC perfidy, presenting irrelevant issues for stalling purposes, and frequently acting in a very discourteous and arrogant manner.

From the beginning of the conferences, the Communists had repeatedly violated the letter and the spirit of the agreements concerning the neutrality of the conference area. They took advantage of the fact that the city of Kaesong was within their lines to place the UNC delegation in an undignified and degrading position, and they portrayed the UNC to the Communist press as representing a defeated command. They attempted to dictate the composition of the UNC delegation party by not permitting newsmen, even though theirs were on hand. They blocked the

passage from the UNC lines to Kaesong. They halted the movement of UNC couriers, and they introduced a body of armed
troops within the demilitarized conference site. When the United
Nations Command protested incidents, the Communists would
retaliate by charging the UNC delegation with a series of alleged
violations of armistice conference agreements. Upon investigation,
these charges invariably proved to be completely unjustified.
Finally, after definitely terminating all meetings following the 22
August incident, they denied having made such a statement.

Dealing with the Communists once again exposed their use
of negotiation to conceal rather than to reveal their true intentions. And just as their spoken words are often contrary to their
real thoughts, their dealings with other countries are characterized
by deceit.

"Sincere diplomacy," Stalin once said, "is no more possible than dry water or iron wood."

4

DEMARCATION LINE

*How laudable it is for a prince to keep good
faith and live with integrity, and not with astuteness, everyone knows. Still the experience of our
time shows those princes to have done great
things who have had little regard for good faith,
and have been able by astuteness to confuse
men's brains and have ultimately overcome those
who have made loyalty their foundation. . . .
Therefore a prudent ruler ought not to keep faith
when by so doing it would be against his interest,
and when the reasons which made him bind himself no longer exist. If men were all good, this
precept would not be a good one; but as they are
bad, and would not observe faith with you, so
you are not bound to keep faith with them.*

MACHIAVELLI, The Prince

*But let your communications be, Yea, yea; Nay,
nay; for whatsoever is more than these cometh
of evil.*   MATTHEW 5:37

For sixty-three days, from 23 August through 24
October, no armistice discussions were held. When the Communists manufactured the 22 August incident, they had not

69

anticipated that the delay would be as prolonged as it was. However, by this time the United Nations Command had become convinced of the impracticality of meeting at Kaesong. The Communists had not dreamed that the meeting place might be changed and were surprised when General Ridgway made such a recommendation. This they sought uneasily to ignore.

The disadvantages of Kaesong had become apparent from the outset of the negotiations. This ancient Korean capital was twenty miles within the Communist lines, yet three miles below the 38th Parallel. This gave the Communists a decided propaganda advantage, for it meant that the UNC would be going to them to negotiate. The existence of the meeting site below the 38th Parallel created the impression that the Communists had made this gain during the war, and added emphasis to the Communists' demands that the 38th Parallel be the military demarcation line.

Meeting at Kaesong, which stood in the route of advancing UNC forces, discouraged and impeded further UNC advances. It is the western area of the Korean peninsula which has the best terrain for military efforts. Eastern Korea is very mountainous. Kaesong is neatly located in this strategic western sector. Had the meetings been held on board the *Jutlandia*, as Ridgway proposed, instead of at Kaesong, the UNC could have pushed forward, thereby making the Communists more receptive to agreeing to an armistice sooner.

Following further Communist allegations of UNC unfaithfulness, General Ridgway on 6 September addressed a communication to Kim Il Sung and Peng Teh-huai in which he suggested the possibility of a new site for the meetings. In this he was supported by General Omar Bradley, Chairman of the Joint Chiefs of Staff, who was visiting Japan and Korea at this time.

I have repeatedly emphasized that my principal concern is to achieve a just and honorable military armistice. Events of the past weeks have made it plainly evident to me and to the world at large that further use of the present conference site at Kaesong will inevitably result in additional interruptions of our armistice talks and further delays in reaching agreement. When you decide to terminate the suspension of armistice negotiations which you declared on 23

August, I propose that our liaison officers meet immediately at the bridge at Pan Mun Jom to discuss the selection of a new site where negotiations can be continued without interruptions.

On 10 September the Communists reported an alleged strafing by a UNC aircraft in the Kaesong neutral zone. Investigation of this incident indicated the UNC had been in error. Admiral Joy, in a message to Nam Il, noted: "The United Nations Command regrets this violation of the agreed neutrality which resulted from the pilot's error in navigation." He offered assurances that "appropriate disciplinary action is being initiated."

In a blatantly conspicuous effort to lay blame for all incidents upon the United Nations Command, the Communists demanded that General Ridgway "promptly bring an end to the ceaseless violation of the agreement [Kaesong neutrality] by your side and take the responsibility to settle every provocative act that has been protested against by our side. The negotiation is possible to be continued on the basis of general equality." The Communists insinuated that if the UNC did not accept full responsibility for acts the UNC did not commit, and thus completely discredit itself, "the whole responsibility and consequences of delaying and hampering the progress of the negotiations will rest on your side."

The Communists at all times sought to lay the blame for delays on the shoulders of the UNC and cover up their own attempts to impede progress.

The United Nations Command positively declined to reconvene the talks at Kaesong while the Communists continued leveling their charges against the UNC.

On 24 September Colonel Chang Chun San, Senior North Korean Liaison Officer reported:

Our delegate wants again to point out with emphasis that Supreme Commander Kim Il Sung and Commander Peng Teh-huai have repeatedly pointed out, in their messages to General Ridgway, that the resumption of the Kaesong armistice talks is eagerly awaited by the peoples of the whole world, and that the Kaesong armistice talks should be resumed immediately without the need to discuss the conditions for resuming talks.

It was becoming obvious that the Communists had not antic-ipated moving the site, and their response to such a suggestion indicated a good deal of anxiety on their part. By moving to a really neutral area they would lose the advantage which Kaesong presented to them. They would have greater difficulty fabricating charges against the UNC.

On 25 September Colonel Chang stomped angrily out of the liaison officers' meeting when Colonel Kinney suggested he obtain broader authority for more fruitful discussions during the meetings. Indeed this reflected how cautious the Communists were in not committing themselves in any way without higher approval.

Because the Communist liaison officers had stated they were not authorized to discuss or arrange satisfactory conditions for resumption of the armistice talks, General Ridgway took the initiative on 27 September to recommend a new site to General Kim Il Sung and Peng Teh-huai:

I propose that both delegations meet as early as possible at a place approximately midway between the battle lines in the vicinity of Songhyon-ni. . . . If you concur, I will arrange to have our liaison officers meet to discuss immediate erection of the necessary physical facilities.

Again, as in their reply of 11 September to General Ridg-way's proposal for discussing a new site, the Communists "con-sider it entirely void of reason." And that "the unreasonable demand proposed by you, if it is not to create a threat, then it merely is to create new pretexts to continue to prolong the negotiations. Our sincere and responsible attitude toward the negotiations is known the world over." They again insisted that the delegations "immediately resume the conference at Kaesong." It was becoming obvious that the reason the Communists were reluctant to accept the UNC proposal was that it might expose their guilt regarding the manufactured incidents at Kaesong. As a result, General Ridgway sought to permit them an escape and still not concede on his demands to change the conference location. On 4 October he offered a new proposition:

Since you reject my suggestion to meet at Songhyon-ni, I propose that our delegations meet at a site selected by you and acceptable to me approximately midway between our respective front lines, where the armistice discussions can be promptly resumed.

Finally, on 7 October the break in the deadlock came. In a message to General Ridgway, Generals Kim Il Sung and Peng Teh-huai, after a lengthy review of their charges and reasons why the site should not be changed, offered the following proposition:

We propose that the scope of the neutrality of the conference site be moved to Panmunjom, and that both sides assume the responsibility of protecting the conference site. At the same time, we propose that the delegates of both sides resume the conference immediately at Panmunjom, and at the first meeting after the resumption of the conference make the regulations concerning expansion of the scope of the neutral zone and the principles concerning expansion of the neutral zone and the principles concerning the security of the conference site; that by establishing appropriate machinery in which both sides participate, concrete and strict regulations be discussed; and that by guaranteeing their enforcement the smooth progress of the armistice negotiations be assured. After you agree to our proposal our liaison officers will immediately meet your liaison officers to discuss matters concerning the resumption of the conference by both delegations.

Inasmuch as the Communists had thus conceded to UNC demands to change the site of the talks, it can be concluded that the military pressure being exerted against them at this time by the UNC forces had a telling effect. There is strong evidence to support the view that, had the meetings not been resumed at this time, UNC forces again could have forged their way to the vicinity of the Yalu and Tumen rivers within not too long a period. This concession by the Communists again illustrated Admiral Joy's contention that "in debating with the Communists there is no substitute for the imperative logic of military pressure." This experience did demonstrate the logic that military pressure applied at vulnerable points at suitable times has caused the enemy to alter his otherwise obstinate stand.

It is of interest that the proposal that the Communists submitted as their own was merely a repetition of Ridgway's recommendations.

In view of increasing United Nations military efforts at this time, enlarging the neutral area would have favored the Communists. To this Ridgway objected:

In regard to your proposed expansion of the neutral zone, it is my view that all that is now necessary is a small neutral zone around the new conference site, with Kaesong, Munsan, and the roads to Panmunjom from Kaesong and Munsan free from attack by both sides.

Meanwhile the Communists had continued to charge violations of the Kaesong neutral zone, and to blame the UNC for delaying resumption of the negotiations.

On 10 October the liaison officers of both sides met at Panmunjom to discuss the matter of resuming full-scale negotiations.

Although it had been agreed that the conference site was transferred from Kaesong to Panmunjom, the Communists continued to insist that the former five-mile neutral zone around Kaesong remained in effect, thus impeding progress of the liaison officers meetings. United Nations Command remained adamant in refusing to accept an enlargement of the neutral zone.

On 22 October, agreement was at length reached by the liaison officers, and the terms were formally signed by the Senior Liaison Officer of each side. The terms specified: 1) naming Panmunjom as the conference site; 2) confining the site to a circular area with a thousand yard radius; 3) decreeing no hostile acts of any kind against the conference site; 4) limiting armed military personnel in the conference area to two officers and fifteen men from each side during meetings, and one officer and five men at other times.[1] 5) permitting free access and movement within the conference site to both delegations; 6) providing for physical facilities; 7) defining the neutral areas as three miles around Kaesong and the UNC camp area near Munsan and two

[1] The Communists were unfaithful in abiding by this agreement. On various occasions high-ranking officers, masquerading as enlisted men or lieutenants, were stationed at the conference site. General Kim Pa, a former Soviet MVD agent, was present at various times at the armistice negotiations disguised as a sergeant or lieutenant.

hundred meters to either side of the Kaesong-Munsan road, and 8) leaving the date and time for resumption of the meetings to be determined by agreement between liaison officers.

On 23 October Nam Il suggested meetings be resumed on 25 October. The UNC immediately accepted. Thus ended the sixty-three-day hiatus.

The new site exhibited marked advantages over Kaesong. By reducing the size of the conference area, it was believed that new incidents, real or alleged, could be avoided. Also, the relocation of the site to a "no-man's land" would ensure equality of responsibility and free access to the zone. Furthermore, it was time to bring an end to the propaganda advantages to the Communists inherent in the Kaesong site, which had lent color to their repeated pretensions that they were "hosts" to the conference.

Panmunjom has become historic. But anyone who has visited this spot, which before the war was only a tiny village on the dirt road to Kaesong and Pyongyang, may wonder of its fame. On the side of the road, opposite two deserted huts, an area of approximately one acre was cleared and leveled. On this plot were placed tents for the meetings of the armistice delegations. The Communists had agreed to supply the conference tents and the UNC light and heat. North and south of the conference tents were the facilities for the respective delegations. The UNC offered further assurances against the instigation of incidents by placing four hydrogen-filled balloons equidistant around the periphery of the site. These were raised to one thousand feet.

The Communists exhibited conspicuous concern over everything being equal in this area over which they were not in sole control. They consistently strove to remain equal or superior in every detail. They seemed to fear appearing inferior in this spotlight of world attention. This was demonstrated in many ways on various occasions. The UNC had erected a small tent behind the UNC assembly tent as a latrine. The Communists watched the progress somewhat bewildered. After they learned what is was, they commenced building a structure of wood in every way superior to that of the UNC. They were satisfied.

During the cold of winter the United Nations Command

constructed wooden sentry posts to protect the guards against the chill Siberian winds, and painted them army olive drab. Several days later the Communists, not to be outdone, copied the UNC efforts, but instead of the drab UNC colors, painted theirs in diagonal red, white, and green stripes. When UNC personnel laughed at this in sheer amusement, the Communists, always sensitive to ridicule, repainted the boxes in the more conservative olive drab color.

In the spring the UNC attempted to beautify its side of the truce site, if one can demarcate area, by planting scrub pines from the surrounding hills and lining the paths with rocks. The Communists, again not to be outdone, transplanted full-grown trees and brought in full-blooming plants to their area, and lined their walks with bricks buried at an angle. They painted the exposed corners of the brick white. The trees did not live, but even after they turned brown, the Communists let them remain— a symbol of their determination to win the propaganda war they were waging at Panmunjom, where they were not the masters of ceremonies, as they had been at Kaesong.

The techniques of the Communist photographers was a further reflection of their eagerness not to be unequal and to win the propaganda war. In taking pictures they always made certain that the result portrayed the Communists in a favorable light. The North Koreans and Chinese, being generally shorter would not create a good impression if photographed together with Americans. Therefore the Communists would wait until their representatives were in a position higher than the UNC members. One is reminded of the pre-World War II film, *The Great Dictator*, in one scene of which Hitler and Mussolini were scurrying to pump themselves higher and higher in the barber chairs so that each would be on a plane higher than the other.

The Communist skill with the camera had been established at the outset. At the first session at Kaesong they had depicted the UNC brandishing the white flag as coming to them to capitulate. This created the false impression of Communist superiority.[2]

---

[2] James Byrnes, Secretary of State in the closing days of and immediately following World War II, tells of having seen a motion picture while in Moscow

One illustration will serve to demonstrate the Communists' adeptness at distortion of the truth through photography at Panmunjom. On one occasion one of the members of the UNC delegation was running from one tent to another to escape getting too wet from the rain. A young Korean boy happened to be in his path. The Communists hurriedly photographed the episode. The picture later appeared in the Communist press, including one in Hongkong. The picture was used to illustrate the Communists' line, that Americans were employing young Korean boys as spies (see Photograph 16).

Occasionally the UNC personnel sought to frustrate Communist cameramen by dodging or covering their faces when the Communists tried to take a picture. Then the Communists would lie in wait for the time when the UNC member was off guard. Each newly arrived UNC member went through this procedure of having his picture taken. He could not avoid it—no matter how he might try as the writer so well discovered.

No description of Panmunjom would be complete without some reference to Mr. Alan Winnington, correspondent for the *London Daily Worker*, organ of the British Communist Party. Winnington lived at Kaesong with the Communists, and it is believed he headed a group of North Korean propaganda writers. The stories he wrote were lies of the most blatant nature directed against the United Nations Command. This individual had been declared a traitor by the British. Certainly it can be said his efforts had a damaging and aggravating effect. The talks would have progressed better without him.

The Communists appeared concerned over being unable to copy or exceed the UNC in the means of transportation used to come to the conferences. UNC delegates and staff were flown to Panmunjom from their Apple Orchard camp near Munsan in helicopters supplied by the United States Air Force and Marine Corps. The Communists eyed these greedily as their

during a foreign ministers' meeting which depicted Russian soldiers pouring into Manchuria in August of 1945, the capitulation of thousands of Japanese, and finally General Derevyankov validating the Japanese surrender by signing the surrender document on board a battleship. The whole scene gave the impression that Russia had won and Japan had surrendered to her! See James F. Byrnes, *Speaking Frankly* (New York: Harper, 1947).

delegates arrived from Kaesong in an eight-passenger black
Chrysler Imperial, a four-door green 1949 Ford, and United
States and Russian jeeps. The Chrysler had become Communist
property as a result of their first assault on the Korean capital
of Seoul. This product of captalism had belonged to one of the
ROK cabinet ministers.

By now conference procedure had become routine. By agreement at the previous meeting, the conferees would gather at the
truce site at the appointed hour. The Communists arrived from
Kaesong to the west by car. The UNC arrived from Base Camp
to the east by helicopter, while the correspondents traveled by
jeep and truck. As soon as the delegates and staffs of each side
arrived, they would go immediately to their respective tents for
final briefing.

Sharply at the agreed hour the delegates filed into the conference tent, the Communists entering at one end, the UNC at
the other. After everyone was seated, the Senior Delegate who
had not opened the previous meeting would speak. Each side
took its turn opening the meetings. The Senior Delegate, sitting
in the center of the other delegates along a long green-felt-cov-
ered table, would read one sentence, stop, and the interpreters
would stand up and translate, first into Korean, then Chinese in
in the case of the UNC, or into English and Chinese in the case
of the Communists. Afterward the Senior Delegate would speak
another sentence, and so on until he had completed what he
had to say. Not knowing exactly what the opponent might say,
all types of refutations were prepared. These were contingency
papers.

After each side had elaborated on its stand to the extent
that it was able and willing, one would exclaim, "If you have
nothing more to say, I suggest that we recess until tomorrow
at this time." To this the other would usually reply, "I agree."
Both sides would then file out of the tent, the delegates first,
followed by their staffs. Meanwhile, for the United Nations Command the stenographers were busy at work transcribing the minutes so that they would be ready for the delegates when they
gathered to discuss the next line of attack after returning to
Munsan. Outside the tent at Panmunjom correspondents always

gathered anxiously to learn what had happened at the conference. Correspondents were not permitted to attend the meetings. The personnel would depart for the points from whence they came, the Communists off in a cloud of dust for Kaesong and the UNC personnel moving swiftly away in their helicopters.

When the delegates entered the conference tent on 25 October, a much more suitable relationship prevailed. Panmunjom was at least in neutral territory. It was only hoped the Communists would not think up new ways to impede the progress of the negotiations.

During the sixty-three-day hiatus United Nations forces had not only repelled strong enemy attacks but had forged new gains on the front lines. Heartbreak Ridge was taken at great cost in human lives. Militarily, the UNC was in a somewhat better position than when the talks were suspended 23 August.

During the three months since the meetings had commenced, little could be shown for its efforts. The UNC faced the new meetings with hopes raised high, against its better judgment.

Item Two was still to be settled. For its part the UNC recognized that international law specifically defined an armistice as a temporary suspension of hostilities, and just as specifically pointed out that hostilities might be resumed by either side if proper notification were given.

With this in mind, it would definitely be foolhardy, and perhaps disastrous, for either commander to expose his forces along a political demarcation line rather than to place them in sound militarily defensive positions, where they could protect themselves in the event hostilities should be resumed.

The objective of the United Nations Command was a military armistice based on military realities. The UNC was aware that the armistice negotiations were an essential prelude to any eventual long-time solution of the Korean problem.

The UNC was aware, as were the Communists, that three military components were employed effectively in Korea by the former: ground forces, air forces, and naval forces. The Communists had only one of these forces at their disposal, namely, land forces. Their other two forces, ineffective even at their peak, had been shot from the sky or driven from the seas.

A military armistice would be applicable to all military components: air, ground, and sea. Therefore, the inexorable pressures UNC air and sea forces were exerting on the Communists' rear would be relieved. An armistice would permit them to refurbish their military machine, regroup and resupply their fighting forces, and thus substantially increase their relative over-all military effectiveness.

On the other hand, the UNC was already at peak efficiency, well organized in combat formations, and well supplied with all of the weapons of war. The net effect of any armistice would be of greater military advantage to the Communists than it would be to the UNC. Thus the UNC, acknowledging these realities and recognizing its obligation to the fighting man to afford him maximum security during the armistice, would not accept the 38th Parallel.

The interval of several months apparently had played its part. The Communists returned to the talks leaving their demand for the 38th Parallel behind them. This demand was never voiced again.

At the Plenary Session on 25 October, Item Two was again referred to the joint Sub-Committee for further study, and the "merry-go-round" was under way.[3]

General Lee: Now we will open the meeting.

General Hodes: OK.

General Lee: Do you have any idea about the military demarcation line?

General Hodes: We ended the last conference before the suspension by asking for your proposal. Do you have one?

General Lee: We would like your opinion first.

General Hodes: We gave our opinion many times, and asked for your proposal based on our proposal. As it was

[3] On 25 October General Nam Il recommended the establishment of a joint office of liaison officers to be "responsible for the determination of details of security arrangements, for the inspection of the observance of the agreement by both sides, for the investigation of violations of the agreement, and for the handling of joint administrative matters." The UNC agreed to this suggestion.

your proposal to have the Sub-Delegation meeting, we expected you to have a proposal. Let's have it.

General Lee: You said you had made a new proposal, but
we have heard nothing new which would break the deadlock.

General Hodes: That's right. You haven't.

And so on, *ad infinitum*. Finally, after fifty minutes, a fifteen-
minute recess was suggested. Then again:

General Hodes: Were you able to find some proposal to
solve the problem while you were out?

General Lee: Did you?

General Hodes: Is the answer that you didn't?

General Lee: We haven't thought of one.

To end such palaver, the UNC suggested a new four-kilometer-wide demilitarized zone based generally on the current
battle positions. In its proposal, the UNC sought to include the
ancient Korean capital of Kaesong within its zone. General Hodes
argued:

We have asked for withdrawal in the Kaesong area for a number
of reasons. First, whether you will admit it or not, if there had
been no armistice negotiations, the Kaesong area would have been
occupied by UNC troops. The only reason UNC troops are not in
the Kaesong area is because it was declared a neutral zone. . . .
We desire the Kaesong area to give more adequately security to
the capital of the Republic of Korea.

Major General Lee Sang Cho presented the Communist proposal the following day with the declaration:

Should the peace-loving people of the world see [your proposal]
they will certainly say it is not just and reasonable. Should we
publish our proposal which we presented today, the righteous people
will certainly see it as a just proposal based on the present contact
line. If the righteous world public sees these two different proposals,
the righteous world public can see who is trying for the armistice
and peace.

Major General Hsieh Fang employed propaganda in his argument supporting General Lee:

The Korean armistice negotiations have been going on for more than one hundred days and the hopes of the people of the world for peace have not been realized. The negotiations have been interrupted with many holdups and now that the negotiations have been resumed I believe it is imperative that we face the realities and try to solve the problem on the basis of realities. . . . In making our proposal, we have been seriously concerned with the interests of the Korean people and the hopes for peace of the people of the world.

The discussions hovered over the accuracies of the line of contact, each side accusing the other of distortion. Finally, on 31 October, at the seventh Sub-Delegation meeting since resuming negotiations, the Communists presented a proposal that the UNC would have accepted at the beginning: a demilitarized zone centered on the battle line. General Lee declared:

In order to eliminate all conceivable pretexts for delaying the armistice negotiations, and to reach speedily an agreement on the second item of the agenda, so that armistice and peace in Korea, so anxiously awaited by all peace-loving peoples of the world, may be realized smoothly, the delegation of the Korean People's Army and the Chinese People's Volunteers will make another great effort and submits the following new proposal. This new proposal of ours proposes that, apart from the necessary adjustments in a few areas, both sides withdraw two kilometers strictly from the existing contact line, with the area evacuated by both sides as the demilitarized zone.

The United Nations Command still wanted Kaesong and attempted as a last resort to have it at least in the demilitarized zone. The Communists dogmatically refused. Finally, on 5 November, the UNC accepted the principle of a four-kilometer-wide demilitarized zone centered on the line of contact, but stipulated that, inasmuch as it had been agreed that the fighting would continue during the negotiations, it must be "the actual line of contact at the time of the signing of the armistice," thus "leaving the finalization of the agreement on Agenda Item Two until such time as it is possible to settle it definitely in order to reach agree-

1.   UNC newsmen and staff arrive for the first meeting at Kaesong. Kaesong was well within Communist territory requiring UNC use of a white flag in order to traverse the front lines. This was portrayed in the Communist press as the flag of surrender.

Jin Min Hua Pao (People's Pictorial), Peking

2.   Until the Armistice meetings were transferred to Panmunjom in October 1951 meetings were held in this house at Kaesong.   *US Army Photo*

3.   On 4 August 1951 a company of heavily armed Chinese troops passed within a few hundred yards of the Staff House used by the UNC. Admiral Joy called off the talks and reported the incident to General Ridgway.   *Wide World Photo*

4.   Communist newsmen photograph the midnight investigation of the alleged bombing of the Kaesong area, 22 August 1951. It was this event that the Communists used as their excuse to call off further meetings.
Jin Min Hua Pao (People's Pictorial), Peking

5.   The Communists exploited their manufactured incidents to the fullest. Here Communists are examining "evidence" of the 22 August incident at Kaesong. The sign reads: "American imperialists dropped bombs at this spot at 10:20 P.M. 22 August in order to obstruct the peace negotiations."

Jin Min Hua Pao (People's Pictorial), Peking

6.   Over-all view of Panmunjom. Formerly a tiny farming village on the road between Munsan and Kaesong, Panmunjom proved more suitable as the site for the armistice talks because of its location between the fighting forces.   *US Navy Photo*

7.   Winter at Panmunjom. Two North Korean security guards patrol the thousand-yard
radius of the conference site.   *US Navy Photo*

ment in all questions related to an armistice in Korea at the earliest possible date." The UNC recommended establishment of a Staff Officers Committee, comprising three officers from each side, "to develop objectively an agreed contact line."

The Communists immediately raised serious objections to such an arrangement, declaring that each item of the agenda should be finalized before proceeding to the next item.

The Communists demanded that the then existing line of contact be made the military demarcation line, and that both sides withdraw two kilometers from this line so as to establish the demilitarized zone.

They accused the United Nations Command of

. . . trying to escape the righteous solution and trying to shirk the duty which has been specified in the agenda item. You use in these discussions and also in your press and radio the sophistic argument that the time of the signing is unknown. By doing so you have truly revealed your true color in refusing to abide by the agenda.

The Communists argued:

Item Two makes it clear that we should determine at the time of discussion as to where both sides are willing to stop fighting. That is to say, Item Two requires that we now write a law to determine where to stop fighting. Once this law is written, it should have, if both sides agree, a binding force. But your side has repeatedly made the unreasonable demand that there should be no binding force. If you could change the situation to a great extent, we have agreed to your viewpoint that it can be revised. But writing the law and revising the law must not be mixed up. The writing of the law is the most important step. . . . The question therefore is, would you rather make a clear proposal that we revise the agenda so that Item Two becomes Item Five?

The UNC retorted that "we have no objection to having a proposal made that items of the agenda be changed, if that is your desire." To this the Communists declared, "To change the agenda is not our desire but it is yours. You must give a clear answer."

To this seemingly protracted circumlocution the UNC pondered:

The line of contact at the time of the signing is where the military demarcation line will be. We do not know where that will be until then. You are reading implications into our proposal for some purpose which we do not understand. . . . Neither are we willing to set up a useless demilitarized zone now whose only purpose is to encourage delay in solution of subsequent items of the agenda.

The Communists sought to force the UNC to decide the question.

Either you make a formal proposal to revise the agenda to postpone Item Two to the end of the discussion or else give a clear indication as to where you are willing to stop fighting. The choice is up to you and is awaited by us.

Again representing themselves as on the side of the "peace-loving people of the world," General Lee Sang Cho concluded:

I sincerely hope and think that you and we are bound in duty to show our sincerity to the peace-loving people of the world by your acceptance of our proposal of establishing a military demarcation line and demilitarized zone in accordance with Item Two.

United Nations' acceptance of the Communist proposal of making the present line of contact the armistice demarcation line would have fixed the demilitarized zone immediately and irrevocably, prior to resolution of other essential agenda items. This would have relieved the Communists from any pressure to reach agreement on other agenda items which from the outset of negotiations were deemed essential by the UNC—in contrast to the Communists—to a full-fledged military armistice.

Admiral Joy noted:

[The enemy] wants all of the advantages of a de facto cease-fire so that he can prolong the armistice negotiations without cost to himself. He wants immediate relief from our inexorable military pressure—the pressure which would be an "incentive" to arrive quickly at agreement on other items.[4]

4 On 14 November Major General Lee had failed to recall the UNC Senior Delegate's name; to which Major General Hodes retaliated the following day by noting: "Your Senior Delegate, whose name I trust you are able to recall . . ."

The United Nations Command on 17 November proposed that the present contact line should constitute the provisional military demarcation line, provided the Armistice Agreement was signed within thirty days. The UNC hoped by injecting the time limit to speed up agreement on the remaining issues. The Communists accepted this proposal, and on 23 November staff officers of both sides commenced the tedious task of determining the actual line of ground contact.

On 23 November the Sub-Delegation on Agenda Item Two agreed to the recommendation to be submitted to the Plenary Session.

The Sub-Delegations of the United Nations Command Delegation and of the Delegation of the Korean People's Army and the Chinese People's Volunteers reach the following agreement on the Second Item of the Agenda, "Fixing a military demarcation line between both sides so as to establish a demilitarized zone as the basic condition for the cessation of hostilities in Korea":

1. The principle is accepted that the actual line of contact between both sides (as determined under either paragraph 2 or 3, as appropriate) will be made the military demarcation line and that at the time specified in the signed armistice agreement both sides will withdraw 2 kilometers from this line so as to establish the demilitarized zone for the duration of the military armistice.

2. In accordance with the above stated principle, the Sub-Delegations will determine immediately the present line of contact so as to fix it as the military demarcation line and as the median line of the demilitarized zone. If the military armistice agreement is signed within thirty days after the two delegations approve in the plenary session this agreement and the specific location of the above military demarcation line and demilitarized zone, the military demarcation line and demilitarized zone shall not be changed, regardless of whatever changes may occur in the actual line of contact between both sides.

3. In view of the fact that hostilities will continue until the signing of the armistice agreement, if the military armistice agreement is not signed within thirty days after the two delegations approve in the Plenary Session this agreement and the specific location of the military demarcation line and the demilitarized zone as determined in paragraph 2 above, the Sub-Delegation shall revise immediately prior to the signing of the military armistice agreement the above military demarcation line and the demilitarized zone in accordance

with the changes which have occurred in the actual line of contact between both sides so that the revised military demarcation line will coincide exactly with the line of contact betweeen both sides immediately prior to the signing of the military armistice agreement and will constitute the military demarcation line for the duration of the military armistice.

On 26 November the staff officers completed agreement on the line of contact, which was drawn on two sets of maps which were initialed by both sides. On 27 November Agenda Item Two was ratified formally by both sides in the first Plenary Session since 25 October.

Thus after sixty-five stormy meetings from 26 July to 27 November 1951, Item Two was completed. Although the Communists failed to achieve all they demanded, they did receive a thirty-day reprieve. The United Nations Command was not going to exert great military effort along the line of contact only to be forced to concede gains. It was during this period that the Communists commenced a concerted effort to construct a fairly impregnable defense line all across Korea, thus precluding further utilization of effective military pressure on the ground by the UNC forces. This is what the Communists had sought from the outset of negotiations. As Nam Il had stated at the second meeting on 11 July: "Without ceasing hostilities in Korea and without carrying out cease-fire in Korea we cannot discuss the armistice."

With this physical barrier to support them, the Communists could delay meetings as long as they pleased. And United Nations Command apprehensions were soon to be confirmed, corroborating General Douglas MacArthur's contention: "There is no substitute for victory."

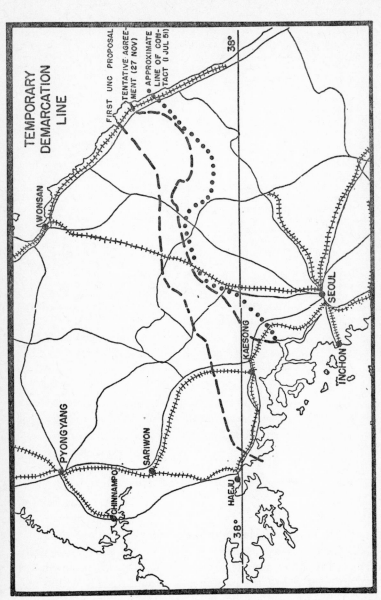

Fig. 2. Map showing the temporary demarcation line agreed upon in November 1951

5

CONCRETE ARRANGEMENTS
FOR A CEASE-FIRE

*A shepherd boy, who tended his flock not far
from a village, used to amuse himself at times
in crying out "Wolf! Wolf!" Twice or thrice his
trick succeeded. The whole village came running
out to his assistance; when all the return they
got was to be laughed at for their pains. At last,
one day the wolf came indeed. The boy cried out
in earnest. But his neighbors, supposing him to
be at his old sport, paid no heed to his cries, and
the wolf devoured the sheep. So the boy learned,
when it was too late, that liars are not believed
even when they tell the truth.*

FABLES OF AESOP

By their fruits ye shall know them.

MATTHEW 7:20

Lord Mahon in his *History of England* describes
an instance such as occurred at Panmunjom where one party
attempted to delay a conference. A British squadron threatened
bombardment unless the participants came to terms within one
hour. "This proceeding, however railed at by the diplomatists
as contrary to all form of etiquette, produced a result such as

88

they had seldom attained by protocols." Within the hour an agreement was reached.

Noticeably lacking at Panmunjom was the existence of a force of sufficient magnitude to induce the Communists to come to a settlement. Nothing the United Nations Command did prevented the Communists from exacting the optimum propaganda harvests from world attention concentrated at Panmunjom.

Following agreement on Item Two, the UNC bent every effort toward consummation of an accord on the remaining items, while the Communists in contrast directed their energies toward creating the impression that they represented the "peace-loving peoples of the whole world" against the machinations of "war-mongering, imperialistic" America and its "puppets." From its experiences, the UNC could but conclude that negotiation to the Communists was only a military and political tactic, not an attempt to reach a ground of common understanding.

To best understand the Communists' motives in the Peace Tent, one must be able to understand their concepts of peace. To the Communists *peace* is the equivalent of *total victory*. The proletariat, by definition, is the peaceful class. Their every act is a peaceful act, whether it involves the employment of a peaceful gun to lodge a bullet in one's warlike brain or the conquest of an imperialistic state by the advance of the forces of peace. The Communists are completely dedicated to peace, i.e., total Communist victory. Their definitions of loyalty, morality, justice, patriotism, and truth itself must be considered in terms of the dialectic.

For six months following the agreement on Item Two, the UNC sparred with the Communists. The UNC's success was measured by its willingness to concede or to force the Communists into a position where they had to accept some solution. It was hoped that the ratification of the thirty-day time limit might pressure the Communists into coming to terms more quickly. It was of no avail, and the Communists accused the UNC of procrastination.

The debate on Item Three commenced on 27 November. This item the UNC regarded as the crux of the armistice and the key to the future. The Communists introduced a plan that would have assumed the good faith of both parties for execution. It provided for no guarantees. According to their plan, after the shooting had stopped, each side would have withdrawn into its respective zone.

The UNC was somewhat more realistic in insisting upon the establishment of certain guarantees against any new eruptions. It wanted a cease-fire, no build-up in the respective military forces, and adequate supervision and inspection.

The United Nations Command offered a seven-point plan:

1. There shall be a cease-fire, effective within twenty-four hours of the signing of the armistice agreement, and adhered to by all forces of any type under the control of either side.

2. There shall be established a supervisory organization, equally and jointly manned by both sides, for carrying out the terms of the armistice agreement.

3. There shall be no increase of military forces, supplies, equipment, and facilities by either side after the signing of the armistice.

4. The Military Armistice Commission in carrying out its supervisory functions shall have free access to all parts of Korea, for itself and for the joint observation teams responsible to the Armistice Commission.

5. There shall be general withdrawal of forces of each side —air, ground, and naval, regular and irregular—from the territory controlled by the other side.

6. There shall be no armed forces in the demilitarized zone except as specifically and mutually agreed by both sides.

7. The military commanders shall administer their portion of the demilitarized zone in accordance with the terms of the Military Armistice Agreement.

In addition, the United Nations Command recommended for inclusion in the concrete arrangements of the final armistice:

1. Details of cease-fire, removal of troops from the demilitarized zone.

2. Measures that will reduce the possibility of resumption of hostilities.

3. The establishment of a supervisory organization to include joint observer teams.

4. The authority for the supervisory organization and its joint observer teams to observe in such parts of Korea as may be necessary

At the same time, to expedite work on Item Four when the time came to discuss this item, the UNC suggested that each side prepare current statistics relating to prisoners of war.

1. The names, nationalities and other identifying data of all prisoners of war held, as of the latest available data.

2. The location of all prisoner-of-war camps.

3. The number, by nationality, of all prisoners of war held at each such camp, as of the latest available data.

This latter was not accepted by the Communists. They, in contrast, offered a five-point proposal concerning Item Three of the agenda:

1. All armed forces of both sides, including regular and irregular units and armed personnel of the ground, naval, and air forces, shall cease all hostilities from the day of the signing of the armistice agreement.

2. All armed forces of both sides shall be withdrawn from the demilitarized zone within three days after the signing of the armistice agreement.

3. All armed forces of either side shall be withdrawn, within five days after the signing of the armistice agreement, from the rear and the coastal islands and waters of the other side, with the military demarcation line as the dividing line. If they are not withdrawn within the stated

time limit, and there is no reason for delaying the withdrawal, the other side shall have the right to take all
necessary action against such armed personnel for the
maintenance of security and order.

4. All armed forces of both sides shall not enter the demilitarized zone and shall not carry out any acts of armed
force against the demilitarized zone.

5. Both sides shall designate an equal number of members
to form an armistice commission to be jointly responsible
for the concrete arrangement and the supervision of the
implementation of the armistice agreement.

The United Nations Command held many offshore islands
in North Korea, which had proved invaluable during the fighting
as air-sea rescue stations. It was not going to give these up unless
"suitable adjustments are made."

General Nam Il immediately raised serious doubts as to the
validity of points 3 and 4 of the UNC's seven-point proposal:

We contend that, in order to achieve a thorough, peaceful settlement
of the Korean question, all forces of foreign countries must be withdrawn from Korea. If all foreign forces are withdrawn from Korea,
there will be no practicable question of the military supplies, equipment, and facilities exceeding the level existing at the time of the
signing of the Armistice Agreement. . . . We oppose the fourth
principle proposed by your side because it is entirely unnecessary
in a military conference.

In point 3 the UNC sought a guarantee against using the
respite afforded by the armistice to build up forces in North
Korea, which the Communists had difficulty doing while the war
continued. The UNC did, however, concede that present forces
could be replenished and replaced during an armistice.

To this latter Nam Il queried:

If armistice is effected in Korea, why should there be introduced
fresh troops, military supplies, and equipment since there will be
no shooting? Your side maintains that the supervisory organ should
have free access to all parts of Korea to carry out inspections. This

is clearly a brazen interference in the internal affairs of the other side. This is unreasonable and impractical, and our side absolutely cannot agree to such a provision. It is entirely unwarranted and unreasonable in any reasonable and practical military armistice. Let me state once more that the third and fourth principles and the related concrete measures proposed by your side are unreasonable, impractical, and unwarranted in a reasonable and practicable military armistice.

The UNC in making its proposals was interested solely in guaranteeing against infractions of the Armistice Agreement by either side. As had been the case with the United States' efforts to guarantee against atomic stock-piling by impartial inspections, the Communists reflected a guilt complex in their adamant refusal to permit inspection.

The UNC carefully pointed out that Item Three covered only the period of the cease-fire, not the period of peace, which would come only after the governments concerned had acted.

To prevent any possibility of new outbreaks, the UNC also made clear that construction, improvement, or rehabilitation of airfields throughout Korea beyond their status at the time the military armistice went into effect should be restricted by both sides.

On 27 November these various proposals were made. By 4 May the following year the main issues were settled. The price for the United Nations Command was patience and an ability to stand up under the avalanche of Communist invective.

On 3 December the Communists submitted their revised list of principles, adding two new points:

6. In order to ensure the stability of the military armistice so as to facilitate the holding by both sides of a political conference of a higher level, both sides shall undertake not to introduce into Korea any military forces, weapons, and ammunition under any pretext.

7. In order to supervise the strict implementation of the stipulation of paragraph six (6), both sides agree to invite representatives of nations neutral in the Korean War to form a supervisory organ to be responsible for con-

ducting necessary inspection, beyond the demilitarized
zone, of such ports of entry in the rear as mutually agreed
upon by both sides and to report to the joint Armistice
Commission the result of the inspection.

This latter was a limited concession to the UNC demands
for inspection teams. Yet both points still did not begin to meas-
ure up to UNC aspirations for establishing waterproof guarantees.

On 4 December the UNC sought to force more rapid progress
in the proceedings by suggesting the discussions be referred to
a subdelegation. This the Communists accepted. The UNC then
proposed that, in order to expedite the negotiations, a second
subdelegation be designated by each side for the purpose of
discussing Item Four of the agenda, the discussions of the two
items to be undertaken concurrently. The UNC continued to make
this latter recommendation every day until 10 December, when
it was finally accepted.

On 7 December the United Nations Command proposed a
revision of the Communists' seven principles and suggested the
inclusion of an additional principle:

1. All armed forces under the control of either side, including regular and irregular units and armed personnel
   of the ground, naval, and air forces, shall cease all hostilities within twenty-four hours after the Armistice Agreement enters into effect.

2. All armed forces of both sides shall be withdrawn from
   the demilitarized zone within seventy-two hours after the
   Armistice Agreement enters into effect.

3. All armed forces under the control of either side shall
   be withdrawn, within five days after the Armistice Agreement comes into effect, from the territory controlled by
   the other side. If they are not withdrawn within the stated
   time, and there is no reason for delaying the withdrawal,
   the other side shall have the right to take all necessary
   action against such armed personnel for the maintenance
   of security and order.

4. All armed forces of both sides, except such armed forces of a police nature as may be specifically and mutually agreed to by both sides, shall not enter the demilitarized zone and shall not carry out any acts of armed force against the demilitarized zone.

5. Both sides shall designate an equal number of members to form an Armistice Commission to be jointly responsible for the supervision of the whole armistice agreement.

6. In order to ensure the stability of the military armistice so as to facilitate the holding by both sides of a political conference of a higher level, both sides shall undertake not to increase the level of units, personnel, war equipment, military facilities, or material existing in Korea, at the time the armistice comes into effect.

7. a) The Armistice Commission and its joint observer teams shall have the authority to observe at ground, sea, and air ports of entry and communication centers throughout all of Korea as mutually agreed to by the two delegations, together with freedom for the above teams over principle lines of communications throughout all of Korea.
b) The Armistice Commission shall have the right of joint aerial observation and photo reconnaissance over all of Korea.
c) The Armistice Commission shall have the right of complete observation of the demilitarized zone.

8. The Armistice Agreement shall not enter into effect until the Armistice Commission has been organized, is staffed, and is ready to begin the exercise of its assigned functions.

The Communists accepted the rewording of principles 1, 2, and 4. They continued to insist upon UNC withdrawal from all coastal islands for acceptance of principle 3. This concession the UNC made on 12 December.

The Communists argued against principle 7 that it did not include the concept of neutral observer teams.

Our stand has been that the ports of entry in the rear should be inspected by neutral nations. Our proposal clearly provides that there be no free access to all parts of Korea but that the places specified—ports of entry for preventing the introduction into Korea of armed forces, weapons, and ammunition—should be inspected. To extend this scope would mean the interference in the internal affairs of the other side.

On 11 December the Sub-Delegation on Item Four commenced discussions in a tent adjoining the one in which the Sub-Delegation on Item Three was meeting. The implications of Item Four are of conspicuous significance, and a discussion of them will be postponed until the next chapter.

On 14 December the Communists offered a new proposal, in which the UNC found "nothing different than your proposal of 3 December." The UNC noted that "you have changed a few words; you have reduced the number from seven to six, but we find not one major change from your former proposal." However, the Communists did accept the UNC provision on a limited basis which would permit the rotation of troops in Korea, "not to exceed five thousand monthly."

The United Nations Command had sought some means of preventing build-ups of military strength in Korea but had recognized the necessity of replacement of equipment and troops. The Communists somehow attempted to impose their own scheming on the UNC:

As long as your side insists upon your unilateral and unreasonable demands of introduction into Korea of military forces under the pretext of rotation and replenishment, while, on the other hand, insisting upon interfering in the internal sovereign state, the negotiations can have no progress at all.

In rejecting the new Communist proposals, Major General H. M. Turner, USAF, UNC Delegate, stated:

You have made a number of statements attempting to show that principles advocated by the UNC are unfair, unreasonable, and unwarranted. You condemn our insistence on prohibiting the rehabilitation and reconstruction of airfields as being interference in your internal affairs. You object to our intention to rotate and replenish our forces in Korea. You complain that our retention of islands threatens your rear. You object to aerial surveillance as being more interference in your internal affairs.

On the other hand, we defend these principles as insuring against an increase of military capabilities during the armistice. Let's look at the situation as it is today. You are not threatening our rear in any way. You are not preventing us from rehabilitating airfields or building new ones. You are not conducting aerial surveillance of our communication centers. You are not preventing unlimited rotation and replenishment of our forces. You do not interfere in the internal affairs of our side in any way. Under conditions as they exist today, you do none of these things. You do none of these things because you cannot—you lack the military capability to do them.

On the other hand, we do hold islands which threaten your rear. We do keep your airfields unusable by constantly attacking them. We do conduct aerial surveillance throughout your rear. We do limit the extent to which you can replenish your forces by our air interdiction program. We do interfere in your so-called "internal affairs" by disrupting your internal communications systems and by destroying communications centers in your rear. We do these things today because we have the military capability to do them. Until the armistice is signed we will keep on doing them.

. . . . we propose only that during the armistice you shall not gain a military capability which you do not now possess. We go even further. We agree to apply the same restrictions to ourselves, even though you lack the military capability today to implement these restrictions by force of arms. But you complain this is unfair—you who are unable to impose any of these military restrictions upon our side by your own strength. You complain that it is unfair for us to insist on continuing restrictions through armistice terms which we are fully able to impose, and are imposing on you by military means during hostilities.

In short, you seek to gain, through negotiation, what you could not win through fighting. You seek to avoid, through negotiation, what you could not avoid through fighting.[1]

On 20 December the UNC sought new means of solving the knotty problems of Item Three by proposing that staff officers of both sides meet to prepare a set of principles incorporating the essen-

---

[1] The italics are the author's.

tial requirements of both sides to be recommended to the Sub-Delegation. The Communists accepted this proposition and hinted they "might consider" the UNC essential of rotation of personnel and replenishment of materiel within the limits existing at the time of the armistice if the United Nations Command would agree to:

1) Communist increase in their military capability through airfield reconstruction and rehabilitation.
2) Inspection by neutral teams at limited points only.
3) Withdrawal of their requirement for neutral team aerial observation in the rear of both sides to insure adherence to the armistice terms.

During the staff officers' meeting on 21 December, the UNC made a major concession by offering to withdraw its military forces from all islands formerly under Communist control off both coasts of North Korea.

By the end of the year there existed four main points of disagreement on Item Three:

1) Restrictions on airfields of both sides.
2) Adequate ground inspection.
3) Aerial observation in the rear of both sides.
4) Rotation of personnel and replenishment of materiel within the ceiling existing at the time of the Armistice.

On 29 December the United Nations Command attempted to reach a solution by offering to withdraw the requirement for aerial observation. The Communists found this new concession "a step forward." However, they were still unwilling to accept any of the remaining points of difference.

On New Year's Day 1952 Admiral Joy was able to report in a special broadcast to America:

In six months we have made some progress toward an honorable, equitable, and stable armistice. That progress has been painfully slow to us here at the armistice camp as it has to the man in the foxhole, to the men in the prisoner-of-war camps, and to you at home. But in dealing with the Communists there is no other way. . . .

On 6 January Major General Turner bluntly informed the Communists that "an air threat to UNC forces would exist in North Korea immediately upon the rehabilitation of any of the Communists' presently inoperable airfields." He revealed that "crated modern combat aircraft already are present in North Korea."

A week later, 8 January, Admiral Joy noted: "With each passing day there is less and less reason to think the Communists really want a stable armistice. Certainly no one can accuse them of being in a hurry to demonstrate good faith."

On 9 January Communist Delegate Major General Hsieh Fang, CCF, offered a counterproposal for solution to Item Three, which again incorporated no major change. The proposal was accompanied by a lengthy and inflammatory statement—typical of the Communist approach to negotiation. It is particularly interesting to note the statements that were simply repetitions of the UNC statements—another technique commonly employed by the Communists. General Hsieh Fang declared in part:

In our revised proposal we have omitted that part of your proposal concerning the restriction on rehabilitation and construction of airfields. Our side absolutely cannot agree to any unreasonable demand to interfere in our internal affairs. . . . You should know that you are unable to interfere in our internal affairs even while you are now carrying out wanton bombings and bombardments and creating widespread destruction with your military force. Yet you now attempt to gain through negotiations what you are unable to gain by military force. I tell you frankly that you will never get what you have failed to gain by military force.

This absurd argument of yours being a failure, you have dished up another absurd argument. You assert that in this world today complete sovereignty is not longer to be found, and that as complete sovereignty does not exist, why be so stingy in calculating about the integrity of sovereign rights and the inviolability of internal affairs. This argument is a naked expression of the wide ambitions of American ruling block for world domination. You attempt to

subject all the nations of the world to your aggression and, therefore, you deny the existence of national sovereignty. It is true that
there are many nations in your aggressive camp which have lost
the integrity of their sovereign rights under the oppression of the
United States of America. But you must not forget that this wild
attempt of yours for world domination has dashed against the
wall at not a few places in the world where there not only exist
nations with complete sovereignty but where some of these nations
have taken up arms to fight in defense of their sovereign rights
and against foreign intervention. One of these nations is the Democratic People's Republic of Korea. . . . Any demand to interfere
in our internal affairs is absolutely impermissible. This is our unshakable—I repeat, unshakable—stand.

At the conclusion of this sixty-minute vituperation, the UNC
delegate, Major General Turner, observed:

It is regrettable . . . that you have seen fit to make the long propaganda statement which has accompanied your proposal. . . . It
would have been just as effective to have handed your propaganda
statement to your controlled press. That would have spared the
time of these delegations. It has no effect upon us.

General Nam submitted these revisions:

In accordance with the spirit of reaching a speedy agreement
our revised proposal reads as follows:

4. In order to ensure the stability of the military armistice
   so as to facilitate the attainment of a peaceful settlement
   through the holding by both sides of a political conference of a higher level, both sides undertake not to introduce into Korea any reinforcing military personnel,
   combat aircraft, armored vehicles, weapons, and ammunition after the Armistice Agreement is signed and
   becomes effective. Such rotation of military personnel
   as within the limit agreed upon by both sides shall be
   reported to the Military Armistice Commission so that
   the supervisory organ of neutral nations may be entrusted
   to conduct on-the-spot supervision and inspection, which
   shall be carried out at the ports of entry in the rear agreed
   upon by both sides.

5. Each side shall designate an equal number of members to form a Military Armistice Commission to be responsible for supervising the implementation of the Armistice Agreement and for settling through negotiations any violation of the Armistice Agreement. The functions of supervision and inspection as stipulated in the Armistice Agreement shall be carried out in accordance with the following provisions:

   a. Within the demilitarized zone, the Military Armistice Commission utilizing joint teams directly dispatched by it shall be responsible.

   b. Outside the demilitarized zone, at the ports of entry in the rear as agreed upon by both sides and at the places where violations of the Armistice Agreement have been reported to have occurred, the supervisory organ of representatives of neutral nations shall be entrusted to be responsible. Upon the request to the supervisory organ of neutral nations by both sides or either side on the Military Armistice Commission for investigation of a violation of the Armistice Agreement, the supervisory organ of the neutral nations shall carry out the inspection.

6. Both sides agree to invite neutral nations *acceptable to both sides*[2] which have not participated in the Korean War to send, upon their consent, an equal number of representatives to form a supervisory organ to be entrusted by the Military Armistice Commission to be responsible for carrying out the functions of supervision and inspection as stipulated in paragraph 4 and paragraph 5b of this proposal. Upon the request by both sides or either side on the Military Armistice Commission for carrying out these functions, the supervisory organ of neutral nations shall dispatch immediately inspection teams to carry out the functions of supervision and inspection as stipulated in the Armistice Agreement at the

[2] The italics are the author's. This proviso is interesting in light of the Communists' 16 February proposal. See pp. 108-110.

ports of entry in the rear as agreed upon by both sides,
and at places where violations of the Armistice Agreement
have been reported to have occurred outside the demilitarized zone, and   shall report on   the results of
supervision and inspection to the Military Armistice
Commission. In performing their above-stated functions,
the inspection teams of neutral nations shall be accorded
full convenience by both sides over the main lines of
communication and transportation as agreed upon by
both sides.

On 22 January the United Nations Command sought another
solution by expressing a willingness to accept the exact phraseology of the Communist-proposed principles if they would add
a proviso for restricting military airfields of both sides during
the armistice. The Communists replied immediately, saying, "our
side firmly rejects any attempt in any form to interfere in our
internal affairs."

In another attempt to expedite the proceedings, the UNC
on 25 January proposed that staff officers of both sides begin
immediately to draft the detailed wording for the Armistice
Agreement for Item Three based on principles thus far agreed
upon. "For this purpose we are prepared to accept and utilize
the agreed principles 1, 2, and 3, principles 5 and 6 as worded
in your proposal of 9 January, and to use your wording of that
portion of principle 4 on which we are agreed." The question
of reconstruction and rehabilitation of airfields, which had not
been resolved, was temporarily held in abeyance.

The staff officers met on 29 January. The UNC had prepared
a draft of points of agreement which it submitted to the Communists, each point of which the staff officers went over word
by word.

One item in the UNC draft the Communists objected to
seriously, "that is, your request to have 75,000 persons be ro-
tated monthly. . . . To add one more remark, I must state that
this figure of rotation is big enough to surprise us."

It will be recalled that the Communists had previously conceded the figure of 5,000. The UNC figure of 75,000 included short rest leaves in Japan and visits of inspecting personnel, in addition to pure rotatees. It noted that of the latter the figure would be 40,000, "and that would be the maximum in any one month, and it is very doubtful that that would ever happen, more than maybe once, depending on shipping."

The UNC delegates illustrated by an example. "Suppose we have a force on either side of 600,000 personnel. Suppose we wish to limit the tour of duty of those personnel to one year. That means we shall have to dispatch from Korea 50,000 men per month. In addition to that figure, we shall have to provide for those who cannot complete their tour of duty due to illness, injury, or wounds, and in addition, we shall have to provide for those who leave Korea for a short period and return, who are not replaced, but themselves constitute their own replacements, so to speak, under a rotation ceiling. In addition to that, we will have visiting personnel . . . making inspections and carrying out other business of the command."

By the end of January, three major points still stood in the way of agreement of Item Three:

1. Restriction on reconstruction and rehabilitation of airfields, which the Communists continued to refuse as being "interference in internal affairs."
2. Rotation of personnel. The UNC wanted a ceiling of 75,000 as opposed to the Communists' 5,000.
3. Ports of entry. The UNC believed the Neutral Nations Supervisory Commission should not be restricted in its ability to determine whether the respective parties were faithful to the terms of the armistice agreement. The Communists maintained a limited number of ports of entry would suffice for inspection purposes.

The Communists had not yet named the USSR as a neutral to be a member of the Neutral Nations Supervisory Commission. On 31 January Admiral Joy directed a message to General Nam Il recommending a subdelegation be appointed on Item

Five, to meet concurrently with discussions on Item Three and Four.

The United Nations Command delegation has furnished to your side proposed draft articles of the Armistice Agreement relating to Items Two, Three, and Four of the agenda. Since Item Five of the agenda was introduced at your initiative, and since the United Nations Command has initially submitted the draft articles for agenda Items Two, Three, and Four, it seems appropriate that your side propose the first draft of articles relating to Agenda Item Five.

On 3 February General Nam Il accepted the proposal, with the suggestion that the Plenary Session handle Item Five.

On 6 February the Plenary Session met to discuss Item Five of the agenda. General Nam Il presented the draft he had prepared:

Draft of the Principle Proposed by the Delegation of the Korean People's Army and the Chinese People's Volunteers on the Fifth Item of the Agenda, "Recommendations to the Governments of Countries Concerned on Both Sides."

In order to ensure the peaceful settlement of the Korean question, it is recommended that within three (3) months after the Korean Armistice Agreement is signed and becomes effective, the opposing sides, the governments of the Democratic People's Republic of Korea and of the People's Republic of China on the one hand, and the governments of the countries concerned of the United Nations on the other hand, appoint five (5) representatives respectively to hold a political conference to settle through negotiation the following questions:

1) Withdrawal of all foreign troops from Korea;
2) Peaceful settlement of the Korean question; and
3) Other questions related to peace in Korea.

In submitting his draft, Nam Il observed *inter alia:*

On 27 June 1950, President Truman . . . publicly connected the war in Korea with other questions of the East and used the Korean war as a pretext for a series of warlike measures in the East. The peaceful settlement of the Korean question calls for a simultaneous solution of these other important problems related to the Korean question. It is only when these problems related to the Korean question are solved simultaneously that peace in Korea can be consolidated; that peace in the East, which has been breached as a result of the war in Korea, can be restored; and that the state of extreme tension into which the world has been plunged as a result of the war in Korea, can turn for the better.

Nam Il failed to add here, as always, that the group he represented was responsible for this "plunge."

The contentions on Item Five related to who was to be represented at the political conference and what was to be discussed. The Communists wanted North Korea and China. They completely ignored the Republic of Korea, to which the UNC objected.

On 9 February the United Nations Command offered a few revisions. Admiral Joy stated in part:

The draft principle proposed by your delegation on the fifth item of the agenda has received our careful consideration. We have found certain matters contained therein with which we are in substantial agreement; others which we had not considered necessary but to which we had no objection; and a few modifications, primarily of phraseology, which we consider advisable for reasons which we believe will be obvious.

The UNC proposal stipulated the Republic of Korea, omitted by the Communists and included in the United Nations as an independent entity, as a participant in the political conference. It also included a significant sentence:

The military commanders have not considered questions concerning a political settlement in Korea, including unification of Korea under an independent, democratic government and other questions arising from but not resolved by this Armistice Agreement. In order to ensure the peaceful settlement of the Korean question the military commanders recommend to the respective governments and authorities concerned, namely to the Democratic People's Republic of Korea and the People's Republic of China on the one hand, and to the United Nations and the Republic of Korea on the other hand, that steps be taken within a period of three months to deal with these matters at a higher level in a political conference for a Korean settlement, or by such other political means as they deem appropriate, including:

1) Withdrawal of non-Korean forces from Korea;
2) Peaceful settlement of the Korean question; and
3) Other Korean questions related to peace.

The Communists objected to the United Nations being considered as an entity for participation in any post-armistice forum which would discuss Korean questions, on the grounds that not all UN members had troops participating in the conflict. Admiral Joy pointed out that this criterion would bar Communist China from taking part in the talks, since they had repeatedly claimed that Chinese units in Korea were "volunteers" and unrelated to any decision by their political authorities.

The Communists also raised strenuous objection to the UNC including in its proposal a statement that the military commanders had not considered in their discussions the question of "the unification of Korea under an independent, democratic government."

The Communists also suggested that the third topic to be recommended for consideration, "other questions related to peace," be modified to read, "other questions directly related to peace in Korea."

The Communists wanted the statement to make a specific recommendation for a political conference convened within a definite time limit.

After haggling over these points for several days, the Communists on 12 February stated they would submit a revised draft at the next session, the date for which they declined to specify. Obviously they required high-level discussions, which took time. On 16 February they presented their "revised draft," which the UNC quickly accepted on 17 February without further argument, knowing that it was on a "recommendation to the governments of both sides." In submitting the revised draft the Communists explained that the first sentence of the UNC proposal went beyond the scope of the agenda, and they absolutely could not agree to it; that the second sentence of the UNC proposal obviously was in violation of the original wording of the agenda item already agreed upon; that the revised draft eliminated UNC "pretexts for haggling" on this point; that the revised draft incorporated the UNC wording regarding the political conference; that the term "foreign forces" means "non-Korean forces"; and that to meet UNC objections to the third question for consideration in the political conference as originally suggested by the Communists the new draft suggested a rewording, "the peaceful settlement of the Korean question, et cetera." [3]

In accepting the Communist revised draft Admiral Joy stated:

The United Nations Command Delegation accepts your proposal of 16 February as the solution of the item of the agenda, subject to the following remarks:

So that there may be no question regarding the understanding of the United Nations Command Delegation as to the meaning of your proposal we deem it advisable to make certain explanations at this time. First, we desire to point out that this recommendation will be made by the Commander-in-Chief, United Nations Command, to the United Nations as well as to the Republic of Korea. Second, in accepting the term "foreign forces" we are doing so on the basis of your statement that this term means "non-Korean forces." And third, we wish it clearly understood that we do not construe the word, "et cetera," to relate to matters outside of Korea.

The rapidity of UNC acceptance caught the Communists completely off balance. They immediately requested a forty-minute recess, only to return to request additional time "to make a careful study of your statement." Two days later the Plenary Session met again, a meeting which again reflected consternation on the part of the Communists over the rapid UNC approval of their "revised draft." The UNC conjectured that the Communists were trying to determine where they had made their blunder: The UNC spokesman, Brigadier General William P. Nuckols, USAF, opined that "they are probably preparing a carefully worded acceptance of our acceptance."

[3] For final draft, see Appendix VI.

Finally, after ninety minutes, Admiral Joy stated: "We agree to recess with the understanding that Item Five is to be turned over to the staff officers to complete any necessary mechanical details." For its part the UNC considered Item Five closed. The hasty conclusion of Item Five, which had been of such concern to the Communists, raised the hopes of the UNC for a quick solution to the other problems.

On 17 February Item Five was completed, but a solution to Items Three and Four was nowhere in sight. Both of these items were now in the hands of staff officer groups. Progress was painfully slow.

On Item Three the two sides were gradually paring down the initial demands of each. The United Nations Command had originally expressed its desire to permit freedom of each side to rotate and replenish its strength during the period of the armistice beyond that existing at the time of the signing of the armistice. The Communists objected on the grounds that this was unreasonable. The staff officers began discussions on Item Three on 29 January. Here progress was made in whittling away at the respective demands. The UNC conceded 75,000 would be the ceiling for troop rotation per month. The Communists offered 5,000 as a maximum. The UNC then dropped its figure to 60,000 and then to 40,000. The latter figure, however, was exclusive of those entering for temporary duty or returning from leave. The Communists then raised their maximum to 25,000, and then to 30,000 by 13 February.

Discussions on ports of entry were held concomitantly. The UNC had reduced its demands for complete inspection of all of Korea by the Neutral Nations Supervisory Commission to the use of certain ports of entry for such purposes. The Communists had declared such inspection as being a flagrant interference in their internal affairs. They finally conceded certain ports of entry for such inspection during the period of the armistice. When determining the exact number of ports of entry to be open for inspection, the UNC asked twelve and the Communists replied with three. The UNC dropped its figure to eight and then to seven. The Communists raised their figure to four.

16 February, the day the Communists submitted their

revised draft on Item Five which the United Nations Command accepted, they also submitted the name of the USSR to be one of the three members for their side on the Neutral Nations Supervisory Commission. This was in complete disagreement with their recommendation of 9 January, and accepted by the UNC, which stated in part: "Both sides agree to invite neutral nations acceptable to both sides which have not participated in the Korean War. . . ."[4]

The injection of the name of the USSR was obviously for bargaining purposes. It also enabled the Communists to stall while they watched to see how discussions on Item Four worked out. The Communists were well aware that the UNC could not accept the USSR as a neutral nation. That this state had contributed to, and in fact initiated, the Korean War had been proved time and again. Perhaps the Communists hoped for UNC acceptance as a means of further absolving the USSR in the eyes of the world from any association with the Korean War. Propaganda-wise, the Communists had always blamed the United States and the ROK for aggression in Korea. They attempted to create the false impression that they were guiltless. The USSR had always sought to display its innocence—to present itself as the fountain of peace. To have accepted this apocryphal demand of the Communists would have confirmed United Nations Command recognition of the neutrality of the USSR.

The Communists' explanation proved ludicrous:

The neutral nations are . . . those nations whose combatant forces have not participated in the hostilities in Korea. The neutral nations nominated by our side are all truly in consistence with this definition. Your side cannot give any reason, nor does it *have* any reason, to object to any of the neutral nations nominated by our side. Your side cannot give any reason, nor does it have any reason, to object to the nomination of the Soviet Union by our side as one of the neutral nations. The Soviet Union is one of the United Nations which is not only most strictly opposed to interventions in the Korean war, but it also is most strongly in favor of a peaceful settlement of the Korean question. If the Soviet Union could not be nominated as a neutral nation, there would be no neutral nation at all existing in the world.

[4] See page 101.

What is more strange is that your side should object to the Soviet Union when it has agreed to Poland and Czechoslovakia. That is an unreasonable attitude which is indeed intolerable. Our side is firmly against this unreasonable attitude of your side.

On 20 February UNC staff officers proposed the monthly personnel rotation figure of 35,000 as an equitable compromise between the 30,000 suggested by the Communists and the 40,000 formerly requested by the UNC. The Communists immediately rejected this figure.

On 22 February the UNC stated it would be willing to modify its requirements for specified ports of entry to six. On this same day the Communists had raised their figure on ports of entry from four to five—their "final compromise proposal." On 23 February the Communists accepted the 35,000 rotation figure, but rejected the UNC proposal for six ports of entry.

On 25 February the UNC suggested reducing the number of neutral nations to be nominated by each side from three to two. This proposal was made in an effort to eliminate the USSR as a neutral nation. The UNC would have eliminated Norway and retained Sweden and Switzerland. The Communists would have retained Poland and Czechoslovakia.

On 16 March the UNC sought again to break the deadlock on Item Three by reducing its demands to five ports of entry. This met the Communist figure. Discussions of the specific ports of entry and their complexes then commenced. On 20 March the specific ports of entry were agreed upon: Sinuiju, Manpojin, Chongjin, Hungnam, and Sinanju in the north, and Pusan, Inchon, Kangnung, Kunsan, and Taegu in the south.

On 25 March the staff officers reached agreement on the detailed areas open to the Neutral Nations Supervisory Commission at each of the ten ports of entry.

This completed agreement on "all of the points which the subdelegates have given us to work out with the exception of one matter—the selection of the neutral nations." The United Nations Command recommended again its solution: "Each side has nominated two neutral nations which are acceptable to both sides. It is our opinion that we could agree on these four neutral nations and solve this problem without further difficulty."

The Communists remained adamant in their demands for having the USSR as a member of the Neutral Nations Supervisory Commission. Thus ensued a deadlock intermingled with lengthy debates on the proper translations for the words United Nations and Korea for use in the "Draft Armistice Agreement."

Finally, after a seemingly irremedial deadlock, the discussions were tossed back on 3 April to the Sub-Delegation on Item Three, which sought to resolve the two remaining issues:

1. Reconstruction and rehabilitation of airfields.

2. Membership in the Neutral Nations Supervisory Commission.

The Sub-Delegation also got nowhere, as reflected by the incredibly short meetings. To illustrate, the meeting of 14 April proceeded as follows:

Meeting reconvened at 1100 hours.

Major General Hsieh: Has your side anything to say?

Major General Harrison: No.

Major General Hsieh: Since your side has nothing to say, I suggest that we recess until the usual time tomorrow.

Major General Harrison: We agree.

Meeting recessed at 1100 hours. (Fifteen-second meeting)

On 20 April the remaining issues of Item Three were referred back to the staff officers after the Sub-Delegation discussions proved fruitless. Finally on 25 April the UNC suggested the question be referred to the Plenary Session in a final attempt to seek a solution.

On 28 April the first Plenary Session since 19 February convened. The meetings were secret, as recommended by the UNC. The UNC proposed an over-all solution for the remaining unresolved issues standing in the way of an armistice in Korea. Admiral Joy observed that the three unresolved issues at this time were:

1. Rehabilitation and construction of military airfields.

2. Basis for exchange of prisoners of war.

3. Composition of the Neutral Nations Supervisory Commission.

Admiral Joy stated that there were two ways to resolve these issues: either one side concede on all issues, or each side concede on all issues, or each side concede on some issues. He asseverated that the UNC categorically would not concede on all the issues, and that the Communists must join in a compromise solution or assume responsibility for the failure of the negotiations. He then submitted the United Nations Command's "package proposal":

In the interest of reaching an early armistice agreement, we are willing to accede to your stand that no restriction be placed on the rehabilitation and construction of airfields. I must make it absolutely clear, however, that our acceptance of your position regarding airfields is contingent upon your acceptance of our positions regarding prisoners of war [i.e., voluntary repatriation] and the composition of the Neutral Nations Supervisory Commission [i.e., omission of Norway and the USSR, thus leaving Poland, Czechoslovakia, Sweden, and Switzerland] . . . . I wish to emphasize . . . that the United Nations Command offer . . . is our final and irrevocable effort.

On 2 May, following a three-day recess, General Nam Il presented the Communists' "package proposal" to the UNC following a lengthy and passionate deluge of propaganda:

In order to reach an armistice in Korea at an early date to meet the foremost wishes of the millions of peace-loving people all over the world, on this question of nomination of neutral nations our side is willing to consider the acceptance of your proposal of the Neutral Nations Supervisory Commission composed of four neutral nations, contingent upon your acceptance of our reasonable compromise solution to question of prisoners of war [i.e., forced repatriation] and your abandonment of the demand for restriction on airfield facilities within Korea, which constitutes interference in our internal affairs.

It need hardly be explained that what the Communists offered as their "concession" was not a concession at all. They had injected the name of the USSR into the discussions knowing full well it could not be accepted, and they persisted in refusing to withdraw the name even though they had originally agreed that the members of the Neutral Nations Supervisory Commission would be states agreeable to both sides.

On 7 May the secret executive sessions were terminated, and the only remaining issue was announced to the world.

The United Nations Command had mustered all its negotiatory weapons in an effort to effect what it considered would be an honorable settlement with the Communists over a war they had started. Of the sixty-two paragraphs comprising the final twenty-eight-page armistice document (dated 27 April 1952), sixty-one were originated by the UNC. It is true that each paragraph was written many times, with each side fighting over every word, phrase, and sentence before final agreement was reached. The UNC was instrumental in exploring every approach to resolve each impasse that arose. If an issue became deadlocked in the Plenary Sessions, the UNC would recommend that a subdelegation, in its less formal atmosphere, attempt a solution. If the sub-delegation reached a dead end, the UNC would suggest the issue be turned over to staff officers. When the staff officers had exhausted all possiblities, the UNC would suggest that the interpreters get together to consolidate the gains that had been made in the three languages: Chinese, English, and Korean. If the UNC suspected more progress might be made in secret sessions where no announcements would be made to the press until such time as agreed upon, it would recommend Executive Sessions. The UNC had made many more compromises of a substantial nature than had the Communists.

In contrast, the Communists obstructed every effort to reach a quick agreement, and then accused the UNC of procrastination. They continually sought to turn the meetings into a propaganda contest, of which the UNC would have no part. They made capital of every opportunity to create the false impression that they were the ones who wanted and worked for an armistice against the odds that the UNC sought to place in their way—

that they were the ones who represented "the peace-loving peoples of the whole world." When the opportunities were not there, they manufactured them. They continued their allegations against the UNC: violations against the immunity of Kaesong, bombing prisoner-of-war camps in North Korea, dumping leaflets in the conference site at Panmunjom, and killing prisoners of war on Koje Island. Their efforts were directed toward developing the impression that the members of the UNC in Korea, and particularly the United States, were the hated, monsterlike doers of evil responsible for all the ills of the world.

Finally, on 28 April, the United Nations Command presented its package proposal. The Communists' rejection of this offer evoked a determined rebuttal by the Supreme UNC Commander, General Ridgway: "The issues are clear; the stakes are manifest. Our position is one from which we cannot and shall not retreat."

8. Representatives of the International Red Cross arrive at Panmunjom in an effort to inspect prisoners of war in Communist custody. Here they are seen conferring with Major General Lee Sang Cho, Communist delegate. *US Army Photo*

9. United Nations delegates at Panmunjom (left to right): Rear Admiral Arleigh A. Burke, US Navy; Major General Harold Turner, US Air Force; Vice Admiral Charles Turner Joy, Commander Naval Forces Far East; Major General Laurence C. Craigie, US Air Force; and Major General Lee Hyung Koon, ROK Army. *US Army Photo*

10.   Members of the Communist delegation (left to right): Rear Admiral Kim Won Mu, North Korean Navy; Major General Lee Sang Cho, North Korean Army; General Nam II, North Korean Army; and Major General Hsieh Fang, Chinese Communist Army. *US Navy Photo*

11.   The conference table inside the peace tent at Panmunjom. The UNC Delegation occupied the seats on the near side of the table and the Communist Delegation the opposite side. The Senior Delegates sat in the center chairs. The staffs, interpreters, and stenographers sat behind the delegations.   *Photo by the author*

12.   Senior Communist Delegate, General Nam II, arrives at Panmunjom in the Imperial Chrysler captured during Communist seizure of Seoul.   *US Navy Photo*

13.   At Panmunjom the Communists constructed sentry boxes similar to those of the UNC with the exception of the striped colors. Later these boxes were repainted because of the amusement they caused among UNC members. Major General Hsieh Fang is seen leaving the conference area.   *US Navy Photo*

14.   Senior UNC Delegate, Vice Admiral C. Turner Joy, US Navy, at a press interview.
US Navy Photo

15.   Staff officers complete agreement on the demarcation line and demilitarized zone 26 November 1951 by initialing two sets of maps. Colonel James C. Murray, USMC, signs for the UNC and Colonel Chang Chun San for the Communists.   *US Navy Photo*

6

PRISONERS OF WAR

"Cheshire-Puss," Alice began . . . "would you tell me please which way I ought to go from here?" "That depends a good deal on where you want to get," said the Cat. "I don't much care where . . ." said Alice. "Then it doesn't matter much which way you go," said the Cat. " . . . so long as I get somewhere," Alice added as an explanation. "Oh, you're sure to do that," said the Cat, "if only you walk long enough . . . In that direction lives a Hatter; and in that direction lives a March Hare. Visit either you like; they're both mad." "But I don't want to go among mad people," Alice remarked. "Oh, you can't help that," said the Cat, "we're all mad here. I'm mad, you're mad." "How do you know I am mad?" said Alice. "You must be," said the Cat, "or you wouldn't have come here."

LEWIS CARROLL, Alice in Wonderland

A Chinese proverb declares: "He who rides a tiger dare not dismount." When the United Nations Command accepted the principle of voluntary repatriation, it was saddled to a fundamental from which it could not escape. The Com-

115

munists were as determined to have all prisoners exchanged as
the UNC was to permit the prisoners to determine for themselves
whether they should return to the land from whence they came.

From 11 December 1951, when discussions on Item Four
commenced, until 27 July 1953, the two sides sparred with each
other in an effort to determine respective strengths and weaknesses. The contest ended in a limited victory for the UNC. The
UNC did not concede on its principle. Yet the Communists were
able to save precious face. In the struggle the Communists mustered every weapon at their disposal to attempt to force the UNC
to concede. But the UNC persistently parried every blow.

The United Nations Command was determined never to
force any man to return against his will to the state from which
he had defected. The Communists, on the other hand, demanded
the total repatriation of all prisoners.

The Communists based their argument on the 1949 Geneva
Convention, especially Article 7 and Article 118.[1]

The UNC, however, contended that the Geneva Convention
was written for the protection of the prisoners of war and not
for the benefit of the state of his origin. As Secretary of State
Dean Acheson subsequently noted: "The United Nations Command would have been quite satisfied to have all prisoners returned, provided no humanitarian considerations entered into
the matter."

The United Nations Command experienced the embarrass-
ments of World War II. At that time many millions had fled
from the Communist orbit, only to be returned to the Communists at the conclusion of hostilities to suffer the indignities of

[1] The wording of these articles is as follows:

Article 7
Prisoners of war may in no circumstances renounce in part or in entirety
the rights secured to them by the present Convention, and by the special
agreements referred to in the foregoing Article, if such there be.

Article 118
In the absence of stipulations to the above effect in any agreement concluded between the Parties to the conflict with a view to the cessation of
hostilities, or failing any such agreement, each of the Detaining Powers shall
itself establish and execute without delay a plan of repatriation in conformity
with the principle laid down in the foregoing paragraph.
In either case, the measures adopted shall be brought to the knowledge
of the prisoners of war.

punishment of one type or another.[2] As a result of this action
by the free world, the message spread quite naturally to those
behind the Iron Curtain that to surrender to the free world was
virtual suicide. By the time the Korean War broke out, the Cold
War was well under way. The UNC knew that the issue of prisoner repatriation was inextricably associated with the ultimate
outcome of that war. It had but one choice—nonforcible repatriation. It recognized that it would be to the long-term interests
of the free world to accept this principle. It was coldly aware,
too, that this principle was one that would not be easy for most
Americans to understand. The concern of most Americans was
to get their own men back. They expressed small concern for
the fate of those who would be returned to the Communists. Emotional response divested them of an understanding of the long-run
problem. Yet the UNC could not dismiss these attitudes lightly.
And the Communists were certain to capitalize on these opinions
to force the UNC's hand into accepting their demands.[3]

The United Nations Command was aware, too, that acceptance of the Communist stand of total repatriation was no guarantee that the Communists would return all prisoners in their
custody. It is significant that the Communists have never in their
entire history fulfilled a pledge or kept a promise in regard to
the return, repatriation, or even a full accounting of civilian
or military personnel falling into their hands. Thousands of
Germans, Austrians, Japanese, and others remain behind the
Iron Curtain to this day, and the Communists refuse even to
discuss their fate.[4]

[2] For an excellent account of the Russians who surrendered to the Germans
during World War II and their fate, see Boris Shub, *The Choice* (New York:
Duell, Sloan & Pearce, 1950).

[3] An example of how the Communists turned American opinion against
UNC principles was demonstrated by a letter to the editor, *New York Times,*
2 August 1952. The letter stated in part: "Important thing now is to stop
fighting, even if at the sacrifice of the principle of prisoner return. . . . We
cannot impose on Asia by military force values and ethical concepts that
underlie our western civilization." This letter was picked up by Radio Moscow
the following day and given the widest dissemination.

[4] On 31 August 1953 the United Nations Commission on Unrepatriated
War Prisoners meeting in Geneva released the following information:

The West German government has submitted to the United Nations the
names of nearly 103,000 German World War II prisoners still held by the
Soviet Union. The Bonn Government also submitted the names of 1,272,000

The 1949 Geneva Convention, taken literally, demands the return of all war prisoners. But the UNC, at times with difficulty, interpreted it differently. It is ironical that at the time the Convention was being written it was the United States that favored total repatriation as specified in Article 118, in contrast to Russian opposition. This was before the Korean War and at a time when the United States was seeking the return of all unrepatriated prisoners in Communist hands. The Communists never pointed to this fact during the negotiations, nor did the UNC mention the Russian stand. It remained one of those unmentionables.

The first consideration in the United Nations Command's position was the fact that it held over ten times as many POW's as did the Communists. The UNC was of the belief that the repatriation of war prisoners should not result in a marked military advantage for either side. Certainly returning nearly 150,000 military personnel to the Communists, in contrast to a little over 10,000 UNC personnel held by the Communists, would work to the advantage of the enemy. Actually, it was from this consideration that the principle of voluntary repatriation evolved.

The Communists reflected the same adamant determination as the UNC not to concede on the position they maintained. They continued to insist that all personnel who had by the fortunes of war fallen into the custody of the enemy during the fighting should be returned at the conclusion of hostilities. Their demands exhibited anxiety over the refusal of so many persons to return to their side. It was scarcely complimentary to their way of life.[5]

In addition, the Communists appeared little interested in

German soldiers listed as missing. Most of these are known to have been held back by the Soviets, and many of them are believed to be still alive in Russian prisoner and forced labor camps. The report added that at least 750,000 German civilians have been deported to the USSR. Of these about 134,000 are believed still alive. The UN Commission has also received reports from the Italian and Japanese governments showing 63,000 Italian and 50,000 Japanese are still held prisoner by the Soviets. The Kremlin also is known to be holding thousands of Austrian, Rumanian, Bulgarian, Greek, Hungarian, and other prisoners.

(For a complete account see the report submitted by this Commission to the Eighth United Nations General Assembly.)

[5] The Republic of Korea government has stated that, since 1946, nearly four million Koreans living within the Communist lines of North Korea crossed over to the Republic of Korea.

consummating an agreement. They had achieved their desired objective of stopping the UNC advance during the thirty-day cease-fire period. The peace talks supplied them with a propaganda sounding board of unparalleled magnitude. The ears of the world were tuned to it.

The Communists exposed their recognition of the importance of the peace talks as a propaganda outlet on various occasions. The following statement by Major General Lee Sang Cho attests to this fact:

All the people of the world are now watching how the conference at Panmunjom is progressing. All the people of the world hear the voice which really wants peace. . . . Which is the right voice they will hear? It is always righteousness and truth which emerge victorious, and before them any such false humanitarianism and false civilization cannot stand.

The Communists knew all too well the impatience of the peoples represented by the United Nations Command. China and Russia were experiencing no destruction to their homelands. They could afford to wait. Time was not of the essence.

One is reminded of the ancient Chinese courtier who fell from the Emperor's favor. After being condemned to death, the courtier asked and received a thirty-day reprieve on the grounds that he wished to teach the Emperor's donkey to talk. A friend visiting the courtier in prison asked what he expected to gain by the reprieve. He replied that three things could happen: the Emperor might die; he might die; or he might teach the Emperor's donkey to talk!

The soldiers that China supplied to the holocaust (about 90 per cent of the Communist forces) and the supplies that Russia contributed (about 90 per cent of those employed) were small cost for such a propaganda harvest.[6] As long as the talks

[6] For an excellent summary of the Russian contributions to the Korean War see United State Department of Defense, *The Truth About Soviet Involvement in the Korean War*, released 15 May 1954. See also the address of Ambassador Henry Cabot Lodge, Jr., to the United Nations General Assembly on 25 February 1953.

produced favorable propaganda results for the Communists, they could not be expected to concede. The Communists reasoned that the Korean War was forcing the free world to bring to bear its forces in an area of the world that caused considerable differences of opinion to be expressed. Possibly the Korean episode would hasten the splitting of Western friendships, to the benefit of the Communists. And it was expected that the tying down of Western forces in Korea would augment Asian antipathy toward the West.

Prior to the commencement of the Sub-Delegation meetings on Item Four on 11 December 1951, there was little discussion of a substantive nature. From the first meeting of the Plenary Session, the UNC sought Communist approval for International Red Cross visits to prisoner-of-war camps, and for the immediate exchange of seriously sick and wounded prisoners.

On 27 November 1951, in anticipation of the discussions on Agenda Item Four, Admiral Joy had suggested an exchange of certain data on prisoners of war. The Communists declined.

On 4 December the UNC recommended concurrent Sub-Delegation meetings on Items Three and Four. The Communists procrastinated. Finally, on 10 December the Communists accepted, and the Sub-Delegation discussions on Item Four began the following day. Rear Admiral Ruthven E. Libby, USN, and Colonel George W. Hickman, USA, headed the UNC Sub-Delegation. Major General Lee Sang Cho, NKA, and Colonel Tsai Cheng Wen, CPV, represented the Communists.

In opening the discussions on Item Four, North Korean Major General Lee Sang Cho noted that "we want a speedy armistice and we have done our best to reach a speedy armistice. . . . We have been insisting that as soon as the armistice agreement is signed the prisoners of war should be released and we should let them go home and enjoy a happy life." He concluded with a note reminiscent of Yakov Malik on 23 June 1951 when he stated: "We think this is a question which is possible." General Lee proposed the carte blanche solution: "Release all the prisoners of war . . . after the signing of the armistice."

For the UNC, Rear Admiral Libby suggested that the following principles be adopted:

1. To effect the early regulated exchange of prisoners of war on a fair and equitable basis and under suitable supervision.

2. To insure humanitarian treatment, safety, and comfort of prisoners preceding and during exchange.

The United Nations Command also brought up the question of visits by the International Committee of the Red Cross, the exchange of pertinent data (such as POW names and nationalities, locations of POW camps, numbers in each POW camp), and the immediate exchange of the seriously sick and injured.

The only progress resulting from this first round was the single Communist statement: "We will release the ill prisoners first, at the time of release."

The tenor of subsequent meetings was established at the first meeting when it became clear that the Communist attitude was going to be one of unreasoning resistance to everything until they received a UNC promise to return all their captured persons.

At the first meeting two other items were mentioned which were later to evolve into major issues: the UNC stated that the repatriation of POW's should not result in a marked military advantage for either side, and that a joint committee should be charged with implementing the details of the exchange of POW's.

At the second meeting the issues became clear. The Communists insisted on agreement to the principle of immediate release of all POW's. The UNC demanded an exchange of data and the immediate opening of the POW camps to the International Committee of the Red Cross. Neither side would discuss the ideas of the other. The UNC pointed out that the Communists had violated the articles of the Geneva Convention (Articles 79 and 88) that pertained to forwarding certain POW information to the headquarters of the International Red Cross. Actually, the North Korean Minister of Foreign Affairs, Pak Heun Yong, had sent a message to the Secretary-General of the United Nations on 13 July 1950 in which he stated that his country agreed to abide by the 1929 and 1949 Geneva Conventions.[7] The Com-

[7] The message read in part as follows: "I have the honor of informing you that the People's Army of the Democratic People's Republic of Korea strictly

munists gave evidence of their agreement to abide by the Geneva Convention by sending telegrams to the international headquarters of the Red Cross on 15 August 1950 and 12 September 1950, in which they reported the names and identification of 50 and 60 UNC personnel respectively in their custody (totaling 110). Those were the only two reports the Communists made, but these acts did indicate their knowledge of the Geneva Convention's principles.

The United States had been a signatory to the 1949 Convention but had never ratified it. The UNC meticulously attempted to honor the principles of the 1929 and 1949 Conventions.

The UNC refused to discuss any substantive matter until it had full information on the prisoners of war held by the Communists. Without the information the talks lacked substance.

Admiral Libby minced no words:

Your side has callously ignored the fundamental right of our side to receive POW data. What you expect to accomplish by holding out this information is not too clear to us. It may be that you think that our desire to achieve a speedy armistice has made us what we call "easy marks." We do hope for an early armistice but not at the price of giving everything for nothing, of "buying a pig in a poke." It may be that you think you can wait us out and that by evasive and nonsensical replies to our questions, you will cause us by sheer frustration to negotiate without knowledge. . . . We refuse to negotiate blindly.

Admiral Libby further noted that his adversaries were violating the Geneva Convention, which they had agreed to follow, by not supplying the information. "Your past actions and concrete demonstration of bad faith are another reason why we insist on the POW data before proceeding further. We have learned by bitter experience."

General Lee offered an uneasy answer to Admiral Libby:

observes the principles of the Geneva Convention, concerning the prisoners of war." Interviews with repatriated POW's disclose that the Communists stated that they had not signed the Geneva Convention and had no intention of abiding by it.

I want to ask you which is the important question, to release the POW's held by both sides or to exchange the data for it? . . . You consistently avoid showing your attitude toward our most fair and reasonable principle of releasing the POW's held at present by both sides. . . . As you know very well, we are not a signatory of the Convention. Accordingly we are not obliged to be responsible for observing the Geneva Convention. However, we respect, we honor, the most good spirit embodied in the Convention.

Admiral Libby refuted General Lee:

I note in your statements that although your Foreign Minister declared to the world that your side will adhere to the provisions of the Geneva Convention relating to POW's, you . . . quibble and indicate that your side proposes to adhere only to such portions of that part . . . as suit your purpose at this time.

In light of UNC revelations of Communist brutality on previous and subsequent occasions toward war prisoners, it is interesting to observe General Lee's expression:

You time and again quote and talk of observing the Geneva Convention, but we must tell you that we not only observe the Geneva Convention, but, more than that, we treat the prisoners more humanely than is provided for in the Geneva Convention.

The Communists were equally dogmatic in their refusal to permit the visits to the POW camps of representatives of the International Red Cross. Their logic reflected anxiety:

As for the visits to the camps by the International Committee of the Red Cross people, that is out of the question, because it is not specified and stipulated in Agenda Item Four. . . . Suppose you have a friend in a POW camp and suppose you are much concerned with his welfare. If I were you, I would rather make provisions for his immediate release than waste a lot of time in trying to arrange visits—if I were sincerely interested in him. . . . I am now going to ask you something. . . . Does your delegation present here represent the military authorities or does it represent the Red Cross society?

The Communists' argument against visits by the Red Cross as a contravention of Agenda Item Four was made despite the fact that the Plenary Session had specifically referred this question to the Item Four Sub-Delegation.

Admiral Libby: The question before the house is not what we think of your principles or what we will or will not do at a later date, but is what I am still trying to find out: In what way is our request for POW data unreasonable? We cannot go on until you do. We will again ask the question.

General Lee: Let us work this problem out this way. Let's not make lengthy statements to each other. Suppose you and I talk together directly. Is it specified in Item Four of the agenda that the Red Cross be invited to visit the POW camps?

Admiral Libby: There is nothing specified in Item Four of the agenda except the general question, "Arrangements relating to POW's." You know that as well as I do. I still asked you a question, General Lee. What is unreasonable about our request for POW data?

General Lee: Let me put it this way. This meeting is called on the basis of Agenda Item Four. We are supposed to negotiate matters contained in Agenda Item Four. Let me ask you this question. Do you put more importance on collecting data, or on releasing POW's? . . .

Admiral Libby recognized the vexations of trying to obtain a direct answer: "You can either answer 'Yes' or 'No' or you can refuse to answer. It is not necessary to ask me a lot of extraneous questions to give me an answer to my question."

The Communists then presented their proposal "for the full settlement of the question of prisoners of war":

1. To decide upon the principle that both sides shall release all the prisoners of war now in the custody of each side.

2. To agree that both sides shall release in groups, and com-

plete the repatriation of all the prisoners of war in their
custody within the shortest period possible after the
signing of the armistice agreement; and to decide upon
the principle that those prisoners of war who are seriously wounded or sick shall have the priority of being
released and repatriated in the first group.

3. To recommend that Panmunjom-Kaesong will be the
place for handing over and receiving the prisoners of
war by both sides.

4. To recommend that both sides will designate an equal
number of members to form a prisoner-of-war repatriation committee under the Armistice Commission, to be
responsible for dealing with matters related to the handing over and receiving of prisoners of war in accordance
with the above stated agreement.

5. Once the above items are mutually agreed and decided
upon, the lists of names of all prisoners of war held
presently by each side respectively will be exchanged.

The Communists carefully placed the exchange of data last
on their list, did not mention the International Committee of the
Red Cross, and put their original principle first.

During the discussions the Communists declared that they
could exchange all prisoners of war within thirty days, the seriously sick within ten days.

The United Nations Command informed the Communists
that it would discuss their proposal "at the appropriate time,"
which would be after it had enough information for substantive
discussions, and after agreement on immediate visits by the
International Committee of the Red Cross.

Finally on 18 December, after seven days of needling the
Communists for POW specifics, lists were exchanged, and meetings were recessed until 22 December to enable the respective
delegations to study the information.

The list that the UNC handed the Communists was broken
down as follows:

North Korean POW's	95,531
Chinese People's Volunteers	20,700
Republic of Korea	16,243
Total	132,474

In exchange the Communists handed the UNC their list:

Republic of Korea POW's	7,142
United States of America	3,198
United Kingdom	919
Turkey	234
Philippines	40
France	10
Australia	6
Union of South Africa	4
Japan	3
Canada	1
Greece	1
Netherlands	1
Total	11,559

The wide discrepancy between the list handed the UNC and the UNC records of men missing in action tended to confirm to the world the earlier announcement by Colonel James M. Hanley, Eighth Army Judge Advocate, on 14 November 1951, which declared that the Communists had killed at least 5,790 POW's, of which approximately 5,500 were United States soldiers, and approximately 250,000 Korean civilians in the Korean campaign. In October 1953, three months following the signing of the Armistice Agreement, the United States Army released a documented account of the Korean atrocities. The account makes Edgar Allen Poe's horror stories seem completely innocuous.[8] Aware of such grim and ghastly atrocities, the UNC faced the Communists in the talks on Item Four with grave misapprehensions.

[8] See *Interim Historical Report*, War Crimes Division, Judge Advocate Section, Korean Communications Zone, APO 234, cumulative to 30 June 1953.

Shocked by the meagerness of the list it received, the United Nations Command on 21 December addressed a stiffly worded note to the Communists. Much of the information on which the UNC based its note was released by the Communists themselves. For example, of the 110 names that the Communists had given to the International Red Cross on 18 August and 14 September 1950, 66 were missing from the 18 December list. From the hundreds of names publicized by the Communists in the course of what they termed "humanitarian broadcasts," in their official releases, and in other sources, more than 1,000 UNC personnel named as POW's were also missing from the 18 December list. The note to the Communists further stated: "Of the tens of thousands of soldiers of the Republic of Korea who are carried in official records as 'missing in action' you listed only 7,142 as captured—a wholly unbelievable ratio under conditions of warfare in Korea." The note ended with a blunt request for a "complete, proper, and satisfactory explanation as to the status of the United Nations personnel noted and the many thousands of ROK army personnel unreported by you as POW's."

On the same day General Ridgway broadcast a message to Kim Il Sung and Peng Teh-huai requesting them to allow Red Cross inspection of the POW camps.[9]

Two days later the Communists replied with the assertion that "our humanitarian care and concern are amply reflected in the detailed and clear list of prisoners of war submitted by our side. Therefore we deem it unnecessary for the International Committee of the Red Cross to visit the prisoner-of-war camps." However, they did suggest that representatives of the Red Cross of North Korea and Communist China and the International Committee of the Red Cross visit the camps "after the armistice agreement is signed and put into effect."

On 22 December the Communists sought to seize the offen-

[9] Shortly after commencing talks on Item Four, the UNC had suggested that the International Committee of the Red Cross send two representatives to Korea to be available if and when the Communists approved their admittance. They arrived in the middle of January, only to be coldly received by the Communists. A letter to the North Korean Prime Minister asking permission to visit the POW camps was flatly declined.

sive by stating in the reopened talks that the information the
UNC had handed them "could hardly be considered as data."
They noted that there was a discrepancy of 1,456 in the list
itself, and that their information from Geneva indicated the
UNC had 44,259 more POW's than presented on the list exchanged. Admiral Libby explained that he was aware that the
UNC list was unsatisfactory and sought to explain the discrepancies. He noted that the major portion of the 44,259 figure
were civilian internees—roughly 37,000. He also accounted for
the 1,456 figure by saying that many prisoners of war gave
more than one name. He also served notice to the Communists
not to expect the civilian internees nor the Republic of Korea
group of 16,243 back. This would leave a balance of approximately 116,000. Admiral Libby called attention to the tremen-
dous military advantage which this exchange would give the
Communists—116,000 for 11,559. On 23 December the UNC
indicated to the Communists that some POW's of the 116,000
group did not wish to be repatriated.

In answer to Admiral Libby's accounting of the 44,259
persons claimed by the Communists to be in UNC hands, General Lee declared:

Today I heard, just now, your new and cute argument. I can hardly
believe your explanation of the 44,259 persons, and I can hardly
believe that the question of 1,456 persons can easily be solved as
you say. We cannot consider that to be a sufficient answer, and we
cannot consider it to be a satisfactory solution.

Puzzled by the Communists' constant allusion to the 44,000
figure, Admiral Libby observed:

Now, I am sorry to waste our time going over and over again this
question, but I am forced to. Let us examine the logic of your
statement that we have failed to account for the whereabouts of
44,259 people. You take a number 176,733, which was the report
you had from Geneva, as of the eighth of June, as to the numbers
of prisoners of war, numbers of people in our custody held as
prisoners of war. From that you substract the figure 132,474 on the
list we gave you on 13 December, over six months later. You sub-
tract one from the other and you produce a figure of 44,259. At
least, that is the only way we can find how you got that number.

The United Nations Command pressed for an explanation of the figure 11,559. The Communists had boasted over their radio and in their press that they had captured some 65,000 UNC personnel. The discrepancy between that figure and the figure the Communists submitted on 18 December was conspicuous. The Communist negotiators squirmed uneasily in seeking a logical reply. Their answer merits a lengthier quotation:

If we had, like you, detained all the persons we captured, it would be possible that we would have the 50,000 you mentioned. But we allowed those who wanted to go back home and who did not want to join a war against their country to go back and lead a peaceful life at home. And we directly released at the front those foreign prisoners of war who did not want to join the war against people who fight for their real independence, who fight for their own people. These measures of ours are perfectly right and I tell you that the righteous people of the world praise this revolutionary policy of ours towards the prisoners of war.[10]

In short, the Communists categorically accepted by this statement the principle of voluntary repatriation—the very principle they were opposing at the conference table.

According to UNC figures, only 177 of those 50,000 (the round-figure difference between 11,559 and 65,000) "released at the front" had returned.

General Lee further declared:

At the front, when we talked with the prisoners of war and found that they are opposed to the war and that they wished to go back home, it was then our policy to release most of them. That we have been continuously doing, and that we will do. We don't think that it is the increase of the military forces, as you think, to return the military forces directly from the front. I tell you that we think it is right. Our policy of releasing the prisoners of war en masse was right; it was for the benefit of the prisoners of war and better than detaining so many prisoners of war. Accordingly, we do not think that the smallness of our list which we handed over to you was inappropriate or not good as you think. On the contrary, we rather think it was a good thing. Those many persons who are released and who have gone back home and are enjoying a comfortable

---

[10] Italics are the author's.

life will certainly know that we are really serving the people, that we are working for the people. Accordingly, you shouldn't ask why we have so few prisoners of war in our prison camps, but you should know that they are leading a family life at home. . . . If you are really humanitarian, you should congratulate the released people on their life at home. . . .

By releasing and repatriating them, we really gave them freedom. There is no coercion such as you want to make. We did not brand on them any such word as "Anti-American" or "Anti-Soviet." We didn't carve on them any such words as "Anti-American" and "Resistance Against America." [11] Of course, we gave them education. But we do not give them any antipopular education, any education, against truth and righteousness as you do. We only educate them to really fight for peace, for humanity, for freedom, and for the welfare of humanity and for their country. There is no such education as that of instigation to war or of depriving one of their freedom an antipopular education. We gave them only the education to serve for truth, righteousness, and the people. We only gave them education to oppose aggression, to safeguard their country, and to fight against an unjust war. In Korea, when we express a big difference, we say "a difference between heaven and earth." The difference between the content of your education and that of our education is something like the difference between heaven and earth. What about accepting our proposal?

General Lee laughed at his own statement during the last five or six sentences, being barely able to say the last sentence because of laughter.

General Lee continually attempted to becloud the issues and insist upon UNC acceptance of their proposition:

The time till the signing of the armistice agreement is very precious because this time is directly related to the lives of so many soldiers on the front. If you give up such untenable arguments of yours and if we speedily reach an agreement on Agenda Item Four, we can save the lives of so many more of the soldiers. At this moment, when the time is being delayed by unnecessary pretexts, I hope you will understand what a misfortune this delaying of time brings to so many families. . . . Whether or not we hear the cannons roar again on the front depends, we think, upon your sincerity for the

---

[11] General Lee Sang Cho was referring to the instances in UNC stockades where the POW's wrote petitions in blood pleading not to be returned to the Communists and tattooing anti-Communist slogans on their bodies.

negotiations. . . . Then what about agreeing to our proposal of releasing the POW's held by both sides?

The Communists offered additional explanations as to the whereabouts of the 50,000-plus discrepancy. Besides those being "released at the front," other POW's were killed by UNC air raids, some escaped, still others died because they "didn't like work and exercise in their daily life" and because they were helpless.

General Lee declared *inter alia*:

We transported many prisoners of war from the front to the rear, mostly at night, and because of your continuous air raids we often shifted the location of the prison camps, so I think it is a natural thing that here many could escape. As to the question of what became of those deserters, you should not ask that question. As I cannot ask Admiral Libby what became of those that deserted from your prison camps, you also cannot ask me that question.

The United Nations Command was not satisfied with this curious adulteration of logic. The Communists stated that this group that had in their conceptions ceased to be prisoners of war should not be so classified. The Communists queried: "Can you call them prisoners of war? It is certain that they are not prisoners of war. Should you insist that such persons are prisoners of war, then what is mentioned in the dictionary as prisoners of war must be changed, or that stand is untenable."

By the first of the new year, the Communists' excuses had become transparent. Admiral Libby summarized the discussions:

Certain areas of agreement and certain differences of opinion have emerged from our exchange of views on the POW problem during the period it has been under discussion. . . .

First, your side wants all the POW's to be released following the signing of the armistice. The UNC agrees that this should be done, under an equitable formula.

Second, your side has incorporated into your army many thousands of our soldiers who fell into your hands as POW's.[12] From your

---

[12] A Communist leaflet directed to ROK troops offers further evidence that the Communists impressed captured South Koreans into their army. The

standpoint, your action in this connection was in accordance with your traditional policy towards POW's. According to you, the POW's were "re-educated" and "released at the front." The fact that practically all of them later reappeared in your own army is explained away by the alleged fact that they exercised their own volition in joining it.

From our standpoint, the wholesale incorporation of POW's into your army is contrary to the rules of warfare and a violation of the rights of the men concerned, since there is reasonable doubt that the prisoners were free from duress in making this decision. The rules of warfare and the rights of the individual under those rules require that you refrain from using POW's in work connected with military operations and that you shelter the prisoners from the effect of military operations. Manifestly, these requirements are not met by incorporating POW's into your own military forces. It is the view of the UNC that all former soldiers of the ROKA who were incorporated into your army through your mechanism of impressment should be returned to their status as POW's.

Moreover, since the outbreak of hostilities on 25 June 1950 your side has conscripted many civilian nationals of the ROK and accepted a certain number of deserters from the ROKA into your army. Both of these practices are consistent with your doctrines of warfare. But both are inconsistent with ours. It is our view that deserters, just as involuntary captives, should be accorded a POW status. The fact that it was with his consent that you placed a deserter from our forces in your army does not change our view that he should now, for the purpose of prisoner-of-war exchange, be placed in a POW status.

Third, your side takes the position that all POW's should be returned to the side with which they were identified when they were captured. The UNC, on the other hand, takes the view that all bonafide residents of the ROK as of 25 June 1950 are nationals of

following leaflet was found between Seoul and Inchon 29 June 1951. It was a testimonial letter from a former ROK soldier. One side of the leaflet is a picture of the author of the letter dressed in a North Korean uniform. The letter on the reverse reads:
"To the officers and men of the ROK army:
"The People's Army always guides those of us who surrendered or were captured from the ROK Army to the road of rebirth. Why? Because the Korean people do not wish to fight among the same people. Their purpose is to annihilate their foes, the Americans, in our Fatherland with the united strength of our people. To be captured or to surrender is the only road to rebirth.

[signed] S/Sgt. Kim Hyun Ok
8th Co., 2nd Bn., 8th Regt., 7th Div.
Korean People's Army."

that state. From that fact they derive certain rights and have certain responsibilities which are not set aside by the accident of war. Consequently, the disposition of persons of this category who have been taken into custody by the UNC while fighting against the ROK is a matter for our side alone to determine. It is of no concern whatever to your side.

Fourth, the tides of warfare in Korea have displaced many civilians of both sides from their homes. Sometimes this resulted from accident; sometimes from military necessity. Whatever the cause, many former residents of the Democratic People's Republic of Korea are now in the territory under the control of the ROK and vice versa. Your side has alluded frequently during these discussions to the conditions under which these refugees are living. You have expressed the thought that these displaced civilians should be permitted to return to their homes as soon as the armistice is signed. The UNC, too, sees no reason why displaced civilians should not return, if they so desire, to their former homes under the Armistice Agreement. Moreover, it considers that failure on the part of the Armistice Delegations to insert a permissive provision in the Armistice Agreement would be to disregard the needs of these people unnecessarily.

Admiral Libby then pointed out that "our proposal provides for the release of all POW's. In this respect it is consistent with the principle advocated by your side." However, Admiral Libby added that "the UNC proposal differs from yours in that it expressly provides that all repatriation will be voluntary." Thus in this statement of 2 January the UNC position on voluntary repatriation had become firmly established.

Admiral Libby then spelled out the United Nations Command proposal:

1. The prisoners of war who elect repatriation shall be exchanged on a one-for-one basis until one side has exchanged all such prisoners of war held by it.

2. The side which thereafter holds prisoners of war shall repatriate all the prisoners of war who elect to be repatriated in a one-for-one exchange for foreign civilians interned by the other side, and for civilians and other persons of the one side, who are at the time of the signing of the armistice in the territory under the control of

the other side and who elect to be repatriated. Prisoners of war thus exchanged shall be paroled to the opposing force, such parole to carry with it the condition that the individual shall not bear arms against the side releasing him.

3. All prisoners of war electing repatriation shall be released from prisoner of war status and shall be paroled, such parole to carry with it the condition that the individual will not bear arms in the Korean conflict.

4. All remaining civilians of either side who are at the time of the signing of the Armistice in territory controlled by the other side shall be repatriated if they so elect.

5. In order to insure that the choice regarding repatriation is made without duress, delegates of the International Committee of the Red Cross shall be permitted to interview all prisoners of war at the points of exchange, and all civilians of either side who are at the time of signing of the Armistice in territory under the control of the other side.

6. For the purposes of paragraphs 2, 4, and 5, civilians and other persons of either side are defined as those who on 25 June 1950 were bonafide residents of either the Republic of Korea or the Democratic People's Republic of Korea.

General Lee, before recessing to study the UNC proposal, objected to practically everything except voluntary repatriation.

The Communists subsequently completely rejected the UNC proposal. In his denunciatory speech General Lee designated the impressed South Koreans as "awakened Korean patriots." The United Nations Command, in defense of its proposal, called attention to the fact that the Communists "released at the front" many thousands of POW's. This was essentially the same as voluntary repatriation. General Lee stated that the execution of the UNC proposal would require interference in their internal affairs. Further, he said that if the Communists should agree to the

UNC proposal "we would have to hand over to your side these deserters who went over to our army in organized groups, those patriots in our army. Our revolutionary ethics do not permit it. Our state would not permit it and could not give an answer to it." Colonel Tsai of the Chinese Volunteers disclosed the real objection. He accused the UNC of trying to turn over the Chinese People's Volunteers to Chiang Kai-shek, which would be dangerous. General Lee added:

So it is apparent that you want to further detain the remaining POW's by the so-called principle of "voluntary repatriation." Then judging by what has been published in your newspapers it is clearly revealed that by force and cruel mistreatment you wanted to deliver them to a certain friend of yours in South Korea and a part of them to a certain friend of yours in Formosa. This is the so-called voluntary repatriation of which you are talking. . . . It's a matter of course that our side, which really wants humanitarianism, which really reveals the democracy, which really represents civilization and really defends the human right, cannot accept and does oppose such a shameful scheme.

At this point it had become obvious that the real issue had emerged and the fight began in earnest.

The UNC categorically denied that it was planning to turn the Chinese POW's over to Chiang Kai-shek. It is, of course, true that at that time such action was not anticipated. As a matter of fact, little thought had been given at this early date to the ultimate disposition of those Chinese who refused to be repatriated. There was no problem as to what would be done with the Korean POW's.

The discussions of the UNC proposals of 2 January convinced the UNC that the Communists, with or without design, misunderstood them. Consequently, on 8 January, a reworded version of the 2 January proposal was given to the Communists. It, too, was immediately and forcefully rejected.

For the next few weeks the meetings were long, bitter, and bereft of solution. There were continual probings for information as to the discrepancies of the POW lists. In answer to the Communists' continuing demands for an explanation of the whereabouts of the 44,000, Admiral Libby asseverated:

I don't know whether you know in Korean what we mean when we say "dead cat," or perhaps you call it a "red herring." We consider the dragging in of the issue of the 44,000 people, plus the discrepancies in the name list, to be very much beside the point.

On 17 January the Communists accused the United Nations Command of bombing its own POW's in North Korea. Admiral Libby asked whether the camp had been properly marked as required by Article 23 of the Geneva Convention. General Lee replied that "it happened at 2100 hours on the fourteenth, so it didn't matter whether it was marked or not. . . . it is a fact that in the beginning we made clear marks at the POW camps, but not a single prison camp which had the mark escaped bombing. Therefore, we had to cancel the marks of the prison camps, and we had to cancel the marks of all the hospitals, because it made your target of attack all too clear."

Admiral Libby replied:

Your answer reveals the disregard your side holds for the basic humanitarian principles of the Geneva Convention. . . . The marking of your POW and civilian internee camps is of the utmost importance, and this responsibility cannot be disregarded by your side. If you refuse to mark them we ask permission for our side to mark them. . . . Even though the incident happened after the hours of darkness, some illuminating means to identify the prisoner-of-war enclosures should have been provided. . . . When your side submitted to us the location of the POW camps, you listed only the names of the towns near which the prison camps were located. You did not furnish us with the exact geographical locations of the POW camps. Proper geographical identifications of the POW installations are necessary to establish adequate safety means around each POW camp. . . . Of course, you are well aware of the fact that two prison camps . . . you reported as located at Pyongyang are in an area which contains military targets. This appears to be an obvious attempt to make the Pyongyang area free from UNC air attack [a violation of Article 23].

On 28 January the United Nations Command produced the controversial data on the 132,474 POW's. In handing the Communists the POW information, Admiral Libby said:

The first roster is of 20,578 Chinese that is the equivalent of the roster of Chinese handed you on 18 December. The increase of twenty in the total figure is the result of a recount. We also hand you a supplementary list of 142 Chinese, bringing the Chinese total to 20,720.

The third roster is of 110,332 Koreans. It is the equivalent of the roster handed you on 18 December except that duplicate names have been removed and the count has been corrected. We also hand your supplementary roster of 1,028 Korean names, bringing the Korean total to 111,360.

The grand total of the four rosters is 132,080. This is slightly less than the total of 132,474, the number of persons actually in our POW camp on 13 December. The difference of 394 represents people that were actually civilian internees on that date and who have since been removed from the POW camp to our civilian internee camp. Their names are now carried on the civilian internee roster. We have completed our work on the 44,000 and on the lists of the dead, the escapees, and the reclassified persons. On seventy-two hours' notice, the UNC is prepared to furnish you this data, which together with that you now have will constitute an over-all accounting for all POW's we ever held, in exchange for a similar accounting for the more than 65,000 POW's captured by you. This exchange will be in accord with our standing agreement.

On 28 January, too, the UNC introduced a proposed draft of Item Four of the Armistice Agreement, expanding the 8 January proposal to include all details considered necessary to a complete draft.

On 29 January, as expected, the Communists rejected the UNC proposal completely, stating that if the major problems were solved the minutia would take care of itself. However, the following day the Communists actually discussed the details of the UNC proposal and tentatively agreed to some paragraphs. They specifically stated that as far as they were concerned the International Committee of the Red Cross was not neutral. Discussions then centered on the possibility of Joint Red Cross Teams. At this point the attitude of the Communists gave the first indication that it might be possible to solve Item Four.

The UNC suggested various changes in its draft as a result of Communist objections. Then, on 3 February, the Communists submitted a counterproposal to the 28 January UNC draft. This was a step forward.

The Communist proposal provided for:

1. Immediate release and repatriation of all POW's.
2. Bilateral parole of all captured personnel.
3. Exchange of seriously sick and injured "with priority."
4. Completion of repatriation within two months.
5. Exchange of POW's to be done at Panmunjom.
6. Establishment of a committee for supervising the execution by both sides of repatriation of POW's.
7. Joint visiting groups composed of representatives of the International Committee of the Red Cross and representatives of the Red Cross of North Korea and Communist China.
8. Exchange of information on deceased POW's.
9. The return of displaced civilians and the establishment of a committee to assist with this program.

On 4 February the UNC proposed turning the work of correlating the two proposals over to the staff officers. This was agreed on 6 February.

During fifty-four meetings of the Sub-Delegates on Agenda Item Four, the issues had been introduced, developed, and refined. It now remained for the staff officers to attempt to resolve them.

On 7 February the staff officers met to resolve the differences between the UNC proposal of 28 January and the Communist proposal of 3 February. The UNC presented for consideration what it termed a "working draft" proposal, which embraced some of the Communists' ideas on wording and general principles. This working draft involved several concessions on the part of the UNC. The United Nations Command dropped the phrases "one-for-one" or "equal numbers" from its repatriation principles. Further, it substituted "no forced repatriation" for "voluntary repatriation" as its basic demand. It also distinguished between prisoners of war and civilian internees. Finally, the UNC conceded its demands for visits by the International Committee of the Red Cross in favor of joint Red Cross teams.[13]

The following day detailed discussion commenced on the working draft. Much of the conversation centered around the meaning of the word "repatriate." The UNC insisted the meaning did not apply to a South Korean transferred to North Korea or a North Korean transferred to South Korea.

On 11 February the UNC submitted a revision of its 7 February working draft. The major difference in this draft was the elimination of interview teams to monitor the return of displaced civilians of both sides in favor of "good faith."

On 14 February the Communists offered a draft proposal for the solution of Item Four. Their draft recognized the UNC viewpoint that the functions and missions of the two committees (Committee for the Exchange of Prisoner of War and Committee for Assisting the Return of Displaced Civilians) and of the joint Red Cross teams should be described in some dettail. The Communist proposal also accepted the UNC recommendation of furnishing supplementary data on POW's. However, their proposal retained the principle of forced repatriation and employed the term "repatriation" in too large a concept.

During the next six days paragraphs were written and rewritten by both sides in an effort to find an answer mutually acceptable. It became quite apparent that the Communist use of the word "repatriation" was the principal obstacle to progress. To eliminate it, the UNC proposed on 20 February that a definition paragraph be included to clarify this point. The Communists at first rejected this suggestion, but conceded the following day. This led the UNC to present a revised proposal on 22 February, which the Communists approved with the exception of the no-forced-repatriation principle.

During the next week both sides made efforts to solve the main issue but with no results. Efforts to solve minor differences in wording and translations, except for the name "United Nations," proved more successful. A deadlock ensued, and the

---

[13] Communist frequent allusion to the "so-called neutral International Committee of the Red Cross" reflected a concern the UNC could be assuaged by suggesting Joint Teams.

discussions were returned to the Sub-Delegation on 29 February.

No progress was made during the Sub-Delegation meetings with the meager exception of the 5 March Communist proposal that the POW issue be settled on the basis of the lists exchanged on 18 December. This, of course, implied that the Communists would forget their "44,000" if the United Nations Command dropped its demands for an explanation of the whereabouts of the "50,000." The Communists rejected also another UNC proposal for the immediate exchange of the sick and wounded POW's held by both sides, and the UNC suggestion that Red Cross packages for the POW's be accepted by both sides. The Sub-Delegation meetings soon degenerated to name-calling bouts, which led the UNC to propose that the discussions be turned back to the staff officers to explore the Communists' 5 March proposal. The Staff officers resumed their talks on 16 March.

On 16 March the Communists repeated their contention that their 5 March proposal was adequate to settle the question. The UNC admitted that it failed to understand how their proposal could settle the differences. However, it stated it would investigate all facets inasmuch as it was not as much interested in the principle as in the "end product" or "end results." This phrase became the basis on which Paragraph 51 of the Draft Armistice Agreement, which pertained to repatriation, was finally drafted.

During the next few days both sides posed written questions in an effort to clarify various points. The questions proved difficult to answer. Each side procrastinated in its effort to outmaneuver its opponent.

On 20 March in answer to a UNC question the Communists amplified their 5 March proposal by substituting numbers for generalities, i.e., the UNC would exchange 132,474 POW's for 11,559 POW's received from the Communists. The Communists admitted that the actual number to be repatriated might be different from this "basic data."

On 21 March the Communists offered their "provision in principle" as a solution. It read:

After the Armistice Agreement is signed and becomes effective, the Korean People's Army and the Chinese People's Volunteers shall release and repatriate all of the 11,559 prisoners of war in their custody and the United Nations Command shall release and repatriate all of the 132,474 prisoners of war in its custody. The lists of the names of the prisoners of war above shall be finally checked by the staff officers of both sides.

On 22 March the Communists made what the UNC considered a very significant statement when they asserted that "adjustments" might be necessary, and that some "particular situations might arise" that would affect the numbers in their "provision in principle." This seemed to offer hope to a hopeless situation. How many "adjustments" would the Communists accept?

On 25 March, after considerable chaffering, the staff officers went into executive session. The negotiations now entered a critical stage. On 27 March the Communists stated that all Chinese People's Volunteers and North Korean POW's must be repatriated, but that South Korean POW's and civilian internees would have their choice. This declaration was reaffirmed on 3 July and again on 8 October.

On 28 March the UNC stated that it appeared possible to solve Agenda Item Four "within the framework of the Communist principle of 21 March."

On 1 April the United Nations Command proposed "what amounts to a revision to some extent of your 21 March proposal," which was essentially the wording used in Paragraph 51 of the final Armistice Agreement. Numbers were omitted.

The UNC declared *inter alia*:

We indicated at the beginning of our executive sessions that we considered that 132,000 failed to take into consideration all pertinent factors and, therefore, was likely to be too high a figure. We indicated that possibly 116,000 would more nearly indicate the magnitude of the exchange, but that we could not say that this number would reflect all considerations. In short, we did not want to mislead you or ourselves in attempting to guess at a figure, the development of which would require several days.

The proposed UNC revision read as follows:

The Korean People's Army and the Chinese People's Volunteers on the one hand, and the United Nations Command on the other, shall release and repatriate all prisoners of war held in custody at the time the Armistice Agreement is signed and becomes effective. The release and repatriation of such prisoners of war shall be effected on the basis of lists which shall be checked by and be mutually acceptable to both sides prior to the signing of the Armistice Agreement.

At the same time the UNC presented two "understandings," one of which stated clearly there would be no forced repatriation. These read as follows:

First, all POW's and civilian internees held by either side whose residence on 25 June 1950 was in the area now under control of the detaining side shall be repatriated, with the exception of those who desire to remain in the area of their original residence.
Second, all other POW's held by either side shall be repatriated except that those who could not be repatriated without the application of force shall be released by the detaining side and resettled, insofar as practicable, in a location of their own choosing where they can lead a peaceful life.

On 2 April the Communists suggested ending the discussions on principles and proceeding with the preparation of the lists. This was done with the knowledge that such preparation would necessitate the UNC's screening those POW's it held. The UNC had apprised the Communists of this on various occasions.

On 4 April both sides agreed to recess to determine the round number of POW's to be repatriated by each side. The UNC requested that the Communists issue a declaration of amnesty which they could present to the POW's before screening was begun. The declaration was delivered to the UNC on 6 April. Hopes were high. It appeared probable that any figure over 100,000 POW's to be repatriated by the UNC would result in an armistice.

During the recess the United Nations Command screened the POW's in its custody in an effort to determine how many wished to be repatriated. Before the screening was initiated, the declaration of amnesty was announced, admonishing the POW's that their individual decisions were most important and advising them that in making their decisions the matter should be carefully considered from every standpoint. They were enjoined to consider the effect of their decisions upon their families. They were specifically notified that POW's who did not oppose repatriation were guaranteed return to their authorities at the time POW's were exchanged, whereas no guarantees as to future disposition were offered to POW's who opposed repatriation.

Following this preparation, each POW was interviewed individually and in private by a UNC military person, who had been carefully instructed and who fully understood the importance in his function. It must be recalled that the Communists had refused the offer of the UNC to make this interview a joint affair or to have it conducted by representatives of an international neutral body.

The series of questions used in the interviews was designed to encourage a maximum number of POW's to return. The first question was designed to identify those who clearly desired to return. In the case of Chinese POW's, the first question was: "Would you like to return to China?" In the case of North Koreans, the first question was: "Would you like to return to North Korea?" If the answer was in the affirmative, the POW was listed for repatriation without further questioning.

Those who replied in the negative were subjected to additional questions designed to determine whether their opposition was nominal or whether they would violently oppose repatriation. The second question was: "Would you forcibly resist repatriation?" If the answer was "No," the POW was listed for repatriation. If the answer was "Yes," the POW was asked four additional questions to fully determine his attitude. These were: "Have you carefully considered the important effect of your decision upon your family?" "Do you realize that you may stay in Koje-do for a long time—even after those who choose repatriation have returned home?" "Do you understand that the United Nations Command has never promised to send you to any certain place?" "Do you still insist on forcibly resisting repatriation?"

Then the most important question was asked: "Despite your decision, if the UNC should repatriate you, what would you do?" The POW was listed for repatriation unless during the questioning he mentioned suicide, fight to death, braving death to escape, or similar intentions.

In the operation only United States military personnel interrogated the Chinese. In the case of the Koreans, United States personnel were largely used. However, in a few cases others assisted. Most of those in the compounds that had become "untouchable" as a result of the Communist-inspired riots were included in those to be sent back.

On 19 April the meetings were resumed. The United Nations Command presented the Communists with the round number it had compiled through the screenings—70,000. And it did so with the feeling that the Communists could not accept such a low figure. Most UNC delegates believed that a figure approaching 100,000 might have been acceptable. But 70,000 would cause too great a loss of face.

Civilian internees	7,200
Republic of Korea POW's	3,800
North Korean POW's	53,900
Chinese People's Volunteer POW's	5,100

The Communists submitted their round figure of "around 12,000": 7,700 Korean POW's and 4,400 non-Korean POW's.

The Communists immediately and forcefully rejected the UNC figure and continued to do so, with many recriminations, until the staff officers recessed on 25 April.

In rejecting the UNC figure the Communists stated:

It is completely impossible for us to consider your estimated number of 70,000 of our captured personnel whom you say your side was prepared to repatriate following the armistice. You said that that figure was the result of the application of the understandings put forth by your side on 1 April. But you should know that our side definitely cannot agree to paragraph 2 of the understandings put forth by your side. Your side averred repeatedly that you were willing to settle the problem within the framework of our proposal of 21 March. Your side also indicated in the executive sessions that the number of our captured personnel whom your side was going to repatriate would be close to 116,000. The round number of 70,000 submitted by your side loses all connection both within the framework of 132,000, which you said you were willing to accept, and with the figure of 116,000, which you specifically indicated.

On 23 April the UNC offered to rescreen all the POW's co-operatively with the Communists. The Communists rejected this offer. "Our side absolutely cannot agree to any such course of action."

It was apparent that the two groups had failed to solve Agenda Item Four by itself. The only remaining hope for an armistice seemed to rest in the possibility of solving Agenda Items Three and Four together. This lead the UNC to submit its compromise "package proposal" on 28 April.[14]

The Communists' rejection of the UNC package proposal and the presentation of their proposal in its stead brought the negotiations to a virtual standstill until 28 March of 1953—eleven months later.

Meanwhile each side struggled uneasily in an effort to dislodge its opponent from his position. The United Nations Command toyed with plans for renewed and forceful military assaults against North Korea—by land, sea, and air—as a means of forcing the Communists to change their tune. The UNC was supported by impatient voices in the United States and elsewhere. The UNC gave the Communists until 8 October to accept its "package proposal," at which time it unilaterally called for a recess.

For their part, the Communists had been frustrated in their plans to engulf all of Korea, and their armies had been decimated by the UNC. They were aware of their inability to realize further military achievements. Yet they had decided not to concede on the repatriation issue. Their only hope was to discredit the UNC and its members, with the chance the UNC might be euchred into capitulating to their demands. They were in no hurry.

The riots among the prisoners on Koje Island, Cheju Island, and Pongam were made to order and were given full play by the Communist propaganda machine to demonstrate that the United Nations Command was really coercing the POW's into refusing to be repatriated. They attempted to show the horrible

[14] See Chapter 5.

treatment the UNC offered its POW's in contrast to their "fair, humanitarian treatment."

It was later revealed that the person who directed these riots was the Communist Senior Delegate at the military armistice negotiations, General Nam Il.[15] He was ably assisted by Major General Lee Sang Cho, also a Communist delegate at the Peace Talks. A forty-four-page intelligence summary which was issued by General Mark Clark's headquarters in Tokyo in February 1953 accused Generals Nam and Lee "and their fanatical followers" of having "exploited a new area of total war." This report noted significantly that "their assignment as delegates was only incidental to their continued performance of their military duties.[16] According to this report, the Communists' aim was "mass mutinies, riots, and breakouts which had as their goal an eventual link-up with the Communist guerrillas and bandits in South Korea," and "direct violence designed to produce propaganda which might influence the armistice negotiations at Panmunjom." In their second objective they succeeded all too well.

By the time the United Nations Command presented its "package proposal" on 28 April the Communists' propaganda sources were running thin. This was well illustrated by the accusation that, at one point, the UNC was training a battalion of monkeys to throw grenades on the front lines. Inasmuch as one

---

[15] See *Interim Historical Report*, Note 8.

[16] The report revealed that General Nam Il was a former Russian army officer and a citizen of the USSR of Korean extraction, and that he had "deliberately planned and master-minded" the riots among the POW's in UNC stockades. The report further disclosed that Major General Lee Sang Cho was Chief of the Military Intelligence Section of the North Korean Army. Major General Pae Chol was described as "a Soviet army officer." This general was Chief of the Korean Guerrilla Guidance Bureau and "responsible for infiltration of agents into South Korea and control of guerrilla operations." Major General Kim Pa was described as a former Soviet MVD (Secret Police) agent who held a high position in the North Korean Political Security Department. The report noted that "he was reported on various occasions to be present at the armistice negotiations disguised variously as a sergeant or lieutenant." Jeon Moon Il, or Pak Sang Hyon, was the leader of the Political Committee inside the UNC prisoner-of-war compound at Koje with the rank of private. Jeon was one of the original thirty-six Soviet Koreans brought into North Korea by the Russians in 1945 to organize the People's Democratic Republic of Korea. Among this group of thirty-six were Kim Il Sung and Nam Il.

of their primary goals at the peace talks was a bountiful propaganda harvest, and inasmuch as the harvest was diminishing, it is not inconceivable that, had the riots not been permitted to occur, or had they not been publicized by the UNC, the Communists might have been amenable to terminating the discussions sooner. The Clark report quotes a Communist document which declares that the disclosures of the riots by the UNC was a great victory. The riots and their publicity provided much grist for the propaganda mills of the UNC's opponents. The capture of Brigadier General Francis T. Dodd, USA, the commandant of the Koje Island stockade, by the POW's in early May served to embarrass further the UNC.

The expected slaughter of the several hundred POW's in UNC camps was of little concern to the Communist leaders. The POW's "lost nothing but their lives in the fight, and these were for liberation and glorious victory." It is an interesting sidelight that the reason the Communists ignored the Geneva Convention which forbids such rioting was that they considered the POW's as still being "fighters" in the war.

To capitalize on the riots the Communists employed every medium. They were assisted by the UNC disclosures of the riots and by subsequent publicity in Western communications media. To illustrate, on 14 May, during the Colson and Dodd debacle, the *Stars and Stripes* newspaper, read by all UNC military personnel in Japan and Korea, carried a two-page spread of pictures showing the good life in a POW camp in North Korea. The photographs had been supplied to the correspondents by the Communists. They were obviously all staged. The previous day the paper carried pictures of the riots in the UNC camp on Koje Island. These depicted death, rioting, and massive propaganda signs erected in the compounds by the POW's. The contrasts of treatment were conspicuous.

Between the time the Communists rejected the United Nations Command "package proposal" and 8 October, the Communists took full advantage of the POW riots by presenting the UNC at Panmunjom with a demand for a full explanation of those killed in a particular riot. The 10 May Plenary Session illustrates Communist exploitation of the riots. Nam Il:

During the time when our captured personnel are in the custody of your side, your side is systematically taking a series of barbarous measures to attain your long-deliberated objective of forcibly retaining our captured personnel. These criminal acts committed by your side under the name of voluntary repatriation thoroughly violate the Geneva Convention relating to prisoners of war and repudiate the minimum standard of human behavior. The resistance of our captured personnel against these unlawful and perfidious acts of your side is entirely justified. The sanguinary suppression, one after another, perpetrated by your side cannot shake the firm will of our captured personnel to demand their right to repatriation. . . . This is not to be tolerated. Your side should be clearly aware that it is the inescapable obligation of the commander of each side to ensure the safety of the prisoners of war under his custody and to respect their personal dignity. Your side must bear the full and absolute responsibility for the safety of our captured personnel.

Again on 5 June, Nam Il, the leader of the riots, declared: "The series of cowardly acts of persecuting and slaughtering our captured personnel carried out by your side for the purpose of retaining them proves conclusively the utter bankruptcy of every fraudulent proposition of retaining war prisoners."

Had the United Nations Command accused the Communists of having perpetrated the riots immediately after they occurred and before Nam Il had a chance to lodge his protest, it would have deflated their propaganda value to the Communists.

On 8 May General Matthew Ridgway brought his successor, General Mark Clark, to Munsan to meet his negotiators. At that time Admiral Joy requested that he be relieved of his duty as UNC Senior Delegate if the Communists failed to accept the 28 April proposal within two weeks. Ridgway approved. Joy named Major General (later Lieutenant General) William K. Harrison, Jr., USA, as his successor. This nomination was subsequently approved by General Clark. Admiral Joy's choice of his successor proved admirable. General Harrison, the "Bible-reading soldier," was not only a capable soldier but was a scholar and an exemplary Christian.

General Harrison, was a descendant of America's "royal family"—of Benjamin Harrison of Virginia who signed the Declaration of Independence, of President William Henry Harrison of Tippecanoe fame, and of President Benjamin Harrison.

General Harrison was well suited to fill Admiral Joy's place. He was an able scholar—well versed in international relations —and equally capable as a soldier. He was self-confident, honest, affable, and deeply religious.

This latter is well illustrated by an experience of the writer. At the end of one meeting, during which the General had presented an eloquent rebuttal to Nam Il's argument, the writer complimented the General on his excellent performance. The General replied, in his Tennesseean drawl, and in complete sincerity, "Vatcher, those weren't my words. It was the Lord that put those words in my mouth."

Not only was the General an ardent reader of the Bible, but he proved adept at pitching horseshoes during the interludes between meetings. As one correspondent put it: "If I were to create a trade-mark for General Harrison, it would be a Bible with a horseshoe emblazoned on it." The many times the writer visited the General, he would find him reading the Bible or some thought-provoking book on history or world affairs. As soon as the writer entered his tent the General would set aside what he was doing and immediately toss out some searching question. This generally set the stage for an hour-long discussion. During his leisure time the General typed a manuscript on military strategy. Before many months had passed he had completed a rather lengthy treatise on the subject. The writer expressed his admiration for the competency of the work when he had read it, and suggested that it should be considered for publication. The General's only reply was, "No. It was just a mental exercise."

General Harrison, like his predecessor, Admiral Joy, was a very human being. He would shun no one consciously. He faithfully answered all the many letters he received as the Senior Delegate—many from mothers or wives of prisoners of war in Communist camps appealing to the General to concede on the POW issue so that their own might be returned. The General's peace of mind was reflected in his happy nature. It was common to see him walking about calmly whistling some tune. When he entered the conference tent, he was cheerful—at times humming—and greeted everyone with a smile. However, his contempt for the Communists, whom he considered as common criminals, was reflected in the stern and cold reception that he gave them and the very matter-of-fact manner that he himself maintained at the conference table.

On 22 May Vice Admiral Charles Turner Joy departed from Panmunjom, but not before he had pronounced his personal indictment against the Communists:

It has become increasingly clear through these long-drawn-out conferences that any hope that your side would bring good faith to these meetings was forlorn indeed. From the very start, you have caviled over procedural details; you have manufactured spurious issues and placed them in controversy for bargaining purposes; you have denied the existence of agreements made between us when you found the fulfillment thereof not to your liking; you have made false charges based on crimes invented for your purposes; and you have indulged in abuse and invective when all other tactics proved ineffective. Through a constant succession of delays, fraudulent arguments, and artificial attitudes you have obstructed the attainment of an armistice which easily lay within our grasp had there been equal honesty on both sides of this conference table. Nowhere in the record is there a single action of your side which indicates a real and sincere desire to attain the objective for which these conferences were designed. Instead, you have increasingly presented evidence before the world that you did not enter these negotiations with sincerity and high purpose, but rather that you entered into them to gain time to repair your shattered forces and to try to accomplish at the conference table what your armies could not accomplish in the field. It is an enormous misfortune that you are constitutionally incapable of understanding the fair and dignified attitude of the United Nations Command. Apparently you cannot comprehend that strong and proud and free nations can make costly sacrifices for principles because they are strong, can be dignified in the face of abuse and deceit because they are proud, and can speak honestly because they are free and do not fear the truth. Instead, you impute to the United Nations Command the same suspicion, greed, and deviousness which are your stock in trade. You search every word for a hidden meaning and every agreement for a hidden trap. . . . That these meetings have continued this long and that we have, after a fashion, resolved our differences to the point where only one major issue remains is testimony to the patience and dedication of the United Nations Command. . . . After ten months and twelve days I feel that there is nothing for me to do. There is nothing left to negotiate. I now turn over the unenviable job of further dealings with you to Major General William K. Harrison, who succeeds me as Senior Delegate of the United Nations Command Delegation. May God be with him.

With these words Admiral Joy left the conference tent and the Korean military armistice negotiations. His patience, persistence and determination to accomplish the mission to which he had been assigned ten months earlier offer sufficient testimony to his greatness.

General Harrison did not inherit a happy responsibility. He faced the task of resolving two seemingly unresolvable issues. The Communists appeared prepared to sit it out in the hope that the UNC would finally concede from sheer fatigue if from nothing else. One correspondent quipped that Mother Nature might be forced to solve the issue if the negotiators did not. Eventually all the POW's would die a natural death. Then there would be nothing left to discuss!

The Communists continued their lengthy invectives at each meeting. Their 20 September statement illustrates such vilification:

It is solely in the interest of a handful of munitions merchants and warmongers of your side that the soldiers of seventeen nations have been driven by your side to come far from their native countries and carry out inhuman destruction and murder against the innocent people of Korea at the cost of their own lives, although people throughout the world who uphold peace and justice, unanimously condemn your side for launching and carrying on this unjust war and demand an early stop to the bloodshed in Korea. And your side has for the interest of that handful of men consistently delayed and even prevented the realization of an armistice in Korea.

The facts of the past fourteen months of the Korean Armistice Negotiations have already inexorably proved and exposed the ferocity and cruelty of an imperialist aggressor which are the true colors of your side.

When your outrageous proposition of forceful retention of war prisoners has gone bankrupt and you can no longer use it as a camouflage to play deceit, your side cannot but resort to vituperation and distortion in these conferences. This only shows how desperate and disreputable—how childish and ridiculous your side has become. . . .

Fig. 3. At least time would be able to solve the knotty prisoner-of-war issue

Fred Packer in New York *Mirror*

And so on *ad nauseam.*

To this General Harrison could but reply:

Some of your language this morning is what we civilized countries associate with common criminals or persons who through ignorance or stupidity are unable to speak logically or convincingly. In their frustration they resort to efforts to insult. . . .

The Communists continued to level their charges against the UNC in an effort to further discredit it. These charges were expanded to include violations of the Panmunjom site in the form of UNC leaflet drops and artillery shells,[17] UNC bombing of POW camps in North Korea, bombing Kaesong and the road from Panmunjom to Kaesong, slaughter of POW's on Koje Island and Pongam, and UNC use of bacteriological warfare. All of these charges were designed to turn Asians against the members of United Nations Command, particularly the United States, fighting Communist aggression in Korea. To illustrate, an editorial in the North Korean newspaper, *Nodong Sinmun,* dated 9 July, described the planned use of five hundred POW's from Koje and other South Korean camps for testing new weapons in Australia. The story declared further that "last year Americans and British took one thousand prisoners of war from Korea . . . to an island in the Atlantic for atom bomb tests. . . ."

The riots were also used by other Communist states to develop the theme of anti-Americanism. An article in *Pravda* had this to say:

[17] The various investigations resulting from the Communist charges did have their amusing side. In June of 1952 the Communists charged that the UNC had violated the neutrality of the Panmunjom site, when an artillery shell landed in the area. The UNC denied the accusation and suggested the site be resurveyed, to which the Communists agreed. On 16 June the resurvey commenced, with United State Engineers doing the job. The Communists insisted on checking every move. The Communist representative followed closely on the heels of the United States Engineer lieutenant. He was short; the American tall. The theodolite was set for the tall American. The Communist was unable to peer through the instrument. He remonstrated. The lieutenant pointed out that he could not move the transit because it was already set. He suggested the Communist get a box and stand on it in order to look through the theodolite. The Communist could not subject himself to such humiliation. Finally he grabbed the transit, pulled it to the angle of his eye, peered through, and exclaimed, "O.K.!"

Koje Island! Again the gloomy shadow of Maidenek [Nazi ex-
termination camp in Poland] has come upon the world, again the
stench of corpses . . . again the groans of the tormented. . . . We
have learned that "civilized" Americans can be yet more inhuman,
yet more infamous than the bloody Hitlerites. Dachau was a death
camp, Maidenek was a death factory. Koje is a whole island of
death. . . . The American hangmen are torturing, tormenting, and
killing unarmed people here. They are trying out their poisons on
them. They have surpassed the Hitlerites; they have turned POW's
into guinea pigs and are testing on them the strength of their germ
"soldiers"—microbes.

Another *Pravda* article stated:

The speeches of orators exhale wrath . . . noble wrath against
these bandits in generals' uniforms, the butchers in white gloves,
the bloody bigots and traders in death who have unleashed the
most inhuman carnage in history, warfare with the assistance of
microbes, fleas, lice, and spiders. . . . The Koje butchers will not
escape!

Russia, who had masterminded the strategy, gave support
to the accusations by demonstrating that Americans were capable of engaging in such atrocities. They built museums to house
various "weapons of torture and death" which Americans had
used upon Russian civilians during the occupation of Murmansk
following the Russian Revolution in 1917, to "prove" Americans
were capable of such acts at Koje. They associated American
leaders with Nazi leaders—a group whose cruelty was widely
known to Europeans.

Communist propaganda attempted to portray the United
Nations Command as completely unfaithful to agreements. For
example, a Peking broadcast of 12 July charged that the UNC
launched attacks on the neutral city of Kaesong "several hundred times in the past twelve months." The Communist forces
"defended zealously to preserve the neutrality of the Kaesong
zone." The report noted that more than 5,800 UNC troops were
killed or wounded in the attacks. Such viciously false propaganda demonstrated further the perfidiousness of the Communists. The Communists also forced prisoners of war in their
camps to write "confessions" stating that they had personally

taken part in disseminating germs. The testimony of Lieutenant Kenneth Enoch, United States Air Force POW, is a case in point:

I have seen the truth as printed by the democratic Chinese press, and all these truths and kind treatment show all the more clearly the lies and untruthful war propaganda of the Wall Street radio and press. .... I am beginning to see very clearly just who is the peace-lover and who is the warmonger responsible for this inhuman war, and I am determined to struggle for peace against Wall Street capitalism, to clear my conscience of past errors. I am filled with determination to join the peace-loving camp.

The various world peace conferences were also directed toward discrediting the Western nations. The conference held in Berlin in the summer of 1952 adopted a resolution calling for the "immediate cessation of the Korean War." Pyongyang Radio blurted on 13 July: "Should America fail to abide by the world peace conference resolution, it must be held responsible for the consequences. Koreans wholeheartedly support the resolution. Korea will fight for the immediate cessation of the Korean War and the withdrawal of all foreign troops from Korea so Koreans can determine their own future by themselves." This persistent line was followed even into the Geneva Conference of April and May of 1954.

The completely fabricated charge of the Communists that the United Nations Command was engaging in bacteriological warfare in Korea was especially insidious, but played its part in the Communists' efforts to discredit the UNC and its members.[18] These charges commenced in 1951 and were carried through to the conclusion of the fighting. Following the old adage that, if one talks long enough and loud enough, eventually

[18] How the Communists distorted UNC statements was illustrated on 4 September 1951. At the Plenary meeting General Harrison stated in part: "The Chinese prisoners are few in number. To recover them it appears that you are satisfied to cause the population of North Korea to suffer the gradual destruction of their economic life in addition to hunger, disease, dislocation of homes, and other troubles which are the inevitable consequences of the military operations which you force them to support and maintain." Radio Peking twisted this statement to imply admission by the UNC of germ warfare. According to the broadcast, Harrison told Nam Il: "The North Korean people will suffer disease among other horrors of the American war unless the Koreans and Chinese abandon their POW's and accept the American ultimatum."

everyone will believe him, the Communists hammered away at
the theme of germ warfare until even the UNC military personnel were beginning to question its falsity. The writer recalls
front-line soldiers and marines asking him in all seriousness
whether the UNC was really engaging in germ warfare. Every
device and technique of the propagandist was employed in the
effort to have these charges believed. The Communists produced
examples of the "actual bombs used to carry the germs." Inter-
estingly enough, these had been used by the UNC to disseminate
leaflets. The Communists forced men to go into the surrounding
hills to find spiders, fleas, and other insects as examples of germ-
spreading instruments of the "capitalistic warmongers" who had
no regard for "humanity." [19]

The Communists forced their doctors to investigate "on the
scene" and come forth with supporting testimony. They organized an International Scientific Commission composed of
doctors and scientists from all Iron Curtain countries to come
to Korea to investigate and report. Even a British doctor was
among the group. The report showed conclusively that the UNC
had engaged in germ warfare. It was given the widest distribution. It was even picked up by American newspapers to show
what the Communists were doing and saying—an act that in
itself assisted in the dissemination of the story.

To find a remedy for the increasing number of cases of the
dreadfully fatal hemorrhagic fever among UNC forces, the
United States set a team of doctors to work on a ship off Korea.
This, the Communists shouted, was where the UNC manufactured
its germs for bacteriological warfare purposes.

The germ warfare charges were based upon a known truth:

[19] A former Chinese Communist soldier in Korea has described how the
Communist leaders had forced their troops to take part in their germ warfare
hoax:

"The Communists sent us out to the mountains to find bugs," he recalls.
"they wanted flies, mosquitoes, and fleas. We had a hard time finding them.
When we brought the bugs back, the Communist officers exhibited them. They
told the men that they had been dropped from American planes. They said
they carried germs and were intended to wipe out the Communist forces.
"Whenever a man became sick, the Communists blamed it on these germs
that the Americans allegedly had dropped. Regardless of whether it was a
cold, fever, or something else, they declared that it was caused by the American
germ warfare. . . ."—*The Korean Republic*, 15 March 1954, p. 1.

epidemics in North Korea. The Communists capitalized on these periodic contagions to support their propaganda line that the members of the UNC, and more especially the Americans, were the demoniac enemies of the people. Such magnification of minutiae again demonstrated the cunning design of the Communists to achieve their ends.

The Communists did not fail to seize every opportunity to pressure the United Nation Command into acquiescing. Recently captured POW's informed the UNC that the Communists were planning to kidnap the entire UNC delegation on 25 June, the second anniversary of the Korean War. Whether this was rumor or fact was never determined. However, it did raise certain certain doubts in the minds of the UNC negotiators as they journeyed to Panmunjom on that day. To squelch such an idea if true, the UNC forces gave North Korean and Chinese forces a particularly heavy pounding the few days prior to the alleged kidnapping. The day and night before 25 June the UNC artillery kept a steady stream of shells directed at Communist positions. In addition, the UNC provided as much support as physically possible to the negotiators on that day. However, inasmuch as Panmunjom was surrounded on three sides by Chinese troops, it would have been difficult to discourage such a plan. General Harrison even informed UNC delegates and staff that he would not force anyone to accompany him to Panmunjom on that particular day. 25 June passed without incident. The UNC could only conclude that it had been a planned hoax.

For its part, the United Nations Command made known its determination not to be coerced into relinquishing a principle that it considered vital. It would never force any man "at the point of a bayonet" to return to Communism. The UNC informed the Communists:

You have repeatedly been informed . . . of the finality of our 28 April proposal. . . . Our stand is unshakable. We will not make further concessions. We are, however, always ready to explain the elements of our proposal.

In May the UNC had recommended to its superiors the release of those POW's who refused to be repatriated. It did so on the assumption that these individuals would not be returned. It recalled the Communists' assertions that the release of their 53,000 POW's was a legitimate act. It recognized that under international law an individual may seek political asylum in another country. The POW's could have been ethically reclassified as political refugees and granted freedom. There would then be nothing left to discuss, and the Communists' propaganda sounding board provided by the peace talks would be destroyed.[20] This recommendation was not approved.

[20] The noted student of international law, Edwin D. Dickinson, gave his views to the *New York Times*, 7 December 1952, in connection with the dispute over the prisoners of war:

Some of the recent discussions on the question of repatriation of prisoners of war seem to me to be based on certain false notions about international law which should be corrected.

In the absence of treaty, the competence of states to grant asylum to political refugees is unlimited. Even Andrei Vishinsky in "The Law of the Soviet State" acknowledges the validity of this principle.

This is no mere moral exhortation. It is a very meaningful and jealously guarded legal power. It is imbedded in the vast network of modern extradition treaties, in the written Constitutions of upward of a score of states, and in the domestic law and practice of the rest. The matter is approvingly and succinctly put in Article 14 of the Universal Declaration of Human Rights, adopted by the General Assembly of the United Nations in 1948:

"Everyone has the right to seek and may be granted, in other countries, asylum from persecution."

States have the power to grant asylum. Everyone has the right to seek it. But there is no generalized obligation to give it—each state must decide on the basis of each request whether or not it will accord it, whether or not under its domestic law it can or should accord it.

Is it nevertheless to be believed that Article 118 of the Geneva Convention was intended to, and did, deprive parties to a conflict of the power to grant asylum? To deprive the very prisoners the convention sought to protect of the right to seek asylum? To deprive the states involved of the power to propose, or agree to, a plan of repatriation under which some prisoners might opt not to go home? The history of the law relating to prisoners of war and the records of the Geneva Conference of 1947 and 1949 supply the answer to these questions. It is an emphatic "no."

As early as the Revolutionary War the option of the prisoner of war not to return was respected by the United States under the Treaty of Paris of 1783, when many Hessian soldiers remained in the United States and became valued citizens of the new Republic. More recent precedents are the Treaties of Versailles, Trianon, and St. Germain and the agreements entered into by the Soviets at the close of the First World War with a large number of states. Still more recently there were the Soviet ultimata at Stalingrad and Budapest and the Anglo-French Accord regarding hostilities in Syria and Lebanon in 1941.

An opinion of the Judge Advocate General of the United States Army in 1945 reflected established law and custom in stating that a detaining

The United Nations Command exerted greater military efforts against the enemy in an attempt to force him into con-

Power was not obliged under international law and the Geneva Convention of 1929 to return a prisoner of war who had strong reason for not wishing to return. The General Assembly itself, in Resolution 427 (V) of December 14, 1950, expressly construed the Geneva Convention and the recognized standards of international conduct as calling not for unconditional return of every prisoner but for an "unrestricted opportunity of repatriation."

The Conference of Government Experts at Geneva in 1947, called in order to consider the proposals of the International Committee of the Red Cross for what became the 1949 Convention, was made aware of the fact that some capturing states had refused to repatriate prisoners against their will, and that in other cases they had repatriated them anyway. The conference decided to make no provision concerning this problem, preferring to leave room for discretion in formulating agreements or plans of release and repatriation, while assuring the principle that the benefits should be accorded promptly.

At the Diplomatic Conference in 1949, there was never any question but that a state might permit an individual who, in its opinion, had valid reasons for not wanting to go home, to benefit from asylum. The only point considered was whether it would be wise to require a state to respect a prisoner's wish. This came up in connection with two articles, 109 and 118. In 109 it was decided to require a state to retain seriously sick and wounded prisoners during hostilities if the person did not wish to be repatriated.

Great Britain and France objected to this requirement on the ground that a state had discretion to retain them anyway, and should be left to itself to exercise this discretion in proper fashion. The winning side, led by Belgium, did not challenge the existence of this discretion, but felt that certain states could not be trusted to exercise it in the appropriate case, and therefore insisted on the requirement.

Article 118 was adopted the same day the conference had made clear its recognition of the power to grant asylum. Previously, an Austrian amendment, under which a detaining Power would have been required to respect the prisoner's wish, had been rejected in committee and never reached the floor of the full conference. An objection to it was offered by General Sklyarev of the U.S.S.R. who said he feared that any expression of will might not be entirely free on the part of a prisoner, so that the question of repatriation ought not to turn entirely on his wishes.

Objections based on immigration law and national policy had been made to similar suggestions in 1947. The most that can be made of this is that it was thought desirable to leave room for the prisoner's state of origin to demand some sort of guarantees that the prisoner's interests would actually be protected. The convention, of course, forbids forcible detention against the prisoner's will and the position of the United Nations Command is precisely to afford unequivocal and impartial guarantees that no force will be exerted to make a prisoner stay or make him return.

The result reached at Geneva, then, was to preserve the right of a detaining Power to afford asylum, in any case where the prisoner genuinely claimed it; to prevent a detaining Power to respect the wish of a sick or wounded prisoner who did not want to return as long as hostilities continued.

Finally, from the record at Geneva, at Panmunjom and recently at the General Assembly, as also from what has been said above, it is

ceding, or at the very least compromising, on the POW issue. It wrought heavy damage in North Korea. However, the principal participants in the war were left untouched, which precluded effective pressure.

The United Nations Command continued to offer the Communists the opportunity to assist in rescreening the POW's. The Communists ignored the offer, preferring instead to make propaganda of this "illegal screening of our captured personnel." The UNC proceeded alone to rescreen the POW's in its camps previously screened to determine whether a larger proportion might not desire to be repatriated, and to screen those prisoners who could not be previously checked because of the riots. On 13 July the UNC announced the results: "Round number of personnel to be repatriated: 83,000 broken down as follows: 76,600 Koreans and 6,400 Chinese People's Volunteers."

The UNC attempted to help the Communists rationalize by presenting supporting arguments. On 21 June the UNC told the Communists how the USSR, "a nation for whom your governments have upon occasion expressed the highest admiration," had in 1943 offered surrendered German soldiers the right to select repatriation to their homeland or alternatively any other country they desired after the war. The UNC then cited from a 1951 official USSR publication, which described the 1943 action as expressing the highest act of humanitarianism.[21]

On 1 July the United Nations Command suggested the possibility of readjusting points of view in an effort to break the deadlock. General Harrison stated: "If there is to be any solution to the issue [of repatriation of POW's], it must be one which in a reasonable degree meets the requirements of both sides. . . . It seems to our side that we actually have a reasonable

perfectly clear that the position of the United Nations Command and of the United States is not that a detaining Power at the end of hostilities must admit to its territory all prisoners of war seeking asylum. Neither the position supported by the United States, nor the Geneva Convention, nor the precedent which would be set in Korea would require the United States or any other detaining Power in any future conflict to permit prisoners of war to remain indefinitely in its territory.

[21] This information was supplied to the UNC by the American Federation of Labor in a letter to General Clark. It tends to reflect the lack of substantive information available for argumentation. The UNC delegation was always grateful for any information which it could use to support its position.

basis for an armistice agreement." In making this statement, General Harrison did not wish to imply the possibility that the UNC might concede. He made it quite clear that "we are not making a new proposal." General Harrison presented the views of the UNC from every possible angle in the hope that one might be acceptable in reconciling the opposing views. The Communist delegation apparently interpreted the General's statement to mean that the UNC would now make a concession which "in a reasonable degree meets the requirements of both sides." On this assumption the Communists asked for a recess on 2 July in order to study the UNC statement and to prepare a reply. On 3 July Nam Il declared that the UNC had altered "the attitude which you have adopted for the last two months." By this Nam Il inferred that the UNC showed signs of a willingness to concede. In practically every meeting until the calling of the indefinite recess on 8 October, Nam Il tossed back those words—"a solution which in a reasonable degree meets the requirements of both sides."

On 3 July General Nam Il asked for executive sessions. Hopes ran high that the UNC had at last proffered a reconciliatory proposition. By a strange coincidence, the UNC assumed that the Communists wanted an armistice and were now willing to make certain concessions, and the Communists believed that the UNC was at last willing to acquiesce.

As a consequence, in subsequent meetings each side tried to determine what his adversary was trying to say. Each read undue meaning into the words of his opponent. Finally on 8 July the Communists disclosed the crux of the problem: "The 20,000 war prisoners of the Chinese People's Volunteers . . . are all to be repatriated." This did redefine the issue, but still it did not meet the UNC requirements of voluntary repatriation. The executive sessions ended on 25 July with little to show for the effort.

The UNC gave the Communists an opportunity to save precious face if that was their particular problem. On 19 July General Harrison showed the Communists how the number of prisoners could be shown to be 121,000. "You have now been informed that the names of 83,000 prisoners of war will appear on the exchange lists to be repatriated to your side. In addition, the lists can show 38,000 Koreans to be released directly, making a total of 121,000 captured personnel to be returned to their homes."

On 26 July the UNC agreed to a Communist proposal that the staff officers meet to go over the wording of the Draft Armistice Agreement. The meetings commenced the following day. When the staff officers completed their work on 4 August, the two sides had still to resolve the "only remaining issue."

Further, the United Nations Command reinforced its determination never to concede the repatriation of prisoners issue by employing the same bold measures in the conference tent that the Communists had employed in their many participations in international conferences in the past: viz., walking out. This was the first occasion that a Western member of the United Nations called the Communists' bluff by walking out on them. What transpired at that 7 June meeting makes interesting reading. A portion is included below:

Nam Il: If you haven't anything new or constructive to offer, I propose to recess until eleven o'clock tomorrow morning.

Harrison: We will agree to recess until 1100 hours on 11 June, or later if you desire, but not sooner.

Nam Il: Your insistence on a recess only indicates that your side is afraid to face the facts, refuses to settle the question, and lacks sincerity toward negotiating an armistice. . . . I propose again that we meet again tomorrow.

Harrison: We will meet at 1100 hours 11 June; not earlier.

Nam Il: There is no reason at all for recessing until 11 June. The conference . . . must proceed regularly. That is not to be escaped. I suggest again to recess until the usual time tomorrow morning.

Harrison: I have nothing more to say.

Nam Il: You mean that we will meet again at 1100 tomorrow morning?

Harrison: 1100 11 June.

Nam Il: 1100 tomorrow for us.

Harrison: If you desire to come tomorrow you may; we will be here at 1100 11 June. I presume that that is all it is necessary to say.

Nam Il: The conference must proceed regularly. It is against precedent that your side unilaterally wants to have a recess. I suggest again that we meet again at 1100 tomorrow. . . .

Harrison: The time of meeting is a matter for agreement between both sides. We will not be prepared to meet again until 1100 11 June.

Nam Il: We are firmly opposed to your attempt to delay the meeting deliberately. There is no reason whatever to have a long recess. I suggest that we meet again at 1100 tomorrow.

Harrison: Since we both agree that there should be a recess, the only difference is the date. We are going to recess now.

General Harrison and his staff then prepared to leave. General Nam Il whitened: "You mean you are leaving the conference site?" The UNC delegation sat down again. Finally, the UNC agreed to recess until 1400 that same day.

When the meeting was resumed at 1400, nothing was accomplished. This prompted General Harrison to declare: "Apparently the only way that I can convince you that I mean what I say is to get up and go out. We will be here at 1100 11 June. The liaison officers, in the meantime, will conduct any necessary business." With that statement the UNC delegation and staff got up and left the conference tent, while the Communists stared after them in abashed amazement.

This was the first United Nations Command recess. It lasted for three days. The UNC delegation's instructions permitted a three-day recess following seven days of meetings. This pattern followed until the recesses lengthened to seven days, then ten, and finally for an indefinite period commencing 8 October.[22] This was the UNC's answer to the Communists' demands to concede on the POW issue. For the UNC, their principle of voluntary repatriation had become "firm, final, and irrevocable."

To further underline its determination not to concede on its stand, the United Nations Command announced plans to release 27,000 Republic of Korea civilians held in protective custody on Koje Island. On 23 June Nam Il lodged a "serious protest" on releasing what it considered "war prisoners." He continued in subsequent meetings to allude to this action "to dispose unilaterally and illegally of 27,000 of our captured personnel."

On 28 September General Harrison restated the UNC proposals that had previously been offered, and then presented three additional alternative proposals, "any one of which will lead to an armistice if you truly desire one."

We have previously proposed that joint teams of Red Cross teams, with or without military observers of both sides, be admitted to the prisoner-of-war camps of both sides to verify the fact that non-repatriates would forcibly resist return to the side from which they came. As an alternative we proposed that all the prisoners of war of both sides be delivered in groups of approximate size to the demilitarized zone and given the opportunity to express their preference on repatriation, the interview to be done by one or a combination of the following:

    a. International Committee of the Red Cross.
    b. Teams from impartial nations.
    c. Joint teams of military observers.
    d. Red Cross representatives from each side.

General Harrison then presented the three new proposals.

a. As soon as the Armistice Agreement goes into effect all POW's in the custody of each side shall be entitled to release and repatriation. Such release and repatriation of POW's shall begin in accordance with the provisions of Article 3 of the Armistice Agreement. Both sides agree that the obligation to exchange and repatri-

---

[22] When the UNC walked out the second time, 17 June, the Communists burst forth in wild, premeditated laughter.

ate POW's shall be fulfilled by having them brought to an agreed exchange point in the demilitarized zone. The POW shall be identified and his name checked against the agreed list of POW's in the presence, if desired, of one or a combination of the International Committee of the Red Cross, Joint Red Cross Teams, or Joint Military Teams. The POW shall thereupon be considered as fully repatriated for the purposes of the Agreement. Both sides agree, however, that any POW who at time of identification states that he wishes to return to the side by which he had been detained shall immediately be allowed to do so. Such former POW shall thereupon go into the custody of the side to which he wishes to go, which side shall provide him with transportation from the demilitarized zone to territory under its control in Korea. Such individual, of course, shall not be detained as a POW but shall assume civilian status, and, in accordance with Paragraph 52 of the Armistice Agreement, shall not again be employed in acts of war in the Korean conflict.

b. As soon as the Armistice Agreement goes into effect, all POW's who desire repatriation will be exchanged expeditiously. All POW's objecting to repatriation will be delivered to the demilitarized zone in small groups where, at a mutually agreeable location, they will be freed from military control of both sides and interviewed by representatives of a mutually agreed country or countries whose forces are not participating in the Korean hostilities, such persons being free to go to the side of their choice as indicated by such interview. The foregoing procedure will be accomplished from each side and under the observation of one or a combination of the following:

1) International Committee of the Red Cross
2) Joint Red Cross Teams
3) Joint Military Teams

c. As soon as the Armistice is signed and becomes effective all POW's who desire repatriation will be exchanged expeditiously. Concurrently, if logistical capability permits, or as soon as possible thereafter, those POW's who have previously expressed their objections to repatriation will be delivered in groups of appropriate size to a mutually agreed upon location in the demilitarized zone and there freed from the military control of both sides. Without questioning, interview, or screening, each individual so released will be free to go to the side of his choice. We will agree, if desired, to have this movement and disposition of nonrepatriates accomplished under the observation of one or a combination of the International Committee of the Red Cross, Joint Teams of Military Observers, or Red Cross representatives from both sides.

After having spelled out the three alternative proposals, General Harrison urged "that you give mature and careful consideration to our proposals. For that purpose I propose a recess of ten days, and that we meet again here at 1100 hours on 8 October."

On 8 October the UNC journeyed to Panmunjom to hear the Communists' answer. The United Nations Command was prepared to bring a halt to the meetings if the Communists failed to accede. At 1100 the two delegations entered the new conference building.[23] General Nam Il spoke first. He repeated his previous proposals that "the captured personnel of the Chinese People's Volunteers . . . must all be repatriated home." However, to this group he added UNC POW's in Communist custody. For the Koreans he stated they "may return to North Korea." He accepted the UNC proposal of visits and classifications under the "observance of inspection teams of neutral nations." He concluded that "your side should agree without delay to this proposal so as to satisfy the peaceful wishes of the world's people including the American people, for a speedy termination of the Korean War." At least it was now clear that the Communists would insist only in the repatriation of all Chinese.

Inasmuch as the Communists still demanded the return of all the Chinese POW's, General Harrison produced the carefully prepared contingency paper summarizing the negotiations on repatriation. At the conclusion of his statement, General Harrison declared:

The United Nations Command has no further proposals to make. The proposals we have made remain open. The UNC delegation will not come here merely to listen to abuse and false propaganda. The UNC is therefore calling a recess. We are not terminating these armistice negotiations, we are merely recessing them. We are willing to meet with you again at any time that you are ready to accept one of our proposals or to make a constructive proposal of your

---

[23] When the conference tents were blown down by a typhoon in August, the Communists offered to construct a wooden building for the meetings. The UNC accepted. This act tended to underline further the Communists' attitude of not being unwilling to extend the meetings *ad infinitum*.

own, in writing, which could lead to an honorable armistice. . . . I have nothing more to say. Since you have nothing constructive we stand in recess.

And on that note the conferences ended. The Communists returned to Kaesong to continue needling the UNC with messages and propaganda over radio and in the press. The UNC delegates and staff returned to their Apple Orchard home at Munsan in preparation for departure for Tokyo. For the UNC, the termination of the conferences brought to an end—at least for the foreseeable future—the steady emissions of calumnies, sophistry, and lies of the Communists.

The UNC delegation had not expected the Communists to accept its principle at that time. The United States was in the throes of the Presidential election. It was not an impossibility that the incumbent party might concede to the Communists in order to enhance its chances for victory at the polls. There did exist a strong "school of thought" in Washington at the time which looked favorably upon such a step. The UNC, however, was not inclined to be moved so easily. It made known its reluctance to acquiesce. And the opposition party had openly pledged for an early peace in Korea.

Too, the Communists would not forget that the UNC had conceded many times in the past. The Communists could assume with some logic that, given time, the UNC could concede again.

The Communists had everything to gain by not accepting the UNC offer; little to gain by accepting it.

The problem had now been reduced to a complete stalemate. Neither physical force, psychological pressure, nor logic could end it. It was not like the negotiations between Russia and China in 1689 at Nertchinsk. In that instance the Russians had one thousand soldiers to reinforce their diplomatic arguments. The Chinese had ten thousand in addition to river boats and artillery. Such disparity in military strength had a favorable effect upon the final treaty.

In Korea, the issue was not between two nations as at Nertchinsk, but involved the entire world. The Korean War was the physical manifestation of the Cold War. Therefore, the answer to the Panmunjom imbroglio would not be found in Korea. It would be found in all the world's capitals. When General Harrison called for an indefinite recess, he was simply tossing the problem back into the laps of the world's representatives for solution.

For the members of the United Nations Command participating in the Korean War, the negotiations on war prisoners had exposed many Communist inconsistencies. Communist objections to the UNC principle of no forced repatriation vacillated constantly. At one time they appeared to have agreed to the principle of voluntary repatriation when they supplied the UNC with an amnesty declaration to be read to the prisoners in UNC custody prior to the first screening. When the results of the screening were announced and it became apparent to the Communists that the riots which they directed did not deter large numbers from renouncing Communism, they contended that the screening had not been fairly conducted. When the UNC offered to have the POW's rescreened cooperatively or by impartial nations, the Communists suddenly announced they would not agree to any type of screening by anybody, anywhere, or under any circumstances. Thus they completely reversed their previous position and denounced the UNC policy as one of "forced retention" of prisoners of war. It was, of course, apparent that the Communists had changed their position because they were not willing to admit the incontrovertible fact that large numbers of their former personnel violently opposed returning to their side.

Further, Communist incongruity was demonstrated by their associating their stand of forced repatriation with the 1949 Geneva Convention. They attempted to create the impression that they were the champions of this document. Their actions belied their words. From the beginning of the conferences the Communists obstinately and quite inhumanely refused to agree to the immediate exchange of seriously sick and wounded prisoners of war. They consistently placed POW camps close to military targets, thereby making strategic areas immune from attack. They refused to turn over the names of captured UNC personnel to the International Committee of the Red Cross, and they refused to allow the International Committee of the Red Cross or other impartial agency to visit their POW camps. They would not even agree to permitting POW's to receive relief packages. They failed to mark, or mistakenly marked, their POW camps. They failed to supply exact locations of POW camps. They religiously conducted an orientation of war prisoners to Communism.[24] They instigated riots and mutiny among POW's in UNC custody and consciously committed acts of barbarity and savagery among the non-conformists. They transferred POW's to China, neither a neutral nor party to the Geneva Convention. They failed to supply their persons with identification cards in case of capture. They impressed POW's into combat units. They forced POW's to testify against their country for propaganda purposes. They subjected POW's at their whim to the most abject forms of cruelty and inhumanity. This was their record. They talked loudly about their humanity, but they failed miserably to translate their words into actions. Yet they were well aware that the Geneva Convention expressly provided for each of these measures that they ignored. They tried to deceive the world into believing that they were concerned with the rights and welfare of individuals. They used the conferences as a forum for the most vicious type of propaganda. They never hesitated to use lies, half-truths, and distortion to further their ends.

The greatest contradiction of the Communists was their insistence that all prisoners of war in United Nations Command custody must be returned regardless of their own desires, where-

[24] Lieutenant Paul T. O'Dowd, Jr., USA, told of his experiences as a prisoner of war in North Korea:

"BRAINWASHING is the process that sent many of our captured soldiers back across the Korean truce line to repatriation singing the International and shouting the praises of their captors.

"It is the process which so twisted the minds of some of these men that they are, even today after returning to the country they have fought for, helpless to deny the sympathy for Communist ideology that has been planted in them.

"The process is not new. It is a perverted application of the process known to psychologists and educators as 'conditioning.'"—From an address delivered to the Commonwealth Club of California, 9 April 1954. For the complete transcript of the speech see *The Commonwealth*, 19 April 1954, pp. 83–85.

as they admitted that they had incorporated into their armed forces many thousands of UNC personnel whom they had captured. They accused the UNC of slaughtering POW's in its camps—acts they themselves perpetrated. Yet the record shows all too clearly the many thousands of UNC personnel they murdered rather than hold them as POW's.

The Communists further exposed their inconsistencies by their insistence that Chinese soldiers in Korea were "volunteers." They strongly supported the right of these individuals to volunteer in the "North Korean venture," but then they adopted the inconsistent position that these same individuals in the custody of the UNC did not have the right to refuse to return to their control.

Finally, after 200 meetings involving 345 painfully long hours, the United Nations Command felt obliged to call a halt to what appeared to be an interminable series of talkathons.

By 8 October 1952 the trees in the Apple Orchard had greatly deteriorated as a result of lack of care. Somehow they reflected the status of the negotiations. But, as Brigadier General William P. Nuckols, USAF, the UNC spokesman, opined on 10 July, the first anniversary of the talks, "At least we are now one year closer to an armistice."

7

ARMISTICE

When he stands up like a tired man, tottering
near and near;
When he stands up as pleading, in wavering,
man-brute guise,
When he veils the hate and cunning of his
little swinish eyes;
When he shows as seeking quarter, with paws
like hands in prayer,
That is the time of peril—the time of the
Truce of the Bear!

RUDYARD KIPLING

Between 8 October 1952, when the United Nations Command unilaterally recessed the conferences and 28 March 1953, when the Communists accepted the UNC proposal for the immediate exchange of the seriously sick and wounded war prisoners, nothing of consequence transpired at Panmunjom nor at the headquarters of the respective commands. Any progress in the negotiations emanated far from the field of conflict—at the sources of that conflict.

Korea had become the tangible expression of East-West differences. Following World War II these differences became more and more pronounced—especially so as a result of the elimination of the forces represented in the Axis powers and the gradual realization that the only two remaining forces in the world were the states surrounding the United States and the Union of Soviet Socialist Republics. The forces of the latter were determined eventually to overcome the former and impose their philosophy upon the peoples of those states. The forces of the West, caught in the path of this struggle, were impelled temporarily to accept a defensive role. In time an East-West balance set in at most peripheral points along the East-West borders. Korea, however, like Indo-China, remained a highly unstable and active area.

The Communists had failed to achieve their military objective of bringing the entire peninsula of Korea under their control. The resulting military deadlock represented an embarrassing blunder, and the Communists squirmed uneasily in an effort to turn a failure into a propaganda victory. Their propaganda success was notable, although it is still too early to offer a full accounting of its extent. Korea crystallized Western thinking and awakened it to the threats from the Communist bloc. In effect, Korea was the pivot of the Cold War, for it forced the West to consolidate its strength and reduce its weaknesses.

The point to remember always is that Korea is bound up inextricably with the East-West struggle. In no way is it divorced from it. When the United Nations Command refused to concede on the principle of voluntary repatriation, which it had to accept, it was defending an issue that was indissolubly associated with its efforts to debilitate Communist vigor throughout the world. It is only in this wider concept that what went on at the military armistice negotiations in Korea can be understood.

Just as it was the diplomatic feeler put out in June 1951 by Yakov Malik, Russian delegate to the United Nations, that led to the beginning of the Korean armistice talks, so in September 1952, when the negotiations had reached a complete stalemate, the problem of peace in Korea once again returned to the United Nations arena.

On 9 September 1952, President Miguel Alemán of Mexico had submitted a plan to the United States designed to solve the touchy prisoner-of-war dilemma. It contained three main points:

1. Prisoners requesting repatriation would be exchanged immediately.

2. Those POW's who refused to be repatriated would be divided among the members of the United Nations and granted asylum with immigration status, so they would be able to work and support themselves.

3. Those POW's who had asked for asylum could be repatriated any time they changed their minds and asked to be sent home, or after restoration of "normalcy" made it possible for their homelands to grant them "facilities and assurances" required for their repatriation.

The United Nations General Assembly took no part in the negotiations in Korea until the breakdown became complete in October 1952. At that time the General Assembly considered a solution to the deadlock that had developed over the POW issue.

The debate in the General Assembly was opened by the United States Secretary of State, Mr. Dean Acheson. Mr. Acheson reviewed for more than three hours the entire history of the Korean question. Additional information that had not been used at Panmunjom was injected into his exposé. Mr. Acheson revealed that the USSR had accepted the principle of voluntary repatriation as early as 3 March 1918 in the Treaty of Brest-Litovsk with Germany. Chapter 5, Section 17 of that treaty reads:

Prisoners of war of both parties will be released into their homelands insofar as they do not, with the consent of the capturing state, desire to remain within the latter's territory or betake themselves into another country.

Mr. Acheson made similar references to fourteen other treaties signed within a few years following World War I, which contained similar provisions. He also alluded to the World War II offers of the Russians to German troops which granted what amounted to voluntary repatriation.

Mr. Acheson concluded with the declaration that "we remain ready to solve this question of the prisoners of war upon any basis whatever that anybody can suggest which preserves the fundamental principle of nonforcible repatriation." [1]

Mr. Vishinsky traversed in his refutation all the arguments of Generals Nam Il and Lee Sang Cho at Panmunjom, with particular attention focused on the 1949 Geneva Convention. But for all his verbal ingenuity, he could not convince the General Assembly that the primary purpose of the Geneva Convention was to ensure not the rights of individual prisoners but the rights of the states that regarded them as chattels.

It was the primary objective of the American delegation, as well as some twenty others, nearly all of those actively participating in the Korean conflict, to obtain the endorsement for the principle that force should not be used in repatriation, and thereby bring the Assembly's weight behind the UNC negotiations at Panmunjom.

As the debate progressed, it became clear that there existed a strong feeling that the Assembly itself should produce a plan for solving the impasse. This feeling was strongest among the Asian delegations, although others were only too willing to consider any plan that, as Mr. Acheson observed, would "preserve the fundamental principle of nonforcible repatriation." The initiative in this matter was taken by India. The Indian resolution, as evolved following discussion and amendment, approved repatriation of all POW's following the signing of an armistice. It provided for sending all POW's to a demilitarized zone, the establishment of a Repatriation Commission composed of Sweden, Switzerland, Poland, and Czechoslovakia, or any other combinations of states not participating in the Korean fighting. In this case two would be named by each side. The Repatriation Commission's first task would be to appoint an umpire to help settle the disputes within the Commission and possibly act as Commission chairman. If the Commission failed to name an umpire within three weeks, the selection of one would be turned over to the General Assembly. The umpire would have the deciding vote. All prisoners of war would be turned over to the Commission, which would make every effort to facilitate their

---

[1] For the text of Acheson's speech, see U.S. Department of State Publication 4771, dated 24 October 1952.

return, but "force shall not be used against prisoners of war to prevent or effect their return to their homelands."

Facilities would have been provided for those POW's who wanted to return to their homelands to do so within ninety days. For those who remained behind, the Commission would make proposals for a "target date" for setting them free. Any POW still in camp thirty days after the start of the conference would be placed under a resettlement agency of the United Nations until the end of his detention.

This resolution did meet the conditions demanded by the Western bloc, yet guaranteed that the rights of the POW's would be protected. In addition, it did afford the Communists a face-saving escape.[2]

Before the views of the Peking authorities had been received by the Indian delegation, Mr. Vishinsky rejected the proposal, which forestalled any possible acceptance by the Chinese Communists. However, the Russian rejection did prove a rallying point in support of the Indian proposals.

It was immediately evident that the Communists regarded the General Assembly's acceptance of the Indian resolution as a diplomatic and propaganda defeat. The very day the Chinese Communist government announced its rejection, a planned revolt broke out among the POW's at the UNC Pongam stockade. Eighty-two POW's were killed. On the final day of the Assembly, the USSR representative attempted to vindicate its position in the manner of Nam Il by calling upon the Assembly to condemn the "American hangmen" for such atrocities, by which "Americans were systematically exterminating those prisoners who desired repatriation." This, according to Mr. Gromyko, proved the falseness of the allegations that POW's were unwilling to be repatriated. It also proved, he added in typical Marxist logic, that "American ruling circles were unwilling to put an end to the bloodshed in Korea," and had decided to detain thousands of POW's in defiance of international law. Hence, he concluded,

[2] The Russian Plan had been rejected by the General Assembly on 5 December by a vote of forty to five. Their Plan provided for an immediate cease-fire, the establishment of an eleven-nation commission to settle the POW and Korean unification issue, and the forcible repatriation of POW's if necessary.

the need for the Indian resolution which the Assembly had rubber-stamped under American pressure.

Mr. Menon, the Indian delegate, pointed out, in confuting Mr. Gromyko, that if the Indian resolution were accepted, there would be no prisoners, no incidents, no killings; and there would be peace in Korea.[3]

Mr. Munro, the New Zealand delegate, assessed the General Assembly's acceptance of the Indian resolution in these words:

> The defeat suffered by the Soviet Union was . . . more than a mere propaganda defeat. The debate served to demonstrate not merely the Communists' lack of interest in a Korean peace, but their essential unconcern with the fate of individual human beings. Their blatant disregard of Asian and world opinion cannot but have its effect. . . . It may well be that the Soviet Union does not want peace under any circumstances. It is even more probable that they cannot afford to admit that thousands of their troops are anxious to escape from their tyrannous rule.[4]

Even more significant was a statement made by the UN Secretary General, Mr. Trygve Lie, in Oslo, 8 December:

> It looks as though those who started the Korean War and attacked the Republic of South Korea are in reality against a peaceful settlement.

Mr. Lie expressed the hope that "world opinion" would influence the Communists to accept the UN General Assembly's resolution pertaining to POW's.

The intervention by the General Assembly at this point and its agreement upon a substantive proposal designed to break the deadlock was a significant contribution to the final success of the armistice negotiations, even though its resolution at that time was not acceptable to North Korea or Communist China.[5]

On 2 to 6 December, President-elect Eisenhower made his

---

[3] The final vote in the General Assembly on the Indian resolution was fifty-four for, five against, and one abstention.

[4] From an address to the Commonwealth Club of California, February 1953.

[5] For an account of the part played by the United Nations in the Korean conflict see Leland M. Goodrich, "Korea: Collective Measures Against Aggression," *International Conciliation*, October 1953.

whirlwind visit to Korea in fulfillment of a campaign promise. His declaration that "much will be done" to "improve our position," modified by a footnote to expect "no panaceas," did renew confidence in United States intentions not only not to concede on the POW issue, but that measures could be expected to be employed to strengthen materially that determination. This visit by the new President of the world's greatest power and subsequent declarations did much to reaffirm the principle of voluntary repatriation.

The Chinese were not, of course, ignorant of American planning. They knew all too well that the United States would not bend to further attacks, and they knew they were in no position to force the United States to bend. They also knew that the United States had decided not to press the attack further. But they were aware that the loudest calls for more concerted action in America had come from Republican elements. The Republicans were now in power. Thus if the Communists dragged out the negotiations too long, these elements would bring great pressure to bear on the Washington authorities to bring the forces of Chiang Kai-shek into the fight.

Likewise the value of the meetings as a sounding board for Communist propaganda had been all but exhausted. The Communists had made full use of the propaganda value of the conferences, and they had reached the point of saturation. Even in America news about the meetings had taken a back page or been forgotten.

Certainly the economic stability of China had been affected by the Korean conflict, and further efforts were seriously hampering more important projects.

And, a factor not to be overlooked, aside from Communism, the Chinese had, through the weight of arms and numbers, stopped the United Nations advance in Korea. This was the first time since Europeans commenced nibbling away at the Chinese melon in 1840 that they were able to stand firm against Western powers. Certainly China's exhibition of power in Korea added considerable prestige to the Communist regime in China. Further fighting in Korea might cost the Chinese the gains they had made.

A further circumstance contributing to the armistice was
the rescinding by President Eisenhower on 2 February 1953 of
the Truman order of June 1950 to the United States Seventh
Fleet, which encompassed prevention of both Communist attacks
against Formosa and Nationalist attacks against the Chinese
mainland. This rescision was intended to end the employment
of the Seventh Fleet "to shield Communist China." However, to
the Chinese Communists it meant freeing Formosa from obstacles
to conquest. To this extent the action did contribute to a more
conciliatory attitude on the part of the Chinese Communists.

An even more substantial contribution to the final armistice
agreement was the demise of Joseph Stalin on 5 March 1953.
It could be expected that the death of an individual who maintained absolute power within the Communist orbit would have
far-reaching repercussions. It could be expected that a new competition for power in the USSR would ensue, as occurred after
the death of Lenin twenty-nine years earlier. The frailties of
men coupled with the absoluteness of the position would permit
nothing else.

The death of such a tyrant demanded an immediate con-
solidation by his successors of strengths at home. The achievement of such an objective necessitated a retrenchment abroad.
However, this did not in any way mean a change of course. It
did not imply that the Communists were now going to accept a
spirit of cooperation with the other members of the community
of nations to accept the formula of "socialism in one country."
Such a notion was midsummer madness. The dynamics of communism conceive of the world revolution—the imposition, by
force or logic, of communism upon all peoples. The coexistence
of Communist and non-Communist philosophies is inconceivable.
The history of the Communist movement since 1917 affirms the
goals of communism to be world domination. The attainment
of that goal never ceases to come nearer. The march from a few
thousand persons under their control in 1917 and nearly one
billion in 1957 attests to the vigor of the movement. A great
force behind that conspicuous accomplishment was Joseph Stalin.
The death of such a power resulted in a temporary readjustment
of focal strength. As Stalin himself opined, "In the course of

16.   An example of Communist-fabricated propaganda printed in the English language (*The Shanghai News,* 13 August 1952, page 1). The man allegedly abducting the Korean boy was running to get out of the rain. The "blanket" was an Army raincoat.

17.   United Nations delegates answer questions of correspondents at Panmunjom immediately following the meeting 25 July 1952 (left to right): the author; Colonel Duncan S. Somerville, US Army; Lt. General William K. Harrison, Jr., US Army; Colonel Lee Soo Young, ROK Army; and Brig. General Frank C. McConnell, US Army.   *US Army Photo*

18.   After high winds blew down tents in August 1952, Communists built this more sub-stantial wooden structure for armistice meetings. White tent on right is Communist delegates' tent. Two dark ones on left are UNC delegates' tent and press tent. *US Marine Corps Photo*

19.   The apple orchard at Munsan where the UNC Delegation set up its headquarters. Note the helicopters in the foreground. The camp was equipped with volleyball courts, baseball diamonds, skeet range, and even a theater where nightly motion pictures and Sunday church services were held. Tents housed the personnel.   *Photo by the author*

20.   In leisurely attire General Harrison, Admiral Joy's successor as Senior UN Delegate, with the author at the UNC Apple Orchard Base Camp.

US Navy Photo

21. Agreement for the exchange of the seriously sick and wounded prisoners of war is signed at Panmunjom, 17 April 1953. Rear Admiral John C. Daniels, US Navy, signs for the United Nations and Major General Lee Sang Cho for the Communists. *US Navy Photo*

this [revolution] there will occur, nay, must occur, ebbs and flows in the revolutionary tide." [6]

Such were the influences on the Korean military armistice negotiations. Amid these contributions to the final achievement of a truce, little transpired in the area of those negotiations in Korea. The Communists continued leveling their charges against the United Nations Command—violations of the Panmunjom site, unfaithfulness in observing the agreement not to bomb truce vehicles moving to and from Kaesong, bombing POW camps in North Korea, slaughtering POW's in South Korea, and employment of bacteriological warfare. These allegations had become routine. Obeying the counsels of effective propaganda, the Communists persisted in repeating the accusations in the hope of discrediting the UNC in the eyes of the world.

The tenor of the Communists' imputations was reflected in a vitriolic note from Nam II to Harrison, dated 12 February, complaining of POW riots at Koje Island:

The endless crimes of persecuting and slaughtering prisoners of war committed by your side completely expose the ugly attempt of your side to retain war prisoners as cannon fodder for your so-called using of Asians to fight Asians, and lay bare the planned design of your side to overthrow the armistice negotiations, extend the Korean War, and further violate peace in the Far East and throughout the world. Your side decidedly cannot escape the serious responsibility for all these war crimes.

The Communists also persisted in pressing their protests over the United Nations Command's initiative in recessing the conferences, even though they offered nothing constructive as a means of ending the impasse.

On 22 February 1953 General Mark W. Clark, Supreme UNC Commander, addressed a letter to Kim Il Sung and Peng Teh-huai. This action was prompted by a resolution adopted in Geneva, Switzerland, by the Executive Committee of the League of Red Cross Societies, on 13 December 1952. This resolution called on both sides in the Korean conflict, as a "gesture of good

---

[6] For an informative analysis of the Communist objective, see Bernard Taurer, "Stalin's Last Thesis," *Foreign Affairs*, April 1953, pp. 367–381.

faith," to take immediate action in implementing the humanitarian provisions of the Geneva Convention by repatriating sick and wounded POW's. In his letter General Clark stated that "the United Nations Command remains ready immediately to repatriate those seriously sick and seriously wounded captured personnel who are fit to travel, in accordance with provisions of Article 109 of the Geneva Convention." Clark concluded with a query:

I wish to be informed whether you are prepared for your part to proceed immediately with the repatriation of seriously sick and wounded captured personnel of the United Nations Command who are in your hands. The United Nations Command liaison officers will be prepared to meet your liaison officers to make necessary arrangements for impartial verification of the condition and for the mutual exchange of such seriously sick and wounded in accordance with the provisions of Article 109 of the Geneva Convention.

Three weeks after the death of Joseph Stalin, on 28 March 1953, the Communists offered a favorable reply to General Clark's letter. The letter in itself is an exemplary piece of propaganda.

Concerning the question of repatriating with priority seriously sick and seriously injured prisoners of war of both sides, the delegates for armistice negotiations of both sides had, as a matter of fact, reached agreement, in accordance with humanitarian principles, on Paragraph 53 of the Draft Korean Armistice Agreement. It was solely because the Korean Armistice negotiations were suspended that there was no way to implement this agreed provision. In consequence, it has not been possible up to the present to repatriate seriously sick and seriously injured prisoners of war of both sides. Since your side now expresses readiness to apply the provisions of the Geneva Convention to sick and injured prisoners of war in the custody of both sides, our side, as an expression of the similar intent, fully agrees to your side's proposal to exchange sick and injured prisoners of war of both sides during the period of hostilities. This proposal should be dealt with in accordance with the provisions of Article 109 of the Geneva Convention. At the same time, we consider that the reasonable settlement of the question of exchanging sick and injured prisoners of war of both sides during the period of hostilities should be made to lead to the smooth settlement of the entire question of prisoners of war, thereby achieving an armistice in Korea for which people throughout the world are longing. Therefore our side proposes that the delegates for armistice negotiations of both sides immediately resume the negotiations at Panmunjom. Furthermore, our liaison officer is prepared to meet your liaison officer to discuss and decide on the date for resuming the negotiations.

On 31 March General Clark replied to the Communists, proposing that liaison groups of both sides, to be headed by a general or flag officer, meet to arrange the exchange of the seriously sick and wounded and to discuss the Communists' proposals for the resumption of the armistice talks. The Communists concurred with General Clark's suggestion on 2 April. With their letter of acceptance, they attached a statement by Mr. Chou En-lai, Premier and Foreign Minister of the People's Republic of China, together with an endorsement by Marshal Kim Il Sung, Premier of North Korea. The statement of Chou En-lai was the more interesting. It was a very lengthy review of the negotiations to date. It concluded with a proposal for the solution to the POW problem. Portions bear quoting:

Regarding the question of prisoner of war, the Government of the People's Republic of China and the Government of the Democratic People's Republic of Korea have always held and continue to hold that a reasonable solution can only lie in the release and repatriation of war prisoners without delay after the cessation of hostilities in accordance with . . . the 1949 Geneva Convention. . . . However, in view of the fact that the differences between the two sides on this question now constitute the only obstacle to the realization of an armistice in Korea, and in order to satisfy the desire of the people of the world for peace, the Government of the People's Republic of China and the Government of the Democratic People's Republic of Korea, in pursuance of their consistently maintained peace policy and their position of consistently working for the speedy realization of an armistice in Korea and striving for a peaceful settlement of the Korean question thus to preserve and consolidate world peace, are prepared to take steps to eliminate the differences on this question so as to bring about an armistice in Korea. To this end, the Government of the People's Republic of China and the Government of the Democratic People's Republic of Korea propose that both parties to the negotiations should undertake to repatriate immediately after the cessation of hostilities all those prisoners of war in their custody who insist upon repatriation and to hand over the remaining prisoners of war to a neutral state so as to ensure a just solution to the question of their repatriation.

In offering this solution, Chou En-lai made it quite clear that his side was in no way relinquishing "the principle of release and repatriation of war prisoners without delay after the cessation of hostilities set forth in Article 118 of the Geneva Convention, nor do we acknowledge the assertion of the United Nations Command that there are among the prisoners of war individuals who allegedly refuse repatriation."

The Communists also suggested 6 April as the date for the initial liaison meetings.[7]

On 5 April General Clark agreed with the Communists' date of 6 April for the commencement of liaison meetings to discuss the immediate exchange of the seriously sick and wounded prisoners "in accordance with the provisions of Article 109 of the 1949 Geneva Convention." General Clark also requested the Communists to furnish a detailed statement of suggestion "on the implementation of the proposal for settling the entire question of repatriating prisoners of war as set forth in the statement of Foreign Minister Chou En-lai, and endorsed by Marshal Kim Il Sung, in order that it may be studied while reasonable settlement of the repatriation of sick and wounded is being effected."

The liaison officers met as scheduled on 6 April at Panmunjom. Rear Admiral John C. Daniel, USN, represented the UNC, and Major General Lee Sang Cho, NKA, represented the Communists. The United Nations Command presented a plan for the orderly exchange of the sick and wounded POW's. The Com-

---

[7] Chou En-Lai's statement of 31 March and Kim Il Sung's endorsement were given further strength by a statement by Russian Foreign Minister V. M. Molotov on 1 April. The latter declaration noted *inter alia*:

I am authorized to state that the Soviet Government expresses its full solidarity with this noble act of the Government of the Chinese People's Republic and the Government of the Korean People's Democratic Republic, and has no doubt that this act will find ardent support among peoples throughout the world. . . . There can be no doubt that the peoples of the whole world, desiring to put an end to the war in Korea and to promote the strengthening of peace and security of the peoples in the Far East and all the world, will welcome this proposal with warm sympathy and offer it full support.

munists, in accepting it, stated they would study it and offer their views the following day. However, the Communists did declare that "our side is prepared to repatriate all the sick and injured prisoners of war entitled to be directly repatriated or accommodated in a neutral country according to the provisions of Articles 109 and 110 of the 1949 Geneva Convention." The following day the Communists agreed to use the UNC draft of the proposed exchange agreement as a basis for discussion, and accepted various points relative to the procedures for delivery and the site where the exchange would take place. They indicated that the number of sick and wounded UNC POW's could be furnished in a day or two. The remaining articles of the UNC exchange proposal continued under Communist study.

On 8 April the Communists and United Nations Command exchanged figures of POW's to be repatriated. The Communists figure of "around 600" included approximately 450 Koreans and 150 non-Koreans. The UNC figures included 700 Chinese and 5,100 North Koreans.

On 9 April the liaison officers established the rate of exchange at 100 UNC and 500 Communist personnel daily.

Finally, on 11 April the work on the exchange agreement was completed, and it was signed by the Senior Liaison Officers.[8] The agreement stated that "repatriation shall commence at Panmunjom not later than ten days after the signing of this agreement."

At 0900 on 20 April the exchange of personnel (popularly known as "Operation Little Switch") began, and it continued through 26 April. By that date the United Nations Command had handed over to the Communists 5,194 North Korean POW's, 1,030 Chinese POW's, and 446 North Korean civilian internees. The UNC had received from the Communists 149 United States, 32 British, 2 Canadian, 6 Colombian, 1 Greek, 5 Australian, 15 Turkish, 1 South African, 1 Filipino, 1 Netherlander, and 471 ROK prisoners of war.

After a careful study of information gleaned from the returned POW's, the United Nations Command informed the Com-

[8] For the text of the "Agreement for the Repatriation of Sick and Injured Captured Personnel," see Appendix.

munists that they held some additional 375 sick and injured UNC personnel, and asked for their return. The Communists replied that all injured and sick captured personnel except those not fit to travel had been returned. That was the last of that![9]

Consummation of the exchange of the seriously sick and wounded POW's marked a significant accomplishment in the course of the negotiations. The United Nations Command had sought such an exchange from the outset of the negotiations on 10 July 1951. After twenty-one weary months of haggling, that goal had been realized. It offered hope that agreement might at last be reached on the "only remaining issue"—the exchange of the prisoners of war.

On 10 April General Nam Il addressed a message to Lieutenant General Harrison, Senior UNC delegate, offering a "full explanation of the new proposal of our side," in answer to General Clark's request of 5 April for a detailed statement "on the implementation" of the Communists' proposal of 30 and 31 March. Nam Il's letter reviewed the proposals of Kim Il Sung and Chou En-lai. It also noted that both Article 118 of the 1949 Geneva Convention and Paragraph 51 of the Draft Armistice Agreement provided for the return of all prisoners. However, "in view of the fact that the differences between the two sides on the question of repatriation . . . have now constituted the only obstacle to the realization of an armistice in Korea, and in order to eliminate the differences so as to bring about an armistice in Korea," Nam Il noted the "obvious concession as to the steps, time, and procedure" of the POW exchange. The remainder of the letter repeated the statement of Chou En-lai with regard to releasing all POW's who insist upon repatriation and turning the remainder over to a neutral nation "so as to ensure a just solution to the question of their repatriation."

---

[9] The Communists' unfaithfulness had again displayed itself in the exchange of the sick and injured POW's. For example, of the twenty-six POW's returned from the Communist camp located at Changsong, four were legitimate cases. The remainder were POW's who had proved themselves in sympathy with the Communist cause and were therefore capable of disseminating a favorable picture when repatriated. This was undoubtedly designed to influence the negotiations and world opinion to the Communists' stand.—Interview with William C. Fleming, 10 April 1954, at San José, California. Mr. Fleming had been a prisoner of the Communists in North Korea for thirty-seven months.

Nam Il reaffirmed that his side was in no way implying a concession on the principle embodied in Article 118 of the Geneva Convention nor their interpretation of Paragraph 51 of the Draft Armistice Agreement.

On 17 April General Harrison's reply to Nam Il's letter offered the following suggestions which could lead to a prompt resolution of the problem of POW's:

That the neutral state be a nation such as Switzerland, traditionally recognized as appropriate in matters of this kind;

That in the interest of practicality, POW's who were not directly repatriated be released to custody in Korea of the neutral state;

That after allowing a reasonable time such as sixty (60) days during which opportunity had been afforded by the neutral state to parties concerned to determine attitudes of individuals in its custody with respect to their status, the neutral state would make arrangements for peaceable disposition of those remaining in its custody.

General Harrison concluded his letter with the proscription: "The United Nations Command is of the opinion that unless meetings of full delegations indicate that an acceptable agreement will be reached in a reasonable time, it will be advisable to recess meetings again."

On 19 April Rear Admiral Daniel, Chief of the UNC Liaison Group, proposed 23 April for reconvening the Plenary Session meetings. He noted that the United Nations Command would be willing to reopen the meetings in the expectation that the new Communist armistice proposal would be "along the reasonable and practical lines set forth in General Harrison's letter." Major General Lee Sang Cho, Chief of the Communist Liaison Group, requested a later date. He added: "Both parties to the negotiations should undertake to repatriate immediately after the cessation of hostilities all those prisoners of war in their custody who insist upon repatriation, and to hand over the remaining prisoners of war to a neutral state so as to insure a just solution to the question of their repatriation."

The date of 25 April was agreed upon for the resumption of Plenary Sessions. On the eve of the meetings the Communists requested a one-day postponement.

On Sunday afternoon, 26 April 1953, the Plenary Sessions reopened. This was the first full-scale meeting of the senior delegations since the recess on 8 October the previous year. General Nam Il presented a six-point proposal for ending the POW impasse:

1. Within two months after the Armistice Agreement becomes effective, both sides shall, without offering any hindrance, repatriate and hand over in groups all those prisoners of war who insist upon repatriation to the side to which the prisoner of war belongs in accordance with the related provisions of Paragraph 51, Article III, of the Armistice Agreement and in conformity with the final name lists exchanged and checked by both sides.

2. Within the time limit of one month after the completion of the direct repatriation of all those prisoners of war who insist upon repatriation, the detaining side shall be responsible for sending to a neutral state, agreed upon through consultation of both sides, the remaining prisoners of war who are not directly repatriated, and then release them from its military control. Such prisoners of war shall be received and taken into custody by the authorities of the neutral state concerned in an area designated by such authorities. The authorities of the neutral state concerned shall have the authority to exercise their legitimate functions and responsibilities for the control of the prisoners of war under their temporary jurisdiction.

3. Within six months after the date of arrival of such prisoners of war in the neutral state, the nations to which they belong shall have the freedom and facilities to send personnel to that neutral state to explain to all

the prisoners of war depending on these nations, so as to eliminate their apprehensions and to inform them of all matters related to their return to their homelands, particularly of their full right to return home to lead a peaceful life.

4. Within six months after the arrival of the prisoners of war in the neutral state, and after the explanations made by the nations to which they belong, the speedy return to their fatherlands of all those prisoners of war who request repatriation shall be facilitated by the authorities of the neutral state concerned, and there should be no obstruction. The administrative details of the repatriation of such prisoners of war shall be settled through consultation between the authorities of the neutral state concerned and the authorities of the nations to which the prisoners of war belong.

5. If, at the expiration of the time limit of six months stipulated in Paragraphs 3 and 4 of the present proposal, there are still prisoners of war in the custody of the neutral state, their disposition shall be submitted, for settlement through consultation, to the Political Conference provided in Paragraph 60, Article IV, of the Armistice Agreement.

6. All the expenditures of the prisoners of war during their stay in the neutral state, including their traveling expenses in returning to their fatherlands, shall be borne by the nations to which they belong.

The Communists' proposal stipulated, then, that all prisoners not directly repatriated would be sent to a neutral state. For six months after their arrival, members of the states to which they belonged would "explain" to them matters related to their return. If after this period any nonrepatriates remained, their disposition would be referred to the political conference.

General Harrison referred to the three points included in his letter to Nam Il as a possible solution. He then pointed out that the United Nations Command did not consider that the physical removal of POW's to a point outside of Korea was justified in any sense. He opined that such a move would afford no material advantage and would entail undesirable delays and many practical difficulties, such as time consumed in transportation, housing, and administrative accommodations. This would delay the release of POW's by months. General Harrison emphasized that the neutral state could exercise adequate custody at suitable locations in Korea, and that six months was an "utterly exhorbitant" time for holding POW's in custody. "It is our firm opinion that sixty days will be ample for this purpose." General Harrison summed up the UNC's reactions to the Communists' proposal by observing that it would force a prisoner to choose between returning to the Communists or facing detention without a foreseeable end. "It is obvious that your side failed to consider our letter of 16 April in which we outlined the nature of a solution that is reasonable and constructive and one which could lead to a prompt resolution of the problem of prisoners of war."

The Communists rejected Switzerland as a neutral state. This argument, to General Harrison, was a strange one indeed. On 29 April the Communists proposed instead an unnamed Asiatic country as a substitute for the United Nations Command's choice of Switzerland as the neutral nation to receive POW's who refused to be repatriated.

On 30 April General Harrison made a statement that was prophetic of Syngman Rhee's releasing of POW's on 18 June, only six weeks later:

It would seem quite appropriate that these Koreans whom we are still holding as prisoners and who want to live in South Korea should be released without further delay to enter into the civilian life of their fellow Koreans rather than be retained indefinitely as they might under your proposal. . . . The obviously humane thing would be to release the Korean prisoners who are now in our hands. Such release would also greatly simplify the whole problem of repatriation and the work of the custodial state.

In view of the advantages to all concerned, a proposal by your side at this time to release in South Korea all Korean prisoners who have refused to return to Communist Korea would greatly facilitate agreement on an armistice and would be received with acclaim by all decent, humane people throughout the entire world.

This, of course, was not out of line with the Communists' earlier demands that all Chinese must be returned, but that the Koreans might make a choice.[10]

On 1 May General Harrison challenged the Communists to "name your candidate for the neutral state. If you are not prepared to do this there is no point in continuing today's discussion." On 2 May the Communists queried the United Nations Command on the possibility of sending POW's to the homelands of the four nations agreed upon by both sides to constitute the Neutral Nations Supervisory Commission, viz., Sweden, Switzerland, Poland, and Czechoslovakia. Nam Il did mention India, Burma, Indonesia, and Pakistan as Asian neutrals. On 4 May General Harrison was prompted to remark that since the Communists were "either unwilling or unprepared" to name their neutral candidate, the United Nations Command had to "take the initiative in the furtherance of an armistice." He said that since Pakistan was one of the four names suggested by the Communists, he expected that its nomination "will be quite acceptable to you and will result in quick agreement on this issue. If so, then this will have been the first indication since these talks began that there may be some justification in our agreement to meet with you again." Nam Il refused to agree to any nation until the question of actually sending the POW's out of Korea to the neutral nations was settled. On 5 May General Harrison asseverated that POW's could not be physically removed to a neutral nation without the use of force and that "many would destroy themselves rather than submit to removal from Korea. . . . Your side might well spare itself the effort of continuing to advocate that unacceptable course of action."

Until 7 May the discussions centered upon the questions of what neutral state should be nominated, of whether nonrepatriates should be removed from Korea, and how long the nonrepatriates would remain in neutral custody.

[10] See Nam Il's statement for 8 October 1952, Chapter 6, page 166.

On 7 May the Communists offered a new eight-point proposal which provided for the establishment of a Neutral Nations Repatriation Commission, to be composed of the four states already nominated for membership on the Neutral Nations Supervisory Commission plus India. This commission was to take custody of the POW's in Korea. Decisions would be reached by majority vote. To this new proposal General Harrison asked how it would solve the POW questions contained in the Communists' 26 April proposal. The initial proposal had contemplated a single-nation custodian. The new proposal provided for a commission made up of five nations, which would raise many questions and difficulties. The new proposal did reduce the "explanation" time from six months to four.

The United Nations Command on 10 May told the Communists that "it was entirely reasonable" that the disposition of POW's who do not desire repatriation after a certain time limit should be handled by the political conference. General Nam Il said that the question of POW repatriation "will naturally not arise at all" as "it is hard to imagine that there should still be prisoners of war [after the explanations] who are filled with apprehensions and who are afraid to return home."

On 13 May the United Nations Command submitted a twenty-six paragraph counterproposal, based upon the Communists' 7 May eight-point proposal. The UNC proposal shortened the period of time in which the nonrepatriates would remain in neutral custody, provided for the release of Korean nonrepatriates immediately after the armistice, and proposed that only Indian forces take actual custody of the nonrepatriates. The Indian representative would also be chairman and executive agent of the Neutral Nations Repatriation Commission. The proposal further stipulated that no force or threat of force was to be used against the POW's to prevent or effect their repatriation, and that no violence to their persons or affront to their dignity or self-respect should be permitted in any manner for any purpose whatsoever.

On 14 May General Nam Il rejected the UNC counterproposal. He declared the proposal "is absolutely unacceptable" and "we absolutely reject it."

On 25 May the United Nations Command, in another effort to obtain Communist agreement on an equitable solution of the POW issue, submitted a new proposal providing for the transfer of both Korean and Chinese nonrepatriates to neutral custody, and for consideration of the disposition of any remaining nonrepatriates by the political conference for a limited period, after which they might either be released to civilian status or the question of their disposition might be referred to the General Assembly.

Before making the proposal, the UNC asked that the delegations go into executive session in order to "reinforce the solemn, nonpropaganda character of the proceedings." The Communists, after a brief recess, concurred.

In presenting the United Nations Command's proposal, General Harrison noted that the Communists' proposals of 26 April and 7 May and their comments on the UNC proposal of 13 May had implicitly indicated mental or physical coercion of POW's:

1) Demanding of excessive time in which explanations would be made;

2) Not providing for the release of POW's to civilian life on their final refusal to be repatriated; and

3) Further deferring final disposition of the POW's to still more conferences, with either side able to indefinitely block a final decision.

General Harrison further declared that the UNC's new proposal contained four major concessions to Communist objections:

1) Withdrawal of the proposal to release to civilian status on the date the armistice became effective all POW's of Korean nationality who were not directly repatriated;

2) Agreement to increasing the period of time during which POW's should be in the care of the custodial organization;

3) Agreement to submit to the political conference the question of disposition of POW's who still refused repatriation; and

4) Agreement that decisions of the POW custodial organization would be by majority vote.

General Harrison declared that the new UNC proposal agreed with the Communists' 7 May proposal on numerous points and differed only in five respects:

1) Armed forces would be provided only by India rather than all five nations represented on the Neutral Nations Repatriation Commission;

2) POW issues would be settled by a majority vote of the Neutral Nations Repatriation Commission, but provisions would be inserted into the agreement guaranteeing that no force or threat of force would be used against POW's;

3) Ninety days would be permitted for explanations to POW's, and at the end of the period those still refusing repatriation would be immediately released as civilians. This was a compromise between the UNC's proposal of 60 days and the Communists' proposal of 120 days. The UNC offered an alternative on this issue in proposing that instead 120 days could be allowed for explanations, and at the end of the period the question of those still refusing would be referred to the UN General Assembly for solution;

4) The state of origin of the POW's would bear the expense of POW repatriation from the point of exchange, as provided for in Article 118 of the 1949 Geneva Convention; and

5) Only three explainers would be permitted per thousand unrepatriated POW's instead of ten per thousand as demanded by the Communists.

At the afternoon session, General Nam Il stated that his side could not agree to turning nonrepatriated POW's over to the United Nations General Assembly as "the United Nations Organization is one of the two belligerents in the Korean War."

The next Plenary Session was 4 June. During the interim General Clark received a letter from the Communists in which they indicated that the United Nations Command's 25 May proposals on the prisoner issue "at their face value are conducive to the progress of the negotiations." At the 4 June meeting the Communists submitted a counterproposal to the UNC's 25 May proposal, which indicated acceptance of all the United Nations Command's points with one minor change. They still insisted on ten explainers per thousand nonrepatriates. They selected the UNC's alternative on postarmistice explanations of ninety days. They added, however, that at the end of the period the question of those still refusing repatriation would be referred to the political conference. At the end of thirty days, those still refusing repatriation would be immediately released to civilian status. Relative to this last point, Article 4, Paragraph 11, of the Communists' proposal read:

The Neutral Nations Repatriation Commission shall declare the release from the prisoner of war status to civilian status of any prisoner of war who has not exercised their right to be repatriated and for whom no other disposition has been agreed to by the political conference within 120 days after the Neutral Nations Repatriation Commission has assumed their custody. Thereafter, according to the application of each individual, those who elect to go to neutral nations shall be assisted by the Neutral Nations Repatriation Commission and by the Red Cross Society of India.

On 6 June the United Nations Command accepted the Communists 4 June counterproposal, with the exception that it would not agree to ten explainers per thousand nonrepatriates. It did say it would allow five per thousand, however.

On 7 June the Communists lowered their figure of ten explainers per thousand to eight, and the UNC countered with a compromise of seven. After a seventeen-minute recess the Communists agreed to the UNC figure. The UNC then recom-

mended that the staff officers review the POW terms of reference
for proper and acceptable wording.

On the afternoon of 8 June the Communist and United Nations Command Senior Delegates signed the completed "Terms
of Reference." [11]

Newspapers throughout the world heralded the signing as
marking the ending of a war. The San Francisco *Chronicle* in
banner headlines proclaimed: "Truce All Set—POW Pact
Signed."

Only minor problems still remained to be settled, such as
revising the demarcation line. On this point, the United Nations
Command suggested adopting the line as agreed to in November
1951. In making this recommendation the UNC recalled that it
had taken two weeks to agree to that line, and until 10 December
1951 to agree to the neutral zone. However, the Communists
insisted upon renegotiating the line. The UNC concurred, and
the question was submitted to the staff officers for settlement.
Actually, the Draft Armistice Agreement did state that the demarcation line would be the line of contact at the time of the
signing of the armistice.

Beclouded by the jubilation over the agreement on the POW
issue was an item in most world papers describing the lack of
concurrence by the President of the Republic of Korea. Such
disaffection was assumed from the outset of negotiations. However, the numerous difficulties arising during the course of negotiations relegated this additional problem to a subordinate position, where it was all but forgotten. It became a bridge to be
crossed when reached. But now, with the resolution of the final
obstacle to the armistice, the bridge was reached. It could no
longer be ignored easily.

Shortly before the 8 June agreement on POW's, Dr. Rhee
became even more vociferous against the impending Armistice
Agreement. The Terms of Reference for the Neutral Nations
Repatriation Commission called for screening the POW's at their
respective camps. Rhee strongly opposed permitting the Communists who would be members of the Commission to enter

---

[11] See Appendix for the complete Terms of Reference.

South Korea. He further objected to the armistice on the grounds that it implied a permanent arrangement, even though it was a mere suspension of hostilities pending the political conference's final resolution. Rhee recognized the fact that too frequently temporary arrangements evolve into permanent solutions. He knew from experience the difficulties in achieving unification of the entire peninsula of Korea. A good portion of his seventy-eight years had been devoted to Korean independence. He did not intend to see his lifelong dream fail of completion at this late date. To Rhee a truce symbolized a stalemated situation. It appeared to him that under the circumstances the goal of complete independence had a meager chance to succeed. To temporize was to admit defeat.

But to a war-weary world, Rhee had become the personification of stubborn recalcitrance. To the United Nations Command, he presented another obstacle to be overcome before an armistice could be realized.

Mr. Eisenhower, as leader of the state that had given the greatest amount of aid in fighting Communist aggression in Korea, and impelled by campaign promises to end the war, sought to modify Rhee's resistance. A series of communications in May and June attempted to achieve this end.

On 6 June Mr. Eisenhower stated in a letter to Dr. Rhee:

The enemy has proposed an armistice which involves a clear abandonment of the fruits of aggression. The armistice would leave the Republic of Korea in undisputed possession of substantially the same territory which the Republic administered before the aggression; indeed this territory will be somewhat enlarged. . . .
The unification of Korea is an end to which the United States is committed, not once but many times, through its World War II declarations and through its acceptance of the principles enunciated in reference to Korea by the United Nations. Korea is unhappily not the only country which remains divided after World War II. We remain determined to play our part in achieving the political union of all countries so divided. *But we do not intend to employ war as an instrument to accomplish the worldwide political settlements to which we are dedicated and which we believe to be just.*[12]

[12] Italics are the author's.

To reassure Dr. Rhee of continued support, President Eisenhower declared the United States would continue to seek unification by all peaceful means, it would enter into a mutual defense pact with the Republic, and it would continue economic aid to the Republic of Korea, which "will permit in peace a restoration of a devastated land."

Stile Rhee remained adamant. "The United Nations . . . is joining hands . . . with the enemy in this matter of armistice terms. . . . There is grave doubt that an armistice reached in such an atmosphere of appeasement can lead to a permanent peace acceptable and honorable to us."

The resistance of Syngman Rhee reached its peak on 18 June 1953, when between midnight and dawn approximately 27,000 "militantly anti-Communist North Korean prisoners of war broke out of United Nations prisoner-of-war camps." The Republic of Korea announced:

The anti-Communist Korean prisoners have been released. . . . The entire population of the Republic of Korea is requested to protect and help these patriotic youths.

On 18 June, following the incident, Mark Clark wrote a letter to Dr. Rhee in which he indicated that the release had clearly "abrogated" several personal assurances by Rhee during "recent weeks" that no unilateral actions would be taken.

It was to be expected that the Communists would make capital of this situation as a means of further embarrassing the United Nations Command. If it could win a propaganda victory, no matter how small, its efforts were well spent. The Communists' protests were not slow in coming. They demanded the return of the escaped prisoners, and guarantees against further defections of the "Syngman Rhee clique." At the Plenary Session on 20 June the UNC received a letter addressed to General Mark Clark from Marshal Kim Il Sung and General Peng Teh-huai accusing the UNC of negligence and placing full responsibility on the UNC for the recapture of all the escaped prisoners.

In view of the extremely serious consequences of this incident, we cannot but put the following questions to your side: Is the United

Nations Command able to control the South Korean government
and army? If not, does the armistice in Korea include the Syngman
Rhee clique? If it is not included, what assurance is there for the
implementation of the Armistice Agreement on the part of South
Korea? If it is included, then your side must be responsible for
recovering immediately all . . . prisoners of war who are now "at
liberty," that is, those who are "released" and retained under coercion and to be press-ganged into the South Korean Army.

On 21 June General Clark denied any collusion in the breakouts. "The entire responsibility rests squarely upon President
Syngman Rhee and the Government of Korea."

The camps had been guarded by ROK personnel in order
to release other UNC units for front-line duty. The unexpected
release, however, forced the United Nations Command to divert
valuable units to the camp areas as POW guards against further
efforts by the ROK to release additional POW's, and to find and
return escaped POW's. Only a small portion of the released
POW's were found.

Aware of the seriousness of Rhee's rebelliousness to the
armistice, President Eisenhower sent the Assistant Secretary of
State for Far Eastern Affairs, Mr. Walter Robertson, to Korea to
explore the nature of Rhee's discomfiture and to find a suitable
solution. Mr. Robertson arrived on 24 June and immediately
commenced discussions with Dr. Rhee.

On 29 June General Clark directed a letter to the Communists concerning the escape of the Korean POW's. In the letter
he acknowledged the incident as serious, and pointed out that
although it was a breakout by the POW's, it was engineered by
the ROK government without the knowledge of the United Nations Command. The letter proposed resumption of the armistice
talks and pointed out that every effort to secure the cooperation
of the ROK government was being and would be employed. The
letter also noted that "you undoubtedly realize that the recovery
of all these prisoners would be as impossible for us as it would
be for your side to recover the fifty thousand South Korean prisoners 'released' by your side during the course of hostilities."

On 11 July the Rhee-Robertson discussions were concluded
by a joint declaration, which stated in part:

These discussions have cemented our determination to continue and extend in the postarmistice period the close collaboration for our common objectives, marking our relations since the Communist aggression commenced three years ago.

In respect to the prisoners of war, we have reaffirmed our determination that no prisoners shall be subject to coercion and that, at the end of the specified period, all prisoners desiring to avoid returning to Communist jurisdiction shall be set free in South Korea, or, in the case of the non-Communist Chinese, to proceed to a destination chosen by them.

Our two Governments are in agreement in respect to entering into a mutual-defense pact, negotiations for which are under way.

We have likewise discussed collaboration along political, economic, and defense lines, and our conversations have disclosed a wide area of agreement concerning these matters.

In particular, we wish to emphasize our determination to work together for the realization within the shortest practical time of our common objective; namely, a free, independent, and unified Korea.

On 8 July the Communists replied to General Clark's letter. The delay in their reply was due to the Rhee-Robertson discussions which were under way. In the reply the Communists stated:

In your letter . . . you admit that the incident of coercing the captured personnel of the Korean People's Army into leaving the prisoner-of-war camps and of forcible retention of them by the Syngman Rhee clique is a serious and unfortunate incident. It is right that you do so. However, your explanation and handling of this incident is not satisfactory.

Following the usual long propaganda harangue intended for the consumption of the world public, the letter concluded:

To sum up, although our side is not entirely satisfied with the reply of your side, yet in view of the indication of the desire of your side to strive for an early armistice and in view of the assurances given by your side, our side agrees that the delegations of both sides meet at an appointed time to discuss the question of implementation of the Armistice Agreement and the various preparations prior to the signing of the Armistice Agreement.

Finally, on 10 July 1953, the second anniversary of the peace talks, and following an interruption in meetings since 20 June, the Plenary Sessions were resumed. The meetings were clouded by additional statements by Syngman Rhee to the effect that if no results were forthcoming from the political conference after ninety days of meeting, he would resume fighting to unify Korea. At the first meeting the UNC suggested moving the non-repatriated Chinese and North Korean POW's to the southern portion of the demilitarized zone, to insure that the Neutral Nations Repatriation Commission might operate unmolested. The Communists continued to express doubt as to the cooperation of the ROK in the armistice. The United Nations Command declared that it stood ready at once to sign an armistice in good faith, and said that in the event of any aggressive action by the ROK Army following an armistice, the UNC would withhold all support. The Communists agreed with the UNC that responsibility for the maintenance of an armistice was an internal matter of each side.

On 15 July General Harrison told the Communists they had delayed progress for the past five days by asking a "farcical repetition of questions which have been answered clearly and positively." Despite comprehensive assurances by the UNC, the Communists continued to delay negotiations and in the meanwhile launched the biggest offensive in more than two years, an offensive which obviously took much planning and preparation and caused heavy casualties. The United Nations Command, aggravated by Communist procrastination, then unilaterally recessed the meetings until the following day.

The 19 July meeting was "most encouraging." In a lengthy statement the Communists informed the United Nations Command that they were willing to commence immediately discussions on "the various preparations prior to the signing of the Armistice Agreement." They qualified this statement with the assertion that they reserved the right to submit the question of the prisoners recently released by the South Korean government to the political conference. General Clark observed: "The progress made in today's meetings should lead to the early signing of an armistice."

Items to be settled prior to the signing included:

1) Agreement as to the effective date of the armistice;
2) Revision of the military demarcation line and demilitarized zone;
3) Preparation of documents including maps;
4) Preparation of suitable facilities for the signing;
5) Reviewing the wording of the Armistice Agreement; and
6) Arrival of the members of the Neutral Nations Supervisory Commission and Neutral Nations Repatriation Commission.

The United Nations Command suggested 1400 hours 24 July as the signing date, and that the armistice should become effective twelve hours later. The Communists tentatively agreed. This date was subsequently advanced to 27 July due to delays in completing final matters.

On 20 July the liaison officers met to iron out some of the remaining problems. The Communists suggested that the "Supreme Commanders of both sides" not attend the signing as previously indicated. They recommended instead that the documents be sent to them for their signatures and returned to Panmunjom for the Senior Delegates' signatures. They based their proposal on "the fact that the Syngman Rhee Government has violated the Prisoner-of-war Agreement and has up to the present still been stating that as the so-called freedom of action."

The United Nations Command wanted the Supreme Commanders present for the signing. The Communists finally consented to the UNC stand on the assumption that the press would not witness the signing, and that the UNC would keep "persons on the side of Syngman Rhee or Chiang Kai-shek" out of the conference site.

This problem was resolved by the compromise that the press and other news media personnel would witness the signing by the Senior Delegates at Panmunjom, and then the documents would be delivered to the Supreme Commanders at their respective headquarters for signatures.

The Communists volunteered to construct a suitable building at Panmunjom for the ceremonies and asked the UNC to supply light for all-night work. This permitted completion of the structure by 27 July.

An interesting side-light arose from the Communists' placing of six-foot Picasso "peace doves," their trade-mark, over the doorway of the new building. These were removed two days before the signing, after the UNC informed the Communists that no UNC officer would enter the structure while these Communist symbols remained.

The Communists proposed, and the UNC agreed to, increasing security personnel at the conference site during the ceremonies to seven officers for each side in the site area and to ten officers for each side inside the building.

The United Nations Command assured the Communists that no representatives of the Republic of Korea or Nationalist China would be present, but that accredited press representatives of those two countries would be among the press present at the signing.

Meanwhile the staff officers completed their work of revising the military demarcation line and demilitarized zone and reviewing the wording of the Armistice Agreement. A supplementary agreement on prisoners of war was also completed. By this agreement the nonrepatriated POW's would be delivered to the Neutral Nations Repatriation Commission at Panmunjom. By this agreement the expressed fears of the Communists about their personnel journeying to the POW camps in South Korea were eliminated, as were Rhee's demands not to permit the entrance of any Communists into South Korea.[13]

By 27 July all details had been resolved. All was in readiness for the signing. The Neutral Nations Supervisory Commission, Neutral Nations Repatriation Commission, and Military Armistice Commission were prepared to execute their respective duties under the terms of the Armistice Agreement.[14]

At 1000 hours Lieutenant General William K. Harrison, Jr., Senior United Nations Command Delegate, and General Nam Il,

[13] See "Supplementary Agreement on Prisoners of War" in Appendix.
[14] For complete text of Armistice Agreement see Appendix.

Senior Communist Delegate, entered the Armistice Building at
their respective entrances, and quietly and with no speeches
affixed their signatures to eighteen copies (six in English, six in
Chinese, and six in Korean) of the Armistice Agreement, while
the representatives of the states fighting in Korea looked on.
Nine of the documents were then delivered to the Supreme
United Nations Commander, General Mark Clark, at Munsan for
his signature. The other nine were delivered to Kaesong for
the signatures of Marshal Kim Il Sung and General Peng Teh-
huai.

In marking the event General Clark opined that "the conflict will not be over until the governments concerned have
reached a political settlement."

President Eisenhower observed the signing with cautious
reflection:

In this struggle we have seen the United Nations meet the challenge
of aggression—not with pathetic words of protest, but with deeds
of decisive purpose. . . . At long last the carnage of war is to cease
and the negotiations of the conference table are to begin. . . . We
have won an armistice on a single battleground—not peace in the
world. We may not now relax our guard or cease our quest.

He added later in a speech at Columbia University:

*The armistice in Korea [has] inaugurated a new principle of free-
dom—that prisoners of war are entitled to choose the side to which
they will be released. In its impact on history, that one principle may
weigh more than any battle of our time.*[15]

On that twenty-seventh day of July 1953 the sixteen nations
that came to the aid of the United Nations–sponsored Republic of
Korea when it was invaded on 25 June 1950 declared jointly:

We, the United Nations Members whose military forces are
participating in the Korean action, support the decision of the
Commander-in-Chief of the United Nations Command to conclude
an armistice agreement. We hereby affirm our determination fully
and faithfully to carry out the terms of that armistice. We expect
that the other parties to the agreement will likewise scrupulously
observe its terms.

[15] Italics are the author's.

The task ahead is not an easy one. We will support the efforts of the United Nations to bring about an equitable settlement in Korea based on the principles which have long been established by the United Nations, and which call for a united, independent, and democratic Korea. We will support the United Nations in its efforts to assist the people of Korea in repairing the ravages of war.

We declare again our faith in the principles and purposes of the United Nations, our consciousness of our continuing responsibilities in Korea, and our determination in good faith to seek a settlement of the Korean problem. We affirm, in the interests of world peace, that if there is a renewal of the armed attack, challenging again the principles of the United Nations, we should again be united and prompt to resist. The consequences of such a breach of the armistice would be so grave that, in all probability, it would not be possible to confine hostilities within the frontiers of Korea.

Finally, we are of the opinion that the armistice must not result in jeopardizing the restoration or the safeguarding of peace in any other part of Asia.

In a message broadcast by radio, the North Korean and Chinese Communist commanders proclaimed a "glorious victory." And Russian Premier Georgi M. Malenkov sent telegrams to the leaders of North Korea and Communist China in which he called the armistice "a great victory [for the Communists] in the cause of defending peace in the Far East and throughout the world."

Here ended the battle for the armistice, the longest truce talks in history.

Here began the battle for the peace, and, if the length of the truce talks were an indication, it augured little for any kind of peaceful settlement. Mr. Lester B. Pearson, President of the UN General Assembly at the time of the signing of the armistice, perceived of the difficulties ahead for Korea:

The signing of the armistice is the end of one chapter—of bloodshed and conflict—but it is only the beginning of a new and difficult one—the making of the peace.

8

IN RETROSPECT

A diplomat's words must have no relation to actions—otherwise what kind of diplomacy is it? Words are one thing, actions another. Good words are a concealment of bad deeds. Sincere diplomacy is no more possible than dry water or iron wood.

                                        JOSEPH STALIN

The most important thing in dealing with a Communist is to remember—and never forget—that you are dealing with a common criminal.

                            WILLIAM K. HARRISON, JR.
                            Lieutenant General, U.S. Army

The armistice negotiations in Korea provide us with further evidence of the trickery and deceit of Communist "diplomacy." For over twenty-four months the Communists suspended the hope of the world between peace and war in Korea. The armistice did bring an end to the fighting that the Communists had started some thirty-seven months before. But the armistice, symbolizing only a temporary suspension of hostilities, was nothing more than a step toward a permanent settlement. It did not imply, nor was it intended, as a final solution to the Korean problem. The peace for Korea was—indeed is—still to be negotiated. The armistice merely reflected a temporary stalemate in the use of physical power in one area of the global conflict. The struggle for the world continues. And if the lessons of the Korean armistice were portentous, they augur little for a peaceful solution to a violently unpeaceful situation.

George Santayana once remarked that "those who cannot remember the past are condemned to repeat it." Our experiences at Kaesong and Panmunjom have increased enormously our knowledge about Communist methods. We have learned much about their strengths and their weaknesses. But knowledge is useful only as it is applied. Major David F. MacGhee, USAF, who spent thirty-three months as a prisoner of war in North Korea, insists: "[We] must get to know the true nature of the enemy right down to his socks. Not just the familiar face of Communist brutality, which anyone can recognize, but the evil masquerading as good which is drawing millions into the Red camp." [1]

What mistakes did the United Nations Command make at the truce talks? What techniques did the Communists employ? What vulnerabilities did they expose? What are the lessons of Korea for the free world? With the experiences of the military armistice negotiations now behind us, we can suggest answers to these questions.

It is a valuable lesson to consider areas in which the UNC failed in whole or in part to take advantage of certain situations. Perhaps the most conspicuous UNC mistake was to assume at the outset that it could deal with the Communists on what it understood as an honorable basis, that a settlement would be reached within a few days or at the most a few weeks, that the Communists were really sincere in seeking a peaceful resolution of differences, that negotiation meant to the Communists what it meant to the UNC: to sincerely and frankly discuss the issues with a view to reaching an equitable and quick ending of the

[1] *Collier's*, 22 January 1954.

war. This initial naïveté on the part of the UNC led to the protracted talkathons and an extension of the war. UNC naïveté was first demonstrated by the acceptance of Kaesong as the site for the talks. This played into the hands of the Communists, for Kaesong's very position forced a halt to advancing United Nations troops by making a large area immune from attack. The location of Kaesong below the 38th Parallel and within the Communists' lines also proved of immeasurable propaganda value to the Communists, for it meant that the UNC had to go to the Communists to negotiate. Had the talks been held instead on some neutral ship or territory outside of Korea, the armistice would have been agreed upon much sooner, for the United Nations forces could have exercised more effective military power against the aggressors. By meeting at Kaesong, the Communists could afford to delay. World attention was focused on Kaesong. The Communists intended to exploit this attention to the fullest. Delay was to them the better part of wisdom.

Following the recess from 22 August to 25 October 1951, the UNC accepted what was in effect a cease-fire. This permitted the Communists the time they had sought from the beginning of negotiations to strengthen their battered forces and to build what amounted to an impregnable defense along their front lines. From that moment the Communists could delay with impunity. Little front-line pressure could be exerted against them. The United Nations Command had accepted the cease-fire on the assumption that it would bring about an earlier armistice. The Communists interpreted the concession as a sign of weakness.

Had the United Nations Command delegation included representation of the other states fighting aggression in Korea rather than just the United States, it would have supplied greater meaning to the term "United Nations," and at the same time would have acquainted other countries with the vexations of negotiating with the Communists. It is true that the Republic of Korea was represented, but it was seldom consulted. Its representatives were merely tolerated. Yet at the time the armistice was signed, the ROK manned two-thirds of the front line with its troops. As Dr. Rhee once told the writer, "If you own 51 per cent of a corporation's stock, you expect to have controlling interest."

Had the United Nations Command beaten the Communists to the draw every time a riot was staged in one of the UNC prisoner-of-war stockades by accusing them before they had a chance to launch an hysterical charge against the UNC, the Communists would have been less willing to continue staging riots. The Communists are distinctly sensitive to unfavorable publicity.

At times the UNC tried to read too much meaning into Communist statements, as though they were trying to say something without actually saying it. This proved false in all instances, and quite rightfully so when considered in the light of Communist purposes in negotiating.

Permitting civilians to remain within the truce area was a mistake. Every time the Communists accused the UNC of violating the neutrality of the conference site, they would produce both material evidence, which if not available was readily fabricated, and witnesses—whether false or not made little difference to them. These "witnesses" were thoroughly indoctrinated as to what to say and what not to say. At times the UNC investigators would catch the witnesses, which tended to embarrass the Communists—but only momentarily, for they would shift the blame quickly or cover up such embarrassment by alleging that the questions were unfair.

Early in the conferences the United Nations Command was quite niggardly in its press information releases. For example, the UNC press release might state that "at 1103 Nam Il lit a cigarette, at 1105 he smiled, etc." This was not substantive, and it forced the non-Communist correspondents to go to the Communists for news about what had transpired at the meetings. The Communists gladly offered their version. As a result, the UNC issued a letter in February 1952 to the correspondents urging them to discontinue such mingling with Communist correspondents.

An early and complete release of news to the press is wise from a public relations point of view. This was done in the latter days of the meetings—after the damage had been done. At that time information about what the UNC intended to cover

during a particular meeting would be handed to the correspondents before the meeting, with the understanding that it would
not be released until the meeting had ended. This enabled the
United Nations Command to get the news out ahead of the
Communists—an important propaganda consideration. The Communists are master propagandists, and they realize its great
importance. They spend billions every year on its dissemination.
And they have come to appreciate more than ever, as a result
of their failure to achieve physical conquest of Korea, the importance of nonmaterial weapons. "We shall conquer the world,"
cried André Vishinsky, "not with atom bombs, but with something the Americans cannot produce—with our ideas, our brains,
our doctrines." Certainly there is nothing immoral about proper
and adequate distribution of the truth.

Interference from Washington tended at times to impede
the progress of the negotiations by restricting the United Nations
Command's ability to act freely. No one could deny the authorities in Washington the right to engage actively in the negotiations. The United States government had been commissioned by
the United Nations to conduct the campaign against the Communist aggressors, and Washington was therefore ultimately responsible. But one would have expected more freedom of action
on the part of those representatives of the Washington authorities at the Korean armistice negotiations. Strong hierarchical
control is certainly the established pattern with, and can be
expected of, the Communists. But such strong command over
the UNC delegates appeared anomalous. Examples are numerous.
On one occasion the UNC submitted to the Communists a proposal that it declared to be "firm, final, and irrevocable." Shortly
thereafter this proposition was countermanded by Washington.
Such action on the part of the American government weakened
the position of those operating in the conference tent, and indeed
made the Communists even more obdurate in their demands. All
too frequently the UNC delegation became nothing more than
a Washington mouthpiece—a "milkman's horse," as one individual described it. The delegation could have accomplished
better results with less interference. When you take a taxi, you
tell the driver your destination and you expect him to drive you

there in the most efficient way. Certainly you would not tell the driver how to shift gears. This is equally applicable to international negotiations. The negotiator should be given as much latitude as possible in order for him to take advantage of immediate situations.

The UNC should have insisted from the outset that the Communists employ the correct terms when referring to the governments of the Republic of Korea or the Republic of China on a *quid pro quo* basis. On no occasion did the Communists use the correct titles for these governments, preferring instead, for propaganda purposes, to employ such cynical appellations as "your friend in South Korea," "your puppet on Formosa," or "the Syngman Rhee clique." Such terminology was in tune with the Communists efforts to discredit the UNC, the United States, and all of its allies. However, the UNC faithfully abided by use of the proper names, "Democratic People's Republic of Korea" when referring to North Korea and "Democratic People's Republic of China" when referring to Communist China. By the same token, UNC good faith in using such terms correctly further contributed to the Communist propaganda effort. "Peace," "people," and "democracy" are glittering generalities the Communists use to seduce unthinking individuals into accepting their schemes, to turn them against any opposition, or at the very least to create serious doubts in the minds of the strong. The Communists convene world peace conferences, have peace appeals, offer peace prizes, employ the dove of peace liberally as their trade-mark. They have "people's courts," "people's police," "people's liberation armies"—and, of course, they insist that only they are the "democratic" people. In effect, they have taken over words for themselves which people in general have commonly accepted as pleasant and desirable. With such intoxicating phrases copiously bandied about, the Communists seek to lull to sleep unsuspecting individuals, and unhappily, when these persons awake to the realities of what they have imbibed, they suddenly suffer from an excruciating hangover.

The United Nations Command even bowed to the Communists' propaganda efforts in the distribution of prisoner-of-war mail, which was exchanged at the conference site. The United

States Post Office instructed all persons sending letters to prisoners of war in Communist custody to "address all mail in care of Chinese People's Committee for World Peace, Peking, China. There is no other correct address." Much of the incoming mail from Communist territory added to the title "Chinese People's Committee for World Peace" the phrase "against American Aggression." This was a clever propaganda device that the Communists employed in support of their propaganda mission of discrediting the United Nations Command and more especially the United States of America. No stone was left unturned in their propaganda war. It was their consistent theme throughout the conference, indeed the war, that the United States was the aggressor in Korea.

The names "Neutral Nations Repatriation Commission" and "Neutral Nations Supervisory Commission" were misnomers, and also contributed to the Communists' propaganda campaign. Poland and Czechoslovakia scarcely measured up to the standards of neutral states. However, dubbing them as such by naming them as members of the two commissions immediately cloaked them in the halo of neutrality, and conveyed the impression that Russia had no part to play in their affairs.

These were some of the mistakes the UNC made. There were others, but these examples serve to illustrate the importance of maintaining constant alertness to every Communist effort. Long experience with Communist "diplomacy" has taught the world that no Communist move is without some secret significance. Too often, in the past, communism's pretensions to peace have been merely disguises for aggressive intentions. Joseph Stalin sanctioned Communist use of peace moves in blunt terms: "Our preparations for war are conducted under cover of paeans to peace. We must take the enemy by surprise—when his forces are dispersed." Any and every Communist proposal, therefore, must be studied for hidden purposes and for its conformity with the pattern of Communist strategy. The circumstances and conditions under which an offer is made always have a bearing on the offer itself.

What techniques did the Communists employ during the Korean military armistice negotiations?

22. Armistice Building, Panmunjom, at the time of the signing of the Armistice Agreement, 27 July 1953.

US Army Photo

23.   The signing of the Armistice Agreement, 27 July 1953. Lieutenant General William K. Harrison, Jr., US Army, Senior United Nations Delegate, signs for the United Nations, while General Nam II, Senior Communist Delegate, signs for the Communists. *US Navy Photo*

24.   Senior UNC Delegate, Lieutenant General William K. Harrison, Jr., US Army, signs
the Armistice Agreement at Panmunjom, 27 July 1953.   *US Navy Photo*

25. Lieutenant General William K. Harrison, Jr., Senior United Nations Delegate, leaves the Armistice Building at Panmunjom after signing the Armistice Agreement, 27 July 1953.

US Army Photo

The Communists made masterly use of propaganda to support their goals at the conference. Every word, every action reflected the high regard they held for this weapon. When they uttered a word in the conference tent, it was only secondarily intended for the ears of those who sat opposite them. The Communists were not genuinely interested in reaching an agreement. The eyes and ears of the world were directed to the talks in Korea. Communist words and deeds were tuned to that audience. Their consistent effort was to capture and hold this audience. Their lengthy tirades exemplified this effort. Their concern for world opinion was admitted by Nam Il on 3 August 1952:

Peace-loving people of the whole world are watching every action of the delegates of our two sides in the armistice negotiations and demanding our two sides to reach a speedy agreement on a reasonable basis . . . so as to bring about an armistice in Korea. However, your side, in disregard of the ardent desire of the people of the world . . .

The Communists had started the war with a purpose, and it follows that they would attempt to salvage as much of their original intentions as possible. For this reason any progress at reaching a settlement was thrust upon the shoulders of the UNC. The Communists were well aware that world communications media would repeat their propaganda blasts for the world public. Even in the United States, a good portion of what the Communists said at the conference table was printed in the newspapers and repeated over the radio and television stations. And, of course, what they said had little or no relationship to what they did. As Joseph Stalin declared, "A diplomat's words must have no relation to actions—otherwise what kind of diplomacy is it? Words are one thing, actions another." What the Communists said was intended to confuse an unaware public, which magnified further the frustrations of the UNC delegates who were desperately seeking to reach an agreement. It is an unfortunate fact that the great mass of individuals base their conclusions on feelings rather than reason, and, of course, the Communists are cunningly clever at appealing to emotions.

The Communists' arguments during the meetings were based

on illogical premises and manufactured incidents. They would state their proposition in such a way as to suggest that it was right and represented the wishes of the people of the whole world. Their presentation reduced all arguments to a black and white basis. Such simplification of complex issues is an important propaganda device. Nam Il's statement of 28 July 1951 illustrates this point:

[Your proposal] is completely groundless and, hence, unworthy of consideration and cannot be considered. On the other hand . . . our proposal is one which is recognized by the whole world and one which is just, reasonable, realistic, and practicable.

Once a stand was taken, the Communists subjected the United Nations Command to a lengthy repetition of bombast, no matter how much or well the UNC would argue against it. The Communists recognized the value of repetition to the ultimate acceptance of their viewpoint. And they talked loud and heatedly. When their interpreter failed to maintain a loud and demanding voice, they would nudge him to let him know his voice had dropped. They injected extraneous issues into the discussions, not alone for bargaining purposes, but for some other sinister intent. They rewrote history to support their arguments. They seldom failed to take advantage of an opportunity, no matter how minute, to further their efforts. They knowingly and purposely delayed the consummation of the armistice in order to reap a greater propaganda harvest. An end of the meetings would do away with their propaganda sounding board.

Over the conference table the Communists cleverly dangled the dove of peace to renew hope when the United Nations delegation became discouraged, like the boy who dangles a piece of meat in front of his dog's nose to make him pull the cart. But, as easily as it was offered, it was taken away. As one cartoonist quipped, "How long can hope spring eternal?"

The Communists always insisted on having the last word—always a lengthy and distorted review of the proceedings. Before making a new proposal, they invariably prefaced it with a painfully tiresome version of why they could never compromise on their "righteous" demands, and concluded with the declaration:

"However, in order to bring about an armistice sooner as demanded by all peace-loving peoples, we now present our absolutely final solution." In most instances these "solutions" were mere rewordings and reshufflings of previous offers.

If the UNC asked a question, the Communists would answer with questions of their own or assert that the question had previously been answered. They never answered a question point-blank. This is an old and effective debating trick to keep the opponent on the defensive. On 15 January 1952 we find this typical conversation:

Admiral Libby: You still haven't answered my question.

General Lee: As to that question, I have given you already my answer. It's in the record.

Such a procedure served to delay the meetings. When the Communists asked questions of the UNC, they would repeat them over and over again, even after the UNC had provided a suitable reply. Reaching agreement was not uppermost in the Communists' minds. Such a technique was frustrating to the UNC, and was also intended to wear down the UNC personnel and to fix charges in the minds of the world's public. If the United Nations Command accused the Communists of contradicting previous statements, they would deny having made them or counter by charging the UNC with perfidy. They caviled over procedural details, as was well illustrated by the length of time they insisted on spending in discussing the agenda. However, even though they were guilty of employing this delaying tactic, they would shift the blame to the United Nations Command and thus attempt to portray the UNC as the procrastinator. They would substantiate all charges with manufactured evidence supported by witnesses who had been carefully briefed. To illustrate, on 7 September 1951 Nam Il announced in support of a charge against the UNC of violating the neutrality of the Kaesong area: "Our side is in possession of adequate witnesses and material evidence to establish the inescapable responsibility of your side." To underscore their charges the Communists de-

HOW LONG CAN HOPE SPRING ETERNAL!

Fig. 4. How long can hope spring eternal!

Milt Morris, Wide World

manded that those responsible be punished. Nam Il, for example, declared on 3 September 1951:

I once more lodge the most serious protest to you and firmly demand that you severely punish the culprits and thoroughly ensure against any further violations of agreement by your side.

The Communists lied without hesitation. They presented fabrications as the truth and challenged the UNC to prove them otherwise—again as another means of keeping the UNC on the defensive. They would ask or agree to secret sessions, thus keeping the conversations from the world's communications media, but would at their own whim release the information in their perverted fashion—like the state that declares war after it has crossed another state's frontiers.

If a statement did contain any substantive information, it was so heavily saturated with propaganda that it was difficult to decipher—like low-grade ore, great quantities of which are needed to get a substantial amount of metal. The Communists generally spoke in vague generalities, which made it difficult to interpret exactly what they did say. General Harrison once candidly observed, "You never know what they mean by what they say!" Frequently they would inject such ambiguities into the conversations as to completely confuse their intent. If asked to clarify their statements, they would suggest rereading the record. "It's in the record," was a common expression.

At times they would denounce a statement made by the United Nations Command and several days later produce it as their own. At other times they would childishly repeat statements or phrases that the UNC had used. Occasionally they would deny the existence of agreements that they had previously made if they did not find the fulfillment to their liking. They would indulge in violently and tempestuously abusive language when all other tactics had proved ineffective. And, as General Ridgway opined:

It is a very difficult thing for a man of integrity and principle to have to deal day after day with men who see little relation between the spoken word and the facts—who resort to intemperate language and deliberately employ known falsehoods as part of their tactics.

The Communists attempted to add support to their efforts at the conference table by manufacturing incidents and then maliciously accusing the United Nations Command of having perpetrated them. Such were the riots among POW's in UNC custody; such were the charges of employing germ warfare, violating the neutrality of the conference site, bombing POW stockades in North Korea, and even training a battalion of monkeys to heave hand grenades at the North Korean lines. If the setting had not been so tragic, this last accusation would have been not only ridiculous but amusing. But the main purpose remained: to embarrass and discredit the UNC.

The Communists claimed the Geneva Convention as support for their stand, but they failed miserably to abide by any of its provisions themselves, even though they had given their word that they would. They went to the extent of threatening the UNC delegation by letting it be known that they intended to kidnap the delegation and staff. They always insisted that everything be equal, but if the UNC were not alert, the Communists would make the UNC appear as the vanquished. As George Orwell would say, under their system everyone is equal, but some are more equal than others.

The Communists approach the resolution of problems through negotiation on a fight-to-the-finish basis—no holds barred. Each step is achieved by brutality. This was illustrated by the surprise they expressed when the United Nations Command on one occasion accepted a Communist proposal carte blanche. The Communists' only remark was, in effect, "You mean you don't want to argue?" They then delayed in accepting the UNC acceptance like the child that does not want what it wants! The Communists expect a knockdown, drag-out fight, and unless one is prepared to accept the challenge he suffers a stinging defeat. Needless to say, the fight requires patience, fortitude, brute strength, and an imperviousness to the types of blows inflicted.

It must be remembered that such methods as the Communists employ in negotiations are to them entirely legitimate. To them the nature of their ultimate end justifies the use of any tactic. The tragedy of Korea was that the United Nations Command did not accept this fact from the beginning. Extending this concept into the postarmistice period makes it clear that the Communists can, with legitimacy by their standards, ignore the agreement they avowed to uphold. Such betrayal of the terms of the Agreement has already been revealed. It becomes clear, in other words, that such tactics must be accepted and dealt with accordingly. Otherwise we are only deceiving ourselves and those whom we represent.

The Communists have clearly revealed that they are not invincible, even though they do attempt to convey that impression. What were the weaknesses they exposed during the long course of the negotiations?

The Communists revealed their extreme sensitivity to the public opinion they were attempting to subvert. They also revealed a sensitivity to opinions among those peoples they controlled. Communism by its very nature demands imposition by force and constant surveillance for its survival. Communism's tyrannical leadership is open to attack. Oliver Wendell Holmes once appropriately remarked that totalitarianism like champagne becomes a stale when exposed to the air. Thus, it behooves the free world to continually expose Communist failures through every known and available communications medium, and to beat them down at all international conferences by unmasking the falseness of their argument and offering a logical presentation in refutation.

Standing up to the Communists—calling their bluff—proved effective on more than one occasion. To deny them the advantages they seek is to make delay less enticing. Walking out of the conference tent when the Communists insisted on continuing their delays was angrily protested, but it was effective in bringing an end to their propaganda blasts. Once having established the precedent of walking out, threats to do it again could be used if the Communists engaged in further efforts to use the meetings for other than their understood purpose. Had the United Nations Command called a halt to the negotiations after submitting its "package proposal" on 28 April 1952 instead of continuing until 8 October, it is possible the Communists might have considered agreeing to an armistice sooner. Likewise, had the UNC released those POW's who refused to be sent back to the Communists on the basis that these were political refugees seeking asylum, an action perfectly legitimate under international law, the Communists would have had nothing more to argue about. One *New York Times* writer has wisely commented that "firmness and fortitude, as the past has shown, have had their influence on the uneasy Communist empire; weakness and indecision, clutching at straws of Red concessions, only lead to new and greater outrages."

The Communists revealed a sensitivity to ridicule and laughter—well demonstrated by their changing the color of their sentry boxes when the UNC members laughed heartily at their original barber-pole design.

Aware of the importance of world opinion, Communists are sensitive to having their side presented as unequal. Because the UNC had naval representation on its delegation, the Communists created a navy so it could be represented. They took photographs only when their side was in a position of prominence. When the UNC beautified its side of the conference site, the Communists overdid themselves to make their side superior in every detail to the UNC effort.

The Communists also exposed their complete reluctance to act without higher approval—no matter how trivial the point. Authority to act came from above. No agreement was forthcoming, nor could be expected to be forthcoming, until some higher authority approved it. If the UNC made a concession as a *quid pro quo* to a like Communist concession, someone would leave the tent and return in about ten minutes or so with an answer—obviously from higher authority.

The lessons of the Korean military armistice negotiations demonstrated once again the discrepancies in attitudes toward diplomacy. To the United Nations Command, in effect the United States as the responsible country, negotiation implied dealing in good faith and complying fully with the results—that is, operating according to accepted standards of procedure. To the Communists, negotiation proved again to be simply one weapon in their arsenal of war. And that weapon, being considered as a weapon of war, could employ, by Communist logic, any device if it contributed to their long-run goal. Lenin, whose pronouncements have profoundly influenced Communist thinking, taught that the Communists, in their struggle to promote world revolution, are justified in using "any ruse, cunning, unlawful method, evasion, concealment of truth." In other words, what is truth to the Communists or what is ethical must be considered in the light of what it contributes to the final goal of world communism. Peace, of course, implies the consummation of their goals. Communist strength lies in the absolute obedience to the consummation of these goals by a small coterie of violently dedicated individuals who accept the use of any means to achieve their ends. Thus any action according to Marxist philosophy is justified if it assists the cause of revolution.

To the Communists, then, any device, no matter how unethical or disreputable it might seem, is legitimate by their standards. And as Lieutenant General William K. Harrison, Jr. wrote in a letter to the writer recently: "Americans generally try to play games according to the rules and expect the opponent to do the same. When they have to play against people like Communists whose only rule is to secure their own end regardless of the means, our people are at a disadvantage." If the Communists cannot achieve their mission on the field of battle, they will attempt to do so at the conference table. If that procedure fails, they will resume fighting or try some other method. Of course, the acceptance of such methods is justification for noncompliance with the results if that aids in achieving their final end. Agreements honored by the pen are valid to the Communists only so long as the terms act as a step toward their objectives. Once that assignment is negated, agreements become invalid and can by this logic justifiably be forgotten. Not long after the Armistice had been signed, its usefulness to the Communists as a step toward their goals terminated, and the UNC was forced to commence its tiresome presentation of fruitless protests. On 12 October 1953 the UNC lodged its first protest against the Communists for violations of the Armistice. A second protest was made on 9 February 1954. On 5 July 1955 the UNC "lodges the strongest and most serious protest against your side since the signing of the Armistice." As of 7 February 1955, sixty-one charges had been made by the UNC, compelling the Swiss mem-

ber of the Neutral Nations Supervisory Commission to remark
at the Commission's 179th meeting: "I think the hand of the
honorable [Communist] Polish member must shake every month
when he signs the evaluation stating that we have established
that both sides have remained within the limits of the Armistice
Agreement!" However, the Communists can be expected always
to make a violation appear as an injustice to them, and falsehoods as the truth.

To the free world, the employment of any means to attain
an end is immoral. To the free world, the rules must be placed
ahead of the winning of the game. Former United States Secretary of State Dean Acheson has described clearly the differences
in the two systems:

It is the nature of democracy to recognize that the means we choose
shape the ends we achieve. In a democracy, there are no final ends,
in the sense of a Utopia.

The followers of Karl Marx endure the dictatorship of a police state
in the delusion that they are ascending to a classless society. But
a democratic society cannot employ means which belie and indeed
destroy the possibility of achieving its goals. Democratic society,
by its conduct from day to day, from week to week, and from year
to year, is creating its own future.

If we continue to move toward our goal of world order in which
peace, freedom and justice may be secure, *the means we choose
to overcome the obstacles in our path must be consonant with our
deepest moral sense.*[2]

It is not in the words we profess, but in what we do, and in how we
do it, that our ends will be found.

To which Sir Hartley Shawcross has raised this question:

Are we to resort . . . to the very weapons . . . which they use who
seek to destroy us? Or should we, and can we with safety, be true
to our own bright weapons and the shining shield of truth?

Whether the free world will be able to persist in its attitudes
toward diplomacy against the relentless and ruthless force of

_____

[2] Italics are the author's.

Communist methods, indeed in a climate of amorality, only time can relate. But to abandon its basic premise is to forfeit that which has been painfully conceived in mankind's historic struggle for freedom.

In times like the present [Abraham Lincoln counseled], men should utter nothing for which they would not willingly be held responsible through time and in eternity. . . . The fiery trial through which we pass will light us down, in honor or dishonor, to the latest generation. We shall nobly save or meanly lose the last best hope of earth.

Certainly the battle for the armistice in Korea, as a manifestation of applied Communist philosophy, challenges those who still live in freedom to bear the most terrifying responsibility history has yet thrust upon them.

APPENDICES

I

MILITARY ARMISTICE STATISTICAL SUMMARY

During the period of negotiation, 8 July 1951 through 27 July 1953, there were 159 Plenary Sessions, 26 of them at Kaesong, 133 at Panmunjom. Of these 41 were held in executive session. There were 37 subdelegation meetings on Agenda Item 2, 71 on Agenda Item 3, and 71 on Agenda Item 4. There were 5 Staff Officer meetings on Item 2, 74 on Item 3, 48 on Item 4 (17 of these in executive session) and 11 Staff Officer meetings on the wording of the Draft Armistice Agreement. Regarding repatriation of sick and injured prisoners of war, there were 11 liaison group meetings and 13 Staff Officer meetings. Following the reopening of the armistice negotiations, 26 April 1953, there were 37 Plenary Sessions and 23 Staff Officer meetings. All of the Staff Officer meetings were held in executive session.

Agenda Item #1: Agenda
    Plenary Session
           Total number of sessions   10
           Total number of hours   23.5

Agenda Item #2: Demarcation Line and Demilitarized Zone
    Plenary Session
           Total number of sessions   17
           Total number of hours   34.3
    Subdelegates
           Total number of sessions   37
    Total number of hours   110.3

Staff officers
    Total number of sessions   11
    Total number of hours   42

Agenda Item #3: Concrete Arrangements for the Cease-fire

Plenary Session
    Total number of sessions   8
    Total number of hours   17.2
Subdelegates
    Total number of sessions   71
    Total number of hours   104.9
Staff officers
    Total number of sessions   77
    Total number of hours   117.5

Agenda Item #4: Prisoners of War

Plenary Session
    Total number of sessions   79
    Total number of hours   48.3
    Total number of executive sessions   23
    Total number of hours in executive session   12.1
Subdelegates
    Total number of sessions   71
    Total number of hours   197.6
Staff officers
    Total number of sessions   50
    Total number of hours   98.6
    Total number of executive sessions   17
    Total number of hours in executive session   29

Agenda Item #5: Recommendations to Governments

Plenary Session (only)
    Total number of sessions   8
    Total number of hours   5.7

On Wording of Draft Armistice Agreement

Staff officers
    Total number of sessions   11
    Total number of hours   10.8

Repatriation of Sick and Injured

    Liaison group
        Total number of sessions   11
        Total number of hours   6.7

Following Reopening of Plenary Armistice Negotiations 26 April 1953

    Plenary Sessions
        Total number of sessions   37
        Total number of hours   31

    Repatriation of Prisoners of War

    Staff officers
        Total number of sessions   5
        Total number of hours   14.2

    Revision of Draft Armistice Agreement

    Staff officers
        Total number of sessions   12
         Total number of hours   36.2

    Military Demarcation Line and Boundaries of Demilitarized Zone

    Staff officers
        Total number of sessions   10
         Total number of hours   49.7

Breakdown by Types of Meetings

    Total number of Plenary Sessions   159
    Total number of hours   159.7
    Total number of subdelegate meetings   179
    Total number of hours   412.8
    Total number of liaison group meetings 11
    Total number of hours   6.7
    Total number of staff officer meetings 189
    Total number of hours   387.1
    Total number of all sessions   538
    Total number of hours   966.3

Breakdown by Agenda Items

    Agenda Item #1
        Total number of all sessions   10
        Total number of hours   23.5

Agenda Item #2
    Total number of all sessions   65
    Total number of hours   186.6

Agenda Item #3
    Total number of all sessions   156
    Total number of hours   239.6

Agenda Item #4
    Total number of all sessions   200
    Total number of hours   344.5

Agenda Item #5
    Total number of all sessions   8
    Total number of hours   10.8

Liaison Officer Meetings

During the period of negotiations there were 227 meetings between liaison officers. These meetings can be broken down into three categories:

1. Seventy-three meetings on administrative and security matters, including those meetings in preparation for meetings at a higher level;

2. One hundred forty meetings called for the purpose of lodging protests, answering protests, or investigations of alleged incidents; and

3. Fourteen meetings called on the general subject of prisoners of war and prisoner-of-war camps.

In many liaison meetings more than one subject came under discussion. In the above breakdown only the principal matter of each meeting was used to determine in which category to place it.

Number of days on which some kind of meeting occurred, (Plenary, subdelegation, staff officer, liaison group, or liaison officer) . . . 520

Recess of Plenary Sessions

The longest recess (8 Oct. 52 thru 25 Apr. 53)   199 days
Number of 19–day recesses   1
Number of 10–day recesses   1

Number of	9–day recesses	1
Number of	8–day recesses	1
Number of	7–day recesses	7
Number of	6–day recesses	1
Number of	5–day recesses	1
Number of	3–day recesses	5

From the beginning of the negotiations in July 1951, nineteen UN officers served as delegates to the conference. Following is a list of those officers and the number of months each served.

Senior Delegates

Vice Admiral C. Turner Joy, USN	10
Lieutenant General William K. Harrison, Jr., USA	12

Delegates

Rear Admiral Arleigh A. Burke, USN	4
Major General Laurence C. Craigie, USAF	3
Rear Admiral John C. Daniel, USN	8
Major General Claude B. Ferenbaugh, USA	1
Brigadier General Lee Han Lim, ROKA	4
Major General Henry I. Hodes, USA	5
Major General Lee Hyung Koon, ROKA	3
Rear Admiral Ruthven E. Libby, USN	7
Brigadier General Frank C. McConnell, USA	4
Brigadier General Joseph T. Morris, USAF	4
Major General Paik Sun Yup, ROKA	3
Major General Howard McM. Turner, USAF	7
Lieutenant General Yu Jai Heung, ROKA	4
Major General Choi Duk Shin, ROKA	2
Brigadier General Ralph M. Osborne, USA	4
Brigadier General Edgar E. Glenn, USAF	3
Major General George G. Finch, USAF	1

Shortest Meetings in Plenary Session

April 11, 1952	1½	minutes
April 12, 1952	1	minute
April 13, 1952	50	seconds
April 14, 1952	15	seconds

II

CHRONOLOGY OF THE MILITARY ARMISTICE CONFERENCE

1951

23 June   Soviet UN Delegate Yakov A. Malik advocated a Korean cease-fire and armistice during a broadcast on the UN radio program "Price of Peace," on Columbia Broadcasting System.

30 June   General Matthew B. Ridgway radioed Commander-in-Chief Communist Forces in Korea that he had been informed that the Communists might desire a military armistice conference. He proposed a meeting aboard a Danish hospital ship in Wonsan Harbor.

1 July   General Kim Il Sung, Supreme Commander of the Korean People's Army, and General Peng Teh-huai, Commander of the Chinese Volunteers, suggested a meeting in the vicinity of Kaesong between 10 July and 15 July.

3 July   General Ridgway accepted the Communist suggestion of Kaesong as a site for a military armistice conference. He suggested a 5 July meeting of liaison officers to make necessary arrangements.

4 July   Communists said liaison officers meeting of military armistice conference must be on 8 July.

5 July   General Ridgway agreed to liaison officers meeting on 8 July.

6 July   Message from Communists to General Ridgway stated that Communist liaison officers, interpreters, and reception personnel would leave Pyongyang at 0500K, 7 July.

7 July   UNC advance headquarters base camp established two miles north of Munsan.

8 July   UNC liaison officers landed at Kaesong at 0922K. In the group were Col. Andrew J. Kinney, USAF; Col. James C. Murray, USMC; Lt. Col. Lee Soo Young, ROKA. The Communist liaison group included Col. Chang Chun San, NKA; Lt. Col. Tsai Cheng Won, CCF; and Lt. Col. Kim Il Pa, NKA. After exchanging credentials, they conferred on arrangement for the first meeting. They decided first meeting would be held on 10 July at same location: Kwangmundong, north of the center of Kaesong.

10 July   First Session of military armistice conference. Admiral Joy proposed that 20 newsmen be permitted, as part of the UNC delegation, to come to the conference area, but not into the conference house. Attending the initial session were:

UNITED NATIONS COMMAND DELEGATES:
Vice Admiral C. Turner Joy, USN
Maj. Gen. Laurence C. Craigie, USAF
Maj. Gen. Henry I. Hodes, USA
Rear Admiral Arleigh A. Burke, USN
Maj. Gen. Paik Sun Yup, ROKA

NORTH KOREAN–CHINESE DELEGATES:
General Nam Il, NKA
Maj. Gen. Lee Sang Cho, NKA
Maj. Gen. Chang Pyong San, NKA
General Tung Hua, CCF
Maj. Gen. Hsieh Fang, CCF

11 July   Second Session military armistice conference. Admiral Joy read General Ridgway's message

concerning the inclusion of newsmen commencing 12 July.

12 July   UN convoy including newsmen en route to military armistice conference stopped by Communists. Convoy returned to Munsan.

13 July   General Ridgway proposed to the Communists that the composition of the delegation party for the military armistice conference be left entirely to the commander.

14 July   Communists accepted General Ridgway's proposals on composition of delegation.
Newsmen accompanied the United Nations Command delegation.

15 July   Third Session military armistice conference. Agenda items were opened for discussion.

16 July   Fourth Session military armistice conference.

17 July   Fifth Session military armistice conference.

18 July   Sixth Session military armistice conference. Admiral Joy reiterated that the UNC stand was that only military matters should be discussed.

19 July   Seventh Session military armistice conference.

20 July   Flooded streams prevented military armistice conference meeting.

21 July   Eighth Session military armistice conference. Adjourned after one hour, forty minutes, until 1100, 25 July, at request of Communists.

25 July   Ninth Session military armistice conference.

26 July   Tenth Session military armistice conference.

27 July   Eleventh Session military armistice conference. Agreement reached upon an agenda for the regulation of the military armistice conference. Points on the agenda were:

    1. Adoption of an agenda;
    2. Fixing a military demarcation line between both sides so as to establish a demilitarized zone as a basic condition for a cessation of hostilities in Korea;

3. Concrete arrangements for the realization of a cease-fire and armistice in Korea, including the composition, authority, and functions of a supervising organization for carrying out the terms of a cease-fire and armistice;

4. Arrangements relating to prisoners of war; and

5. Recommendations to the governments of the countries concerned on both sides.

28 July   Twelfth Session military armistice conference.

29 July   Thirteenth Session military armistice conference. Discussions on Item Two of agenda.

30 July   Fourteenth Session military armistice conference. Definite understanding reached that hostilities would continue during negotiations.

31 July   Fifteenth Session military armistice conference.

1 August   Sixteenth Session military armistice conference.

2 August   Seventeenth Session military armistice conference. UNC group limited to twenty-three members because of helicopter lift over Imjin River. One newsman present.

3 August   Eighteenth Session military armistice conference.

4 August   Nineteenth Session military armistice conference.

5 August   General Ridgway protested violation of the neutral zone by armed Communist troops in a message to Generals Kim Il Sung and Peng Teh-huai; Admiral Joy in turn informed General Nam Il, referring to this communication, that UNC delegation would remain within UN lines until further notice.

10 August Twentieth Session military armistice conference. Communist delegation refused to discuss any line of demarcation other than the 38th Parallel and any agenda item other than Item Two.

11 August Twenty-First Session military armistice conference.

12 August Twenty-Second Session military armistice conference.

13 August   Twenty-Third Session military armistice conference. Communists claimed that three supply vehicles were strafed by UN aircraft southwest of Sibyon-ni while en route from Kaesong to Pyongyang.

14 August   Twenty-Fourth Session military armistice conference.

15 August   Twenty-Fifth Session military armistice conference. UNC delegation proposed that a joint subcommittee be appointed to make recommendations to the delegations as to ways and means of breaking the deadlock.

16 August   Twenty-Sixth Session military armistice conference. Communist delegation accepted UNC proposal on formation of a subcommittee. They agreed that it be composed of two delegates, one staff assistant, and one interpreter for each group. UNC representatives appointed were General Hodes, USA, Admiral Burke, USN, Colonel G. C. Mudgett, USA, and Lieutenant Horace Underwood, USN.

17 August   First subcommittee meeting of military armistice conference.

18 August   Second subcommittee meeting of military armistice conference.

19 August   Third subcommittee meeting of military armistice conference. Lieutenant Colonel H. S. Levie replaced Colonel Mudgett.

20 August   Fourth subcommittee meeting of military armistice conference.

21 August   Fifth subcommittee meeting of military armistice conference.

22 August   Sixth subcommittee meeting of military armistice conference.

23 August   Colonel Chang declared all the meetings off from that time on. He also included the subcommittee meetings.

24 August   Generals Kim Il Sung and Peng Teh-huai sent

message to General Ridgway protesting an alleged incident.

29 August   General Ridgway informed the Communists that
when they were ready to terminate suspension of
negotiations, the UNC delegation would be directed to meet with the Communist delegation.

2 September   Major General Lee Hyung Koon was named as
alternate ROKA member of UNC delegations,
replacing Major General Paik Sun Yup.

17 September   General Ridgway notified Reds UNC liaison officers were prepared to discuss resumption of
talks.

20 September   The Communists agreed to a resumption of the
liaison discussions.

21 September   General Ridgway informed the Communists the
UNC liaison officers would be at Panmunjom the
next day to discuss resumption of armistice talks.
Military liaison officers met at Panmunjom. UNC
asked for new site for talks.

24 September   Military armistice conference liaison officers met.

25 September   Military armistice conference liaison officers met.

26 September   Military armistice conference liaison officers met.

27 September   Military armistice conference liaison officers met.
A message from General Ridgway to the Com-
munists proposed a new meeting place approximately midway between the battle lines in the
vicinity of Songhyon-ni.

4 October   The Communists rejected the UNC proposal for
a change of conference site and advocated the
immediate resumption of meetings.

5 October   General Ridgway proposed that the military
armistice conference meetings be resumed at a
place approximately midway between the battle
lines.

7 October   The Communists counterproposed that hence-
forth both sides should assume responsibility
for maintenance of the neutral zone; the scope
of the neutrality zone be expanded to Kaesong
and Munsan; the conference site be moved to

	Panmunjom; and at the first meeting the security of the neutral zone be agreed upon.
8 October	General Ridgway reiterated that the conference site be midway between the front lines and that only a small neutral zone be maintained.
10 October	The Communists stated that the question of extension of the neutral zone should be settled in an immediate resumption of the talks at Panmunjom.
11 October	UNC and Communist liaison officers met at Panmunjom.
12 October	At a liaison officers' meeting at Panmunjom, the Communists proposed that small neutral areas be set up around the new conference site and UNC base camp.
14 October	Military armistice conference liaison officers met at Panmunjom.
15 October	Military armistice conference liaison officers met at Panmunjom.
16 October	At a liaison officers' meeting, the Communists proposed increasing the size of the neutral zone. UNC opposed the increase.
17 October	Military armistice conference liaison officers met at Panmunjom.
18 October	Military armistice conference liaison officers met. Senior Communist members said that "there was very little difference between us" on conditions for resumption of talks.
19 October	Military armistice conference liaison officers met. Agreement reached on 18 October UNC neutral zone proposal.
20 October	Military armistice conference liaison officers met. Agreement reached on neutral zone "corridor" dimensions.
21 October	Military armistice conference liaison officers met.
22 October	Military armistice conference liaison officers met. Agreement signed for resumption of talks. It contained eight points:

        1. Named Panmunjom as conference site;

2. Confined the site to a thousand-yard radius;

3. Decreed no hostile acts of any kind;

4. Limited armed military personnel in conference area to two officers and fifteen men from each side during meeting and one officer and five men at other times;

5. Permitted free access and movement within the conference site to both delegations;

6. Provided for physical facilities;

7. Defined the neutral areas as three miles around Kaesong and UNC camp area and two hundred meters to either side of the Kaesong-Munsan road; and

8. Left date and time for resumption to be determined by agreement between liaison officers. Admiral Joy ratified the agreement later the same day.

24 October   The Communists ratified the liaison officers' agreement of 22 October and asked for resumption of talks on 25 October.

25 October   Twenty-Seventh Session of military armistice conference.

26 October   Eighth subcommittee meeting of military armistice conference. The Communists presented their proposed line of demarcation, which had little relation to the battle line.

27 October   Ninth subcommittee meeting of military armistice conference.

28 October   Tenth subcommittee meeting of military armistice conference. Communists agreed generally to the UNC concept of the battle line as the demarcation line.

29 October   Eleventh subcommittee meeting of military armistice conference.

30 October   Twelfth subcommittee meeting of military armistice conference.

31 October   Thirteenth subcommittee meeting of military armistice conference. The Communists submitted a map showing a slight change on their line of demarcation and proposing Kaesong in their territory.

1 November   Fourteenth subcommittee meeting of military armistice conference.

2 November   Fifteenth subcommittee meeting of military armistice conference.

3 November   Sixteenth subcommittee meeting of military armistice conference. Longest to date—four hours. Negotiations still concerned with line of demarcation. Reds rejected UNC proposal that Kaesong be placed in an adjusted demilitarized zone.

4 November   Seventeenth subcommittee meeting of military armistice conference. Afternoon session shortest to date—five minutes.

5 November   Eighteenth subcommittee meeting of military armistice conference. UNC introduced new proposal calling for:

    1. A demarcation line the same as the battle line;

    2. A demilitarized zone four kilometers wide;

    3. A committee to determine actual contact line at any time; and

    4. A recommendation that the main delegations continue with negotiations of other items while a bilateral committee developed an agreed contact line.

6 November   Nineteenth subcommittee meeting of military armistice conference. The Communists rejected the UNC proposal of 5 November.

7 November   Twentieth subcommittee meeting of military armistice conference. Communists offered a new proposal for Item Two of the agenda.

8 November   Twenty-First subcommittee meeting of military

armistice conference. UNC rejected the Communist proposal of 7 November.

9 November   Twenty-Second subcommittee meeting of military armistice conference.

10 November Twenty-Third subcommittee meeting of military armistice conference. UNC proposed line and zone be based on line of contact at time of signing.

11 November Twenty-Fourth subcommittee meeting of military armistice conference.

12 November Twenty-Fifth subcommittee meeting of military armistice conference.

13 November Twenty-Sixth subcommittee meeting of military conference. Session indicated Reds were seeking in effect a cease-fire upon agreement on Item Two.

14 November Twenty-Seventh subcommittee meeting of military armistice conference. The Communists for the past few meetings had been arguing for a *de facto* cease-fire upon agreement of a line of demarcation.

15 November Twenty-Eight subcommittee meeting of military armistice conference.

16 November Twenty-Ninth subcommittee meeting of military armistice conference.

17 November Thirtieth subcommittee meeting of military armistice conference. UNC proposed the establishment of a provisional line of demarcation which would be included in any armistice signed within thirty days.

18 November Thirty-First subcommittee meeting of military armistice conference.

19 November Thirty-Second subcommittee meeting of military armistice conference. Communists proposed a two-day recess, after which they would reply to the UNC proposal of 17 November.

21 November Thirty-Third subcommittee meeting of military armistice conference. The Communist submitted a counterproposal for a solution of Item Two.

22 November Thirty-Fourth subcommittee meeting of military armistice conference. Reds indicated tacit agreement to UNC "line of contact."

23 November Thirty-Fifth subcommittee meeting of military armistice conference. Agreement was reached on the following points:

  1. The actual line of contact will be the demarcation line. At a specified time, both sides will withdraw two kilometers; and

  2. The subcommittees would immediately determine the line of contact. If an armistice were signed within thirty days after the delegations approve agreement, the line should not be changed regardless of changes in the battle line during the thirty days.

24 November In second staff officers' meeting of military armistice conference, agreement was reached on one-half the location of the line of contact.

25 November Thirty-Sixth subcommittee meeting of military armistice conference. Agreement reached in staff officers' meeting on three-fourths the location of the line of contact.

26 November In staff officers' meeting, agreement was reached on location of the entire line of contact. Officers on both sides initialed maps, indicating acceptance.

Rear Admiral Arleigh Burke replaced by Rear Admiral Ruthven E. Libby as UNC delegate.

27 November Twenty-Eighth Session of military armistice conference.

Agenda Item Two was formally ratified by the delegations in the first Plenary Session since 25 October. Seven principles for a detailed solution of Item Three were introduced by the UNC.

28 November Twenty-Ninth Session of military armistice conference. Communists opposed limitation on size of military forces and any inspection to enforce

such limitation. They advocated immediate withdrawal of all "foreign" troops.

29 November — Thirtieth Session of military armistice conference.

30 November — Thirty-First Session of military armistice conference.

1 December — Thirty-Second Session of military armistice conference. UNC reiterated its stand that the construction, rehabilitation, and improvement of airfields, beyond their status at the armistice signing, should be restricted by both sides.

2 December — Thirty-Third Session of military armistice conference. Communists insisted on improvement of airfields during an armistice.

3 December — Thirty-Fourth Session of military armistice conference. Communists introduced two new principles:

1. Agreement not to introduce into Korea any military forces; and
2. The inviting of neutral nations to conduct inspections during the armistice.

4 December — Thirty-Fifth session of military armistice conference.

Thirty-Eighth subcommittee meeting on Item Three held. UNC proposed that joint subcommittee meetings on Items Three and Four be held.

5 December — Thirty-Ninth subcommittee meeting of military armistice conference. Discussed the Communists' proposal introduced in Plenary Session on 3 December.

6 December — Fortieth subcommittee meeting of military armistice conference. UNC proposal to hold concurrent subcommittee meetings on Item Four.

7 December — Forty-First subcommittee meeting of military armistice conference.

8 December — Forty-Second subcommittee meeting of military armistice conference.

9 December	Forty-Third subcommittee meeting of military armistice conference.
10 December	Forty-Fourth subcommittee meeting of military armistice conference. UNC said it had formed another subcommittee to meet on Item Four, and it would be at Panmunjon the following day to receive the Communist reply to the UNC proposal for such a meeting.
11 December	Forty-Fifth subcommittee meeting of military armistice conference. First concurrent meeting of both Items Three and Four subcommittees.
12 December	Forty-Sixth subcommittee meeting of military armistice conference. Both subcommittees met.
13 December	Forty-Seventh subcommittee meeting of military armistice conference. Both subcommitttees met.
14 December	Forty-Eighth subcommittee meeting of military armistice conference. Both subcommittees met.
15 December	Forty-Ninth subcommittee meeting of military armistice conference. Both subcommittees met.
16 December	Fiftieth subcommittee meeting of military armistice conference. Both subcommittees met.
17 December	Fifty-First subcommittee meeting of military armistice conference. Both subcommittees met. Major General Claude B. Ferenbaugh replaced Major General Henry I. Hodes on the UNC delegation.
18 December	Fifty-Second subcommittee meeting of military armistice conference. Both subcommittees met. UNC and Communists exchanged POW lists. UNC list contained 132,472 names. Reds provided UNC with the list of 11,559 POW's held by them. List included 7,142 ROK; 3,198 US; 919 British; 234 Turks; 40 Filipinos; 10 French; 6 Australians; 3 Japanese, 1 Canadian, 1 Greek, 1 Netherlander. UNC listed over 10,000 missing in action. ROK listed 70,000 as POW's and 88,000 MIA. UNC troops captured by Reds held in eleven camps—three near Pyongyang and eight along the Yalu River.

UNC asked for and received an indefinite recess to study the list.

19 December   Fifty-Third subcommittee meeting of military armistice conference.

20 December   Fifty-Fourth subcommittee meeting of military armistice conference.

21 December   Staff officers of both delegations at military armistice conference met to consider principles for the solution of Item Three.

General Ridgway broadcast a message requesting the Communists to allow Red Cross inspection of Communist POW camps.

22 December   Fifty-Fifth subcommittee meeting of military armistice conference. UNC invited Reds to inspect UNC POW camps to see that 37,500 Koreans previously listed as POW's had been removed from POW status after being investigated. UNC told Reds their POW list omitted 1,000 soldiers (mostly U.S.) previously reported held by Reds; demanded explanation. UNC proposed immediate exchange of all sick and wounded POW's.

23 December   Fifty-Sixth subcommittee meeting of military armistice conference. Reds rejected POW exchange until armistice was signed. UNC said 65,363 UN soldiers were held as POW's by Reds through first nine months of war according to accumulated information demanded explanation of 50,000-plus not on Red list (mostly ROK).

24 December   Fifty-Seventh subcommittee meeting of military armistice conference.

25 December   Fifty-Eighth subcommittee meeting of military armistice conference. Both subcommittees met.

26 December   Fifty-Ninth subcommittee meeting of military armistice conference. Both subcommittees met. Reds said that of the 1,058 UNC soldiers not on the 18 December list, but previously reported informally, 571 died, 152 escaped, and 3 were released. They claimed they were trying to locate the other 332.

27 December	Sixtieth subcommittee meeting of military armistice conference. Both subcommittees met. Reds intimated that the 50,000 POW's unaccounted for might be dead. They claimed that the ROK and US MIA and POW lists were inaccurate, and that ROK and US soldiers were unable to withstand the hardships of captivity.
28 December	Sixty-First subcommittee meeting of military armistice conference. Reds said that International Red Cross reported to them that 9,007 Red soldiers held by UNC had died.
29 December	Sixty-Second subcommittee meeting of military armistice conference. Both subcommittees met. UNC offered a compromise for the solution of Item Three in which it would withdraw its demand for aerial observation during the armistice. On Item Four, the Communists agreed to exchange list of prisoners of war who had died or escaped from UNC POW camps.
30 December	Sixty-Third subcommittee meeting of military armistice conference. UNC submitted a list of fifty-five non-Korean cvilians believed to be in Communist hands, requesting they be released when POW's were exchanged.
31 December	Sixty-Fourth subcommittee meeting of military armistice conference. Both subcommittees met.

1952

1 January	Nineteenth subcommittee meeting on Item Four. Twenty-Eighth subcommittee meeting on Item Three. Communists agreed in principle to repatriation of civilians, and to supply additional information on 50,000 UN soldiers not on Red POW list of 18 December.
2 January	Twentieth subcommittee meeting on Item Four. Twenty-Ninth subcommittee meeting on Item Three. The UNC proposed:

1. Exchange of 11,559 or more UNC-held prisoners for an equal number of Communist-held POW's;

2. Exchange of 105,000 more UNC-held prisoners on a man-for-man exchange for ROK civilians held by the Communists;

3. Unlimited exchange of displaced civilians; and

4. Supervision by IRA to insure all repatriations are voluntary.

The UNC scaled down its list of UNC-held POW's from 132,474 to about 116,000, explaining that the difference was persons who had been reclassified as civilian internees.

The ROK government estimated that 113,000 ROK civilians had been abducted by the Communists. The Communists claimed that the UNC had taken 500,000 North Koreans to the South.

3 January   Twenty-First subcommittee meeting on Item Four. Thirtieth subcommittee meeting on Item Three. A categorical rejection of 2 January's UNC proposal on Agenda Item Four matters indicated that the Reds either misunderstood the proposal or were deliberately misinterpreting it. Communists categorically rejected UNC proposal of 2 January.

4 January   Twenty-Second subcommittee meeting on Item Four. Thirty-First subcommittee meeting on Item Three. Further discussions on Item Four concerning the 2 January UNC proposal indicated Reds' misunderstanding of the proposal was deliberate. They also ignored another request for the immediate repatriation of the seriously sick and injured POW's.

6 January   Twenty-Fourth subcommittee meeting on Item Four. Thirty-Third subcommittee meeting on Item Three.

7 January   Twenty-Fifth subcommittee meeting on Item Four. Thirty-Fourth subcommittee meeting on

Item Three. Reds repeated allegations that UNC position of airfields is "intentionally delaying the negotiations" and a deliberate attempt to "wreck" the conference.

8 January   Twenty-Sixth subcommittee meeting on Item Four. Thirty-Fifth subcommittee meeting on Item Three.

9 January   Twenty-Seventh subcommittee meeting on Item
(Six months of   Four. Thirty-Sixth subcommittee meeting on Item
negotiations)   Three. Truce talks reached half-year mark.

10 January   Twenty-Eighth subcommittee meeting on Item Four. Thirty-Seventh subcommittee meeting on Item Three.

11 January   Twenty-Ninth subcommittee meeting on Item Four. Thirty-Eighth subcommittee meeting on Item Three.

12 January   Thirtieth subcommittee meeting on Item Four. Thirty-Ninth subcommittee meeting on Item Three.

13 January   Thirty-First subcommittee meeting on Item Four. Fortieth subcommittee meeting on Item Three.

14 January   Thirty-Second subcommittee meeting on Item Four. Forty-First subcommittee meeting on Item Three.

15 January   Thirty-Third subcommittee meeting on Item Four. Forty-Second subcommittee meeting on Item Three.
Dr. Otto Lehner and Mr. Albert de Cocatrix, IRC representatives, accompanied UNC convoy to Panmunjom and requested transportation from the Communists to deliver a message to the North Korean government. Request refused.

16 January   Thirty-Fourth subcommittee meeting on Item Four. Forty-Third subcommittee meeting on Item Three. GHQ PIO released the text of a preliminary statement on Communist charges that UNC planes bombed the Red POW camp Kangdong on the night of 14 January.
IRC representatives again requested transporta-

tion from the Communists. When refused, they handed the Communist delegate a letter from IRC president to North Korean prime minister.

17 January   Thirty-Fifth subcommittee meeting on Item Four. Forty-Fourth subcommittee meeting on Item Three. The UNC charged the Reds with a violation of the Geneva Convention, Article 23, for failure to mark properly its POW enclosures, and proposed the creation of a joint committee of staff officers to study the problem and make recommendations.

23 January   Major General William K. Harrison, Jr., Deputy Commander of Eighth Army, replaced Major General Claude B. Ferenbaugh as a member of the UNC delegation at the military armistice conference.

27 January   Forty-Fifth subcommittee meeting. UNC presented a fifty-four-paragraph military armistice document in draft form for Item Three staff officers to study.

28 January   Forty-Sixth subcommittee meeting. The UNC turned over to the Communists four rosters with the names of 132,080 POW's held by the UNC.

31 January   Admiral Joy in a letter to General Nam Il proposed that a subdelegation begin talks on Item Five of the Agenda.

6 February   Thirty-Sixth Plenary Session (First Plenary Session on Item Five). Tenth staff officers' meeting on Item Three. Fifty-Fifth subcommittee meeting on Item Four. Communist submitted proposal containing three recommendations to be made to governments concerned, including withdrawal of all foreign forces from Korea, peaceful settlement of the Korean question, and other questions related to peace in Korea.

9 February   Thirty-Seventh Plenary Session (Second Plenary Session on Item Five).

10 February   Thirty-Eighth Plenary Session (Third Plenary Session on Item Five). Item Three UNC staff

officers offered to reduce the number of ports of entry required from twelve to eight for each side. Reds rejected and insisted on only three ports.

11 February   Thirty-Ninth Plenary Session (Fourth Plenary Session on Item Five).

12 February   Fortieth Plenary Session (Fifth Plenary Session on Item Five). Sixteenth meeting of staff officers on Item Three offered to permit rotation at the figure of 30,000 monthly, and to allow each side four ports of entry instead of three they formerly insisted upon.

13 February   Seventeenth meeting of staff officers on Item Three. Seventh meeting of staff officers on Item Four. Both sides agreed upon sixty days as the time allowance for return of prisoners during the Item Four staff officers' meeting. UNC officers on Item Three continued to press for a minimum rotation figure of 40,000 but offered to reduce their requirement for eight ports of entry to seven.

16 February   Forty-First Plenary Session (Sixth on Item Five). The Reds named Poland, Czechoslovakia, and Russia as their nominations for the neutral nations inspection teams. UNC stated that Russia was unacceptable. "Freedom Gate Bridge" opened across the Imjin on the road to Panmunjom. Built in a record time of one month and two days, the bridge was to be used by American soldiers returning from Communist prison camps.

17 February   Forty-Second Plenary Session (Seventh on Item Five). UNC accepted Communist proposed solution for Agenda Item Five.

19 February   Forty-Third Plenary Session (Eighth on Item Five).

20 February   Twenty-Fourth meeting of staff officers on Item Three. Fourteenth meeting of staff officers on Item Four. The UNC proposed a monthly personnel rotation figure of 35,000, which was rejected by the Reds.

23 February   Twenty-Seventh meeting of staff officers on Item Three. Seventeenth meeting of staff officers on Item Four. Reds accepted 35,000 rotation figure but rejected UNC proposal of six ports of entry. The Reds handed over a protest on the Koje riot of 18 February.

26 February   Thirtieth meeting of staff officers on Item Three. Twentieth meeting of staff officers on Item Four. The Reds "categorically rejected" the UNC proposal concerning the reduction of the number of neutral nations from three by each side to two.

27 February   A fire started by a defective voltage regulator caused considerable damage to a storage car on the press train used by newsmen covering the military armistice conference at Panmunjom. This was the second fire on the train in about two months.

1 March   Thirty-Fourth meeting of staff officers on Item Three. Fifty-Seventh Item Four meeting of subdelegates. The Reds repudiated their agreement of 29 December and 1 January to exchange supplementary data on prisoners. They said UNC was unilaterally obligated to account for the 44,000 which the UNC had reclassified as civilian internees, but disclaimed any responsibility to account for some 53,000 ROK soldiers who were admitted to have been captured. The Reds also rejected the UNC proposal for immediate exchange of sick and wounded prisoners, and refused the UNC suggestion that Red Cross packages for prisoners be accepted by both sides.

17 March   Fiftieth meeting of staff officers on Item Three. Four. Discussion on the port of entry complexes to be used by each side began in today's Item Three session. The Reds contended again that the city limits of the port cities named should constitute the limits of inspection team activity.

20 March   Fifty-Third meeting of staff officers on Item Three. Twenty-Seventh meeting of staff officers

on Item Four. The names of the five ports of entry for each side were agreed upon today, after the UNC had dropped the controversial Chinnampo-Pyongyang airfield complex.

25 March   Fifty-Eighth meeting of staff officers on Item Three. Thirty-Second meeting of staff officers on Item Four. Item Three staff officers reached general agreement on the ports of entry question. Discussion began on the composition of the neutral nations inspection teams, with the UNC suggesting that only four nations furnish representatives rather than six. Item Four staff officers agreed to hold executive session until further notice.

28 March   Sixty-First meeting of staff officers on Item Three. Thirty-Fifth meeting of staff officers on Item Four. Advance preparations for Red Cross assistance in the eventual exchange of prisoners of war were announced in Tokyo by Gail Galub, assistant director of the American Red Cross Foreign Operations Division.

8 April   Sixtieth subcommittee meeting on Item Three.

14 April
(Nine months of
negotiations)   Today's meeting marked the ninth month of the negotiations, but no progress resulted during a four-minute meeting of the Item Three subdelegates. Sixty-Sixth subcommittee meeting on Item Three. Subdelegates set a record for brevity when they remained in session only fifteen seconds.

25 April   Seventy-Second staff officers' meeting on Item Three. Forty-Eighth staff officers' meeting on Item Four. The Communist staff officer on Item Four abrogated further executive sessions on this agenda item.

28 April   Forty-Fourth Plenary Session. The UNC proposed an over-all solution for the remaining unresolved issues standing in the way of a military armistice at today's forty-fourth plenary meeting of the full delegations. The Communists

proposed an indefinite recess, and the UNC agreed.

2 May   Forty-Fifth Plenary Session. Plenary meeting of the full delegations were in executive session after three-day recess. Communists rejected UNC solution. Proposed instead that they would withdraw name of Soviet Union if the UNC would in turn forcibly repatriate 132,000 prisoners held in exchange for 12,000 men, and would also accede to airfield build-up. This proposal was summarily rejected by Admiral Joy.

3 May   Forty-Sixth Plenary Session. Full delegations held twenty-four-minute meeting at Panmunjom in executive session.

7 May   Fiftieth Plenary Session. Termination of the executive nature of the Plenary Session proposed yesterday by the UNC, became a fact with Communist acceptance after an overnight recess. It was announced that the POW question was the only remaining issue not agreed upon.

General Ridgway made a statement, reiterating UN stand on Panmunjom talks. "Our position is one from which we cannot and shall not retreat," he said.

8 May   Fifty-First Plenary Session.

9 May   Fifty-Second Plenary Session.

10 May   Fifty-Third Plenary Session. Reds continue their rejection of the UNC's over-all solution of 28 April at the Plenary Session.

11 May   Fifty-Fourth Plenary Session.

12 May   Fifty-Fifth Plenary Session. The Reds launched their most vicious propaganda tirade of the entire armistice proceedings.

13 May   Fifty-Sixth Plenary Session.

14 May   Fifty-Seventh Plenary Session.

15 May   Fifty-Eighth Plenary Session.

16 May   Fifty-Ninth Plenary Session.

17 May   Sixtieth Plenary Session.

18 May   Sixty-First Plenary Session. Admiral Joy told the Reds at today's Plenary Session that not even they believed their fantastic, trumped-up charges.

19 May   Sixty-Second Plenary Session.

20 May   Sixty-Third Plenary Session. In today's Sixty-Third Plenary Session the Communists unleashed one of the most vituperative outbursts of the negotiations in an attempt to discredit the UNC rescreening of prisoners. Brigadier General F. C. McConnell named UNC delegate.

21 May   Sixty-Fourth Plenary Session.

22 May   Sixty-Fifth Plenary Session. Major General William K. Harrison succeeded Vice Admiral C. Turner Joy as Senior UN Delegate.

23 May   Sixty-Sixth Plenary Session.

27 May   Sixty-Seventh Plenary Session.

28 May   Sixty-Eigth Plenary Session. For the first time the UNC revealed at the Plenary Session the questions asked POW's in the screening program. Brigadier General Lee Han Lim, ROKA, replaced Lieutenant General Yu Jai Heung, ROKA, on UNC delegation.

29 May   Sixty-Ninth Plenary Session. General Harrison pointed out that the screening actually was performed at the Communists' suggestion.

30 May   Seventieth Plenary Session.

31 May   Seventy-First Plenary Session.

1 June   Seventy-Second Plenary Session.

2 June   Seventy-Third Plenary Session. General Harrison said the Communist fear of facing the truth which would be disclosed by an impartial rescreening of captured personnel stood in the way of armistice agreement.

3 June   Seventy-Fourth Plenary Session.

4 June   Seventy-Fifth Plenary Session. UNC delegates were subjected to a particularly vicious and emotional type of Communist propaganda. Reds

still charged "slaughter" of their prisoners at Koje. They insisted on meeting every day.

5 June   Seventy-Sixth Plenary Session.

6 June   Seventy-Seventh Plenary Session.

7 June   Seventy-Eighth Plenary Session. General Harrison walked out of the meeting with the comment that he was declaring a recess until 11 June. The Reds opposed this move, but General Harrison departed, saying he would not return until 11 June.

9 June   General Clark received a letter from Kim Il Sung and Peng Teh-huai regarding conference session. Contents of letter same as talks.

11 June Seventy-Ninth Plenary Session. General Clark replied to Communist letter. He backed up the truce delegation's actions and said they could recess when they wanted to.

12 June Eightieth Plenary Session.

13 June Eighty-First Plenary Session.

14 June Eighty-Second Plenary Session.

15 June Eighty-Third Plenary Session. Reds continued to reject UNC offer for impartial rescreening.

16 June Eighty-Fourth Plenary Session. A UNC engineering team, with Communist observers in attendance, began a survey of the Panmunjom conference site to determine the exact location of the neutral area boundaries. The Communists claimed that UN artillery fire had fallen inside the zone, while UN liaison officers maintained that the Reds had three infantry observation posts within the neutral zone.

17 June Eighty-Fifth Plenary Session. General Harrison told Red delegates that the UNC would take a "unilateral recess" until 21 June despite their objections.

21 June Eighty-Sixth Plenary Session. General Harrison disclosed that in 1943 Soviet Russia offered voluntary repatriation to German soldiers as an

inducement to surrender during the battle of Stalingrad.

22 June   Eighty-Seventh Plenary Session.

23 June   Eighty-Eighth Plenary Session. Rear Admiral John Daniel, former commander of Destroyer Flotilla III in the Pacific, replaced Rear Admiral R. E. Libby on the UN delegation. Major General Howard Turner also left the delegation on reassignment. He was replaced by Brigadier General Joseph Morris, Commanding General, Spokane, Washington, Air Depot Air Material Command.

24 June   Eighty-Ninth Plenary Session.

25 June   Ninetieth Plenary Session.

26 June   Ninety-First Plenary Session.

27 June   Ninety-Second Plenary Session. The UNC delegation walked out of the meeting despite Communist protests. General Harrison announced that UNC delegates would return on 1 July. This was the third recess in less than a month.

30 June   Recess at Panmunjom. United Nations officials identified as Russian-made a shell that had almost struck the main tent at the truce site on Friday. The tent had been empty at the time. The Communists were warned of possible "serious consequences."

 1 July   Ninety-Third Plenary Session. The twenty-nine-minute meeting involved a review by the UNC Senior Delegate of both sides' positions on the POW question and an attempt to adjust divergent views.

 2 July   Meeting canceled at Panmunjom. The Communists requested that the truce talks be recessed for one day, apparently to study the UN proposal that prisoner lists be revised to exclude those POW's who do not desire to be repatriated.

 3 July   Ninety-Fourth Plenary Session. The Communists proposed a reclassification of POW's and sug-

gested that the conference enter into executive session.

4 July   Ninety-Fifth Plenary Session. The UNC accepted the Communist proposal to conduct the armistice negotiations in executive session.

5 July   Ninety-Sixth Plenary Session. This was the second day in which the session was held in secret. Credentials for Brigadier General Joseph T. Morris, USAF, were presented to the Communists.

6 July   Ninety-Seventh Plenary Session. This was the third secret session.

7 July   Ninety-Eighth Plenary Session. This was the fourth secret session.

8 July   Ninety-Ninth Plenary Session. This was the fifth secret session. In a meeting of liaison officers the UN representative handed the Communists ten maps pin-pointing exact locations of UN POW camps.

9 July   One Hundreth Plenary Session. This was the sixth secret session.

10 July (One year of negotiations)   One Hundred First Plenary Session. This was the seventh secret session and the first anniversary of the Korean truce talks.

11 July   One Hundred Second Plenary Session. This was the eighth secret session.

12 July   One Hundred Third Plenary Session. This was the ninth secret session.

13 July   One Hundred Fourth Plenary Session. This was the tenth secret session. Prior to the meeting, the Reds handed a note to General Harrison from Nam Il claiming that UN bombers had hit a POW camp near Pyongyang during record air strikes. The Communists said thirteen Allied prisoners were killed and seventy-two wounded.

17 July   Recess at Panmunjom. UNC liaison officers delivered a list of 1,014 Communist POW's whose names were submitted to the UNC on 11 March and 4 April.

18 July   One Hundred Fifth Plenary Session convened at Panmunjom in executive session after a four-day recess. This was the eleventh secret session and lasted forty-one minutes.

19 July   One Hundred Sixth Plenary Session convened at Panmunjom in executive session for the twelfth time in the current series. The meeting adjourned after twenty-nine minutes.

20 July   One Hundred Seventh Plenary Session convened at Panmunjom in secret session. This meeting, the thirteenth executive session, lasted twelve minutes. Brigadier General William P. Nuckols, USAF, official UN spokesman for the UNC delegation since the truce talks started, ended those duties and was replaced by Lieutenant Colonel J. J. Borchert, USA.

21 July   One Hundred Eighth Plenary Session convened at Panmunjom for secret talks for the fourteenth time in the current series. The session lasted twenty minutes.

22 July   One Hundred Ninth Plenary Session convened at Panmunjom. This, the fifteenth executive session in the current series, was the shortest of the group, as it lasted only five minutes.

23 July   One Hundred Tenth Plenary Session was conducted at Panmunjom, lasting seven minutes, as delegates concluded their sixteenth secret session in this series

24 July   One Hundred Eleventh Plenary Session was completed at Panmunjom in twenty-six minutes of secret talks, the seventeenth secret meeting in the current series.

25 July   One Hundred Twelfth Plenary Session met at Panmunjom, marking the end of secret sessions which had run since 4 July. The Communists requested the cessation of executive talks after eighteen fruitless sessions in which the Communists refused to accept the UNC's firm objection of forced repatriation of prisoners of war.

26 July   One Hundred Thirteenth Plenary Session convened at Panmunjom, and meetings were then recessed for one week by Major General William K. Harrison, Senior UNC Delegate, after he told the Communists the recent Plenary Sessions had been futile and that he hoped staff officer meetings, to get underway at once, would be more productive.

27 July   Recess of Plenary Sessions at Panmunjom, but General Nam Il dispatched a lengthy letter to General Harrison expressing condemnation of UNC's "unilaterally deciding on a seven-day recess" and reiterating demands for full repatriation of prisoners of war—forced or otherwise. Staff officers met at Panmunjom, with Communists acceding to UNC request that alleged unresolved points of draft armistice agreement be submitted in writing.

28 July   Recess of Plenary Sessions at Panmunjom. Staff officers met forty minutes in "rewording" efforts on Draft Armistice Agreement.

29 July   Recess at Panmunjom. Staff officers met again in discussions of wording of draft armistice agreement.

30 July   Recess at Panmunjom. Staff officers' meeting of forty minutes said taken up with "minutiae."

31 July   Recess at Panmunjom. Staff officers continued sessions on rewording of Draft Agreement. General Harrison dispatched a letter to General Nam Il, via liaison officers, requesting information as to status of 45 UNC individuals on "Supplemental List VI" and 1,881 others on whom information had been sought earlier. General Harrison's letter stated evidence indicated all had been taken prisoners of war by the Communist forces. General Van Fleet told newsmen "present trends show less chance for an armistice than ever before."

2 August   Recess at Panmunjom. UNC and Communist staff

officers signified agreement on the wording of all but two paragraphs in the Draft Armistice Agreement. UNC senior staff officer withheld a statement of agreement on the Communist-proposed revised wordings of Paragraphs 52 and 60 pending further study.

3 August   One Hundred Fourteenth Plenary Session met for thirty-two minutes and recessed for seven days at UNC delegate request.

4 August   Recess at Panmunjom. Staff officers held a thirty-nine-minute meeting in which they agreed to wording in Paragraph 52. UNC resubmitted to the Communists a request for permission to ship individual packages to prisoners of war in Communist custody.

5 August   Recess at Panmunjom. Staff officers' meetings terminated following agreement by both sides to text of paragraph 60. Session lasted forty-four minutes. Letter from General Harrison again requested Communists to permit POW's on both sides to receive comfort packages.

8 August   Recess at Panmunjom. General Harrison sent a letter requesting Communists to clarify status of their POW camps Numbers 6 and 9.

11 August   One Hundred Fifteenth Plenary Session met for thirty-five minutes with no apparent progress in the negotiations for an armistice. Seven-day recess was requested by the UNC delegates and accepted by the Communists.

13 August   UNC requested information as to locations and number of POW camps from the Communists.

19 August   One Hundred Sixteenth Plenary Session met at Panmunjom. No progress reported. General Harrison proposed another seven-day recess and Communists agreed.

22 August   UNC liaison officers apprised the Communists of new designations of thirteen POW camps.

27 August   One Hundred Seventeenth Plenary Session met

for thirty-three minutes with no apparent progress in the negotiations for an armistice. The question of repatriation of prisoners of war was still in a deadlock. Recess proposed by the UNC to 4 September was agreed to by the Communists. General Harrison again proposed POW's of both sides be permitted to receive comfort packages.

28 August   A letter was received from the Communists at a liaison officers' meeting protesting the killing of five and wounding of sixty-four POW's during the recent disturbance at the Koje Island Camp.

30 August   Recess at Panmunjom. The Communists sent a protest to the UNC liaison officers regarding the killing of one and wounding and injuring twenty-six Communist POW's.

31 August   The Communists lodged a protest to UNC regarding the killing of six and wounding of twenty-two captured personnel by a strafing UNC aircraft.

1 September   A letter trom the Communist truce delegation insists that on 20 August UNC troops fired on prisoners and wounded twelve.

2 September   In a letter to UNC truce team, Communists claimed that UNC forces killed one and wounded sixteen prisoners on 30 August.

4 September   Truce delegates met again at Panmunjom in One Hundred Eighteenth Plenary Session and fifty-two minutes later called a recess until 12 September.

6 September   Major General W. K. Harrison was promoted to Lieutenant General and assigned Deputy Commanding General of the United States Army Forces Far East.

12 September   Truce delegations met in One Hundred Nineteenth Plenary Session at Panmunjom after a recess since 4 September. Delegations agreed to a recess until 20 September.

15 September   Recess at Panmunjom. UNC and Communist liai-

son officers exchanged letters. UNC protested marking of prisoner-of-war camps. The Communists charged violation of conference site neutrality by dropped leaflets, and also mistreatment of Communists in prison camps.

20 September UNC and Communist truce delegations met in One Hundred Twentieth Plenary Session. The Communists protested the injury of twenty-three prisoners of war on 17 September. After a fifty-two-minute discussion, the delegates agreed to a recess until 28 September.

24 September UNC liaison officers were handed a letter by Communist delegates protesting the proposed release of 11,000 prisoners now classified as civilian internees by UNC.

28 September UNC and Communist truce delegations met in One Hundred Twenty-First Session at Panmunjom today. General Harrison presented the Communists three alternative proposals for a solution to the prisoner-of-war question. The Communists held firm for no voluntary repatriation of prisoners, and protested the wounding of four Communist prisoners at the Cheju-do Camp on 27 September. The two delegations agreed to a ten-day recess until 8 October.

2 October Communist liaison officer delivered a note of protest from General Nam Il on death and injury of prisoners of war in disorder at Chejo-do yesterday. The death toll had risen to fifty-two.

6 October Recess at Panmunjom. Lieutenant General William K. Harrison, Jr., Senior UNC Delegate, in a letter to General Nam Il reiterated UNC proposals to permit prisoners of war to receive comfort packages as described in Article 72 of the Geneva Convention. The letter proposed a specific plan for exchange of parcels by both sides.

7 October One Hundred Twenty-Second Plenary Session convened at Panmunjom and after sixty-three minutes went into indefinite recess called by the

United Nations Command. Lieutenant General
William K. Harrison, Jr. Senior UN Delegate,
after a lengthy statement concerning fruitless
efforts to resolve the prisoner-of-war issue, informed the Communist delegates the UNC was
not terminating the talks and would be readily
available should the Communists accept one of
the UNC proposals on the POW's or submit in
writing a constructive proposal of their own.
General Mark W. Clark also issued a statement
on the Panmunjom impasse, pointing out that
the UN had "made repeated and earnest efforts
to settle this [POW] question." He reiterated
that the UNC continued to stand ready to "conclude an armistice acceptable to the conscience
of the free peoples."

11 October   General Nam Il, Senior Communist Delegate,
sent a letter of protest to Lieutenant General
William K. Harrison expressing displeasure with
the UN in unilaterally declaring an indefinite
recess to the peace talks but offered nothing
constructive to break the impasse over the
prisoner-of-war issue.

16 October   Recess at Panmunjom. Lieutenant General William K. Harrison informed the Communists by
letter that the Allies had not terminated the
truce talks and would resume when they accepted
Allied views or made a constructive proposal
of their own.

19 October   Recess at Panmunjom.

20 October   Recess at Panmunjom. General Clark, in a letter
delivered by UNC liaison officers at Panmunjom,
replied to the Reds that the peace talks would not
resume under their terms, but the UN was "ready
and willing" to continue the talks when the Reds
began to show evidence of good faith.

24 October   Recess at Panmunjom. William C. Foster, United
States Deputy Secretary of Defense, speaking in
Seoul, praised teamwork of UNC forces, said,
"We cannot expect to pull out and leave the

ROK's alone in the foreseeable future." Letters were exchanged by Communist and UNC liaison officers at Panmunjom.

28 October   Recess at Panmunjom. Lieutenant General Harrison received a letter from the Communist Senior Delegate accusing the UNC of "plotting to extend the war" and "slaughtering prisoners."

31 October   Recess at Panmunjom. A letter in which prisoner-of-war camps were redesignated was handed to UNC liaison officers by a Communist liaison officer.

1 November   Recess at Panmunjom. The Communist Senior Delegate sent a long, vituperative letter protesting prisoner-of-war incidents to the UNC Senior Delegate.

10 November   Recess at Panmunjom. The Communist liaison officer at Panmunjom affirmed that a prisoner-of-war camp listing by their side on 31 October superseded all previous lists, but delayed answering a query as to whether the previously listed POW collecting points still existed.

14 November   Recess at Panmunjom. The UNC handed a letter of protest to the Communist liaison officer at Panmunjom on the fatal shooting of a United States Medical Corpsman on 14 November in the truce zone.

20 November   Recess at Panmunjom. The Communists declined to assume responsibility for the death of a United Nations Command medical aid man killed by small-arms fire in the Panmunjom restricted area on 14 November, stating an "internal investigation" had established "beyond doubt" that the bullet was not fired by their troops.

4 December   Recess at Panmunjom. The Communists were informed of the establishments of a POW camp at Taegu by the United Nations Command, in a letter delivered at Panmunjom by UN truce negotiators.

16 December   Recess at Panmunjom. General Nam Il sent a

strong letter of protest to General Harrison on the death of eighty-three Communists on 14 December at Pongam during a riot by civilian internees.

17 December   Recess at Panmunjom. Commander James A. Masterson, USN, was named to the UNC liaison officer group for the armistice negotiations, to serve with Colonel Charles McCarthy and Lieutenant Colonel Earl H. Robinson.

1953

15 January   In a letter from UNC senior liaison officer presented to Communists at meeting, UNC reduced the number of convoys to be granted immunity from air attack between Kaesong and Pyongyang.

21 January   By letter, Communists charged UNC with "undermining various administrative agreements relating to armistice negotiations." Letter was in reply to letter of 15 January.

19 February   At liaison officers' meeting, UNC delivered a letter to Nam Il from General Harrison rejecting flatly a "deliberate fraudulent" charge that UN aircraft bombed area of Communist POW camp at Sunchon. Lieutenant Colonel Harry M. Odren, USAF, replaced Lieutenant Colonel Earl H. Robinson as UNC liaison officer.

22 February   At Panmunjom meeting UNC liaison officers delivered letter from General Mark W. Clark to Kim Il Sung and Peng Teh-huai requesting immediate exchange of all sick and wounded prisoners of war and proposing liaison officers meet to prepare for such action.

23 February   At Panmunjom meeting UNC senior liaison officer received letters of protest from Colonel Ju Yon protesting various deaths of their captured personnel.

13 March   In letter reply to Nam Il's protest of 23 February that UN aircraft bombed and strafed POW camp

at Sunchon on 26 November 1952, General Harrison stated that primary responsibility for POW's in their custody attached to their side. Protest labeled "fraudulent" by General Harrison, since UN aircraft had expended no ordnance in that area at time stated.

23 March   At liaison officers' meeting UNC delivered letter from General Harrison to Nam Il informing of new POW camp location.

24 March   General Nam Il informed UNC of several Communist changes of POW camps in letter to General Harrison delivered at liaison officers meeting.

28 March   Communists replied to General Clark's letter of 22 February, stating agreement with proposal to exchange sick and injured prisoners during the period of hostilities.

31 March   By letter General Clark acknowledged "with pleasure" receipt of Communist letter of 28 March and requested Communists propose date for liaison groups to meet on exchange of sick and injured prisoners.

1 April   At liaison officers' meeting UNC asked if several POW camps were still in existence. UNC also requested location of collecting points at Suan. Communists confirmed the camps still existed at same locations.

2 April   Communist letter to General Clark suggested liaison group on sick and injured exchange meet on April.

5 April   Letter from General Clark to Communists agreed to 6 April meeting of liaison group.

6 April   At liaison group meeting at Panmunjom, Rear Admiral John C. Daniel stated UNC was prepared to repatriate personnel according to Article 109 of Geneva Convention. General Lee Sang Cho stated they were prepared to repatriate according to Articles 109 and 110.

7 April   Liaison group met at Panmunjom. Communists

reported their figures on sick and wounded would be ready in day or two. Groups agreed on three points of UNC proposal for handling exchange.

8 April   Liaison group meeting. Both sides gave first figures of sick and wounded to be repatriated.

9 April   Liaison Group meeting. Agreed ratio of exchange of 500 Communist sick and wounded to 100 UNC per day until repatriation completed. Agreed to begin repatriation no later than ten days after signing of agreement.

10 April Liaison group meeting. Communists gave partial breakdown of non-Korean prisoners to be exchanged. Admiral Daniel requested complete breakdown. Nam Il sent "full explanation of new proposal to our side" in letter to General Harrison.

11 April Admiral Daniel reiterated request for complete breakdown of exchange prisoners, and asked broad interpretation of "sick and injured." Agreement for repatriation of sick and injured captured personnel signed by both sides.

12 April Staff officers' meeting at Panmunjom. Communists report repatriation convoy to start movement 14 April.

13 April Staff officers' meeting at Panmunjom. Communists name more nationalities represented by exchange prisoners, but no figures.

14 April Staff officers' meeting at Panmunjom. UNC informed of Communist convoy movements.

15 April Staff officers' meeting. UNC requested Communists to repatriate proportionate numbers by nationality on first day of exchange.

16 April Staff officers' meeting. UNC was informed that first-day exchange would include fifty Koreans, fifty non-Koreans.

17 April At liaison officers' meeting, a letter from General Clark to Nam Il stating our side was prepared to establish reopening date for Plenary Sessions was delivered. At staff officers' meeting the

Communists were informed that Colonel Edward Austin, USA, had been designated as UNC Control Officer for repatriation, and Colonel Soo Young Lee, ROKA, his assistant.

18 April   Staff officers' meeting. Communists stated they would begin repatriation at 0900 hours 20 April and designated Colonel Lee Pyong Il, NKA, as control officer.

19 April   At liaison group meeting Admiral Daniel proposed 23 April as reopening date for armistice negotiations. Communists proposed 25 April.

20 April   Repatriation proceedings of sick and injured POW's commenced.

21 April   Repatriation proceedings.

22 April   Repatriation proceedings.

23 April   Repatriation proceedings. At liaison group meeting UNC was informed Communists would repatriate all sick and injured during current exchange.

24 April   Repatriation proceedings. At liaison group meeting Communists requested postponement of opening date of resumed Plenary Sessions to 26 April. Admiral Daniel stated repatriation should be continuing process in accordance with Geneva Convention.

25 April   Repatriation proceedings.

26 April   Repatriation proceedings. At One Hundred Twenty-Third Plenary Session of armistice negotiations, Nam Il presented a proposed pattern for discussions and stated that UNC's earlier proposal that Switzerland serve as neutral nation to supervise repatriation of prisoners was unacceptable.

27 April   One Hundred Twenty-Fourth Plenary Session. General Harrison stated Communist pattern for discussions did not give acceptable solution to POW question and that they had proposed no reasonable basis for armistice agreement.

28 April   One Hundred Twenty-Fifth Plenary Session.

29 April   One Hundred Twenty-Sixth Plenary Session. Communists proposed unnamed Asiatic nation as their choice to take custody of POW's not wishing repatriation.

30 April   One Hundred Twenty-Seventh Plenary Session. General Harrison indicated understanding on neutral nations should precede other elements of Communist proposal in discussions and requested Communists announce their nominee.

1 May   At One Hundred Twenty-Eighth Plenary Session General Harrison reiterated request that Communists name their nominee for neutral nation to serve as nonrepatriated POW custodian. At liaison group meeting, Admiral Daniel accused Communists of holding 375 UNC sick and wounded POW's eligible to return.

2 May   At One Hundred Twenty-Ninth Plenary Session Communists asked UNC to consider sending nonrepatriated POW's to homelands of Neutral Nations Supervisory Commission, (Sweden, Switzerland, Poland, Czechoslovakia). UNC reaffirmed stand that custody by neutral nations should be maintained in Korea. Communists mentioned, but did not nominate India, Burma, Pakistan, and Indonesia as Asian neutrals as POW custodians, and charged UNC had rejected Asian nation as neutral. General Harrison denied the charge. At liaison group meeting, Admiral Daniel insisted 375 remaining sick and wounded POW's be repatriated.

3 May   Repatriation operations completed for both sides; 6,670 Communists and 684 UNC personnel repatriated. Communists had not yet replied to Admiral Daniel's charge.

4 May   One Hundred Thirtieth Plenary Session. UNC nominated Pakistan as neutral nation to handle nonrepatriated prisoners after armistice signing.

5 May   One Hundred Thirty-First Plenary Session. General Harrison stated POW's refusing repatriation should not be moved out of Korea by force.

6 May One Hundred Thirty-Second Plenary Session. UNC renominated Pakistan as neutral POW custodian. General Harrison stated that further discussion of the POW handling was premature until neutral nations were selected. Communists reiterated stand that nonrepatriated POW's should not be sent to neutral nation homelands.

7 May One Hundred Thirty-Third Plenary Session. In a new group of proposals the Communists agreed to UNC stand on not removing nonrepatriated prisoners from Korea by force. Communists suggested five countries to act as Neutral Nations Repatriation Commission, including Switzerland, Poland, Sweden, and Czechoslovakia, already agreed upon as Neutral Nations Supervisory Commission, and adding India.

8 May No meeting.

9 May One Hundred Thirty-Fourth Plenary Session. New Communist proposals discussed.

10 May One Hundred Thirty-Fifth Plenary Session. Communists defended their proposal that political conference handle nonrepatriated prisoners after certain time limit.

11 May One Hundred Thirty-Sixth Plenary Session. UNC stated that answers to UNC questions on Communist proposals necessary before agreement on Communist proposal could be worked out.

12 May One Hundred Thirty-Seventh Plenary Session. UNC reiterated statement of previous day. UNC also stated there was no guarantee that political conference could settle repatriation problem.

13 May One Hundred Thirty-Eighth Plenary Session. UNC submitted counterproposal to Communists proposal, naming India to supply armed forces for Custodial Commission.

14 May One Hundred Thirty-Ninth Plenary Session. Communists completely rejected UNC counterproposal of 13 May.

15 May One Hundred Fortieth Plenary Session. General

Harrison told Communists they "either misunderstood or deliberately misinterpreted" UNC counterproposal.

16 May   One Hundred Forty-First Plenary Session. UNC Chief Delegate stated Communists should read Allied terms more carefully and called criticism "completely unjustified."

25 May   One Hundred Forty-Second Plenary Session. Executive.

4 June   One Hundred Forty-Third Plenary Session. Executive session of delegates.

6 June   One Hundred Forty-Fourth Plenary Session. Executive session of delegates.

7 June   One Hundred Forty-Fifth Plenary Session. Executive session of delegates.

8 June   One Hundred Forty-Sixth Plenary Session. Executive session of delegates. General Harrison and Nam Il signed "Terms of Reference" for Neutral Nations Repatriation Commission.

9 June   One Hundred Forty-Seventh Plenary Session. Delegates and staff officers met in executive session.

10 June   One Hundred Forty-Eighth Plenary Session. Delegates and staff officers met in executive session.

17 June   One Hundred Forty-Ninth Plenary Session. Senior Delegates met in executive session.

18 June   Letter from General Harrison to Nam Il announcing escape of 25,000 North Korean POW's was delivered to Communists at Panmunjom.

20 June   Delegates met at Panmunjom; One Hundred Fiftieth Plenary Session. Nam Il read letter from Marshal Kim Il Sung to General Clark in answer to UNC 18 June letter concerning escaped POW's, which included several questions regarding further UNC intentions.

29 June   Liaison officers' meeting. UNC delivered letter to Communists from General Mark W. Clark in

answer to 20 June letter from Marshal Kim Il Sung concerning escaped POW's.

8 July   Liaison officers' meeting. Communists delivered letter from Kim Il Sung and Peng Teh-huai to General Clark in reply to letter of 29 June concerning POW's.

9 July   Liaison officers' meeting. Plenary session scheduled for 10 July.

10 July   One Hundred Fifty-First Plenary Session in executive session.

11 July   One Hundred Fifty-Second Plenary Session in executive session.

12 July   One Hundred Fifty-Third Plenary Session in executive session.

13 July   One Hundred Fifty-Fourth Plenary Session in executive session. At liaison officers' meeting Communists protested by letter an alleged incident at Suan POW collecting point.

14 July   One Hundred Fifty-Fifth Plenary Session in executive session. At liaison officers' meeting Communists protested alleged violation of Panmunjom neutral zone.

15 July   One Hundred Fifty-Sixth Plenary Session in executive session.

16 July   One Hundred Fifty-Seventh Plenary Session in executive session.

19 July   One Hundred Fifty-Eighth Plenary Session meeting, and liaison officers' meeting in executive session.

20 July   Liaison and staff officers met in executive session at Panmunjom.

21 July   Liaison and staff officers met in executive sessions.

22 July   Staff officers met in executive sessions at Panmunjom.

23 July   Liaison and staff officers met in executive session at Panmunjom.

24 July   Liaison and staff officers met in executive session.

25 July   Liaison officers met in executive session at Panmunjom.

26 July   Liaison officers met in executive session at Panmunjom. General Mark W. Clark announced that UNC and Communists had reached agreement on terms of armistice and that signing was scheduled for 27 July.

27 July   One Hundred Fifty-Ninth Plenary Session at 1000 hours at Panmunjom. UNC Senior Delegate Lieutenant General William K. Harrison, Jr., and Communist Senior Delegate General Nam Il signed the Armistice Agreement. General Mark W. Clark, Commander-in-Chief, United Nations Command, signed the agreement in the afternoon at Munsan Base Camp.

III

MR. YAKOV A. MALIK STATEMENT, 23 JUNE 1951

THE PRICE OF PEACE

Settlement of Korean Question

by

Yakov A. Malik

23 June 1951

It is perfectly obvious that radio broadcasts on the subject of "the price of peace" should serve the cause of strengthening peace and assisting the forces which stand for peace in their noble struggle to prevent war. All the nations of the world realize the supreme value of peace to mankind.

It is not yet six years since the conclusion of the Second World War, in which millions of persons lost their lives but peace, for which such a high price was paid, is once again threatened.

The ruling circles in the United States of America, the United Kingdom, and France are endeavoring to convince their peoples that, in order to maintain peace, it is necessary to arm, to create a so-called "position of strength" which will supposedly make the outbreak of a new war impossible.

It should, however, be clear to all that whoever desires peace should seek to resolve by peaceful means the problems arising out of mutual relations with other countries.

The government of the Soviet Union has repeatedly declared that the policy which is being pursued by the United States, the United Kingdom, France, and a number of other countries is profoundly vicious, will inevitably lead to fresh international conflicts, and contains within itself the seeds of a new world war. It is precisely this policy of the Western powers which has brought about the present serious international tension.

The chief reason for the deterioration in relations between the USSR and the three Western powers was the establishment of the North Atlantic Military Alliance. The political leaders of the countries participating in this bloc make no secret of the fact that this military alliance is directed against the USSR and the peoples' democratic republics. It is sufficient to point out that American newspapers and magazines are daily publishing maps and diagrams showing a ring of United States military bases in Europe and the Near East surrounding the Soviet Union, and indicating the air routes of United States bombers from those bases to the industrial centers of the USSR.

It is well known that at the preliminary conference of the deputy foreign ministers of the four powers in Paris, the representatives of the United States, the United Kingdom, and France offered every resistance to the adoption of the Soviet proposal that the urgent question of American military bases and the Atlantic pact should be placed on the agenda of the council, whose task it is to consider all the more important question concerning the safeguarding of peace. This policy of the government of the United States, the United Kingdom, and France cannot be regarded otherwise than as an endeavor to maintain the existing international tension.

The conclusion of the North Atlantic pact, the establishment of American military bases abroad, the remilitarization of Western Germany and the creation of West German armed forces, the encouragement of a revival of Japanese militarism, the mad armaments race, and the expansion of armed forces in the countries of the North Atlantic pact and especially in the United States—these are all current features of the aggressive policy of the Western powers.

The most flagrant manifestation of this policy is the armed intervention in Korea of the United States and a number of other countries dependent upon the United States. The Soviet Union, the Chinese People's Republic, and a number of other states have repeatedly submitted proposals for the peaceful settlement of the Korean dispute, and the only reason why the war still continues in

Korea is that the United States has prevented the adoption of these peace proposals.

The seizure of the Chinese island of Taiwan (or Formosa) and the bombing of Chinese territory provide irrefutable evidence of the United States endeavor to extend the war in the Far East. As we know by experience, however, this can have only the effect of drawing more closely together the peoples of Asia, who justly regard this policy of the ruling circles in the United States as a threat to their security and independence.

The peoples of the countries members of the North Atlantic bloc are themselves suffering all the consequences of the policy of an armaments race and the preparations for a new war. Whereas in 1938–39, before the Second World War, the per capita military expenditure of the American government was about $8, in 1950 the per capita expenditure of the American government on war preparations rose to $147 and in 1951 it will rise to $307.

The only people to benefit from the armaments race are those who make enormous profits from military contracts. The National City Bank letter, a publication of American capitalists, has admitted that the American economy is moving every month at an ever faster rate toward making armaments its chief business and subordinating to armaments all civilian activities and the peacetime way of life.

In order to mask this policy of an armaments race and the creation of centers of aggression, the ruling circles of the Western powers are trying to represent as aggressive the peaceful policy of the Soviet Union, the People's Republic of China, Poland, Czechoslovakia, Rumania, Hungary, and Bulgaria, while declaring that their own policy of actual aggression is a policy of peace. Both these assertions, however, are refuted by the facts, which cannot be concealed.

The Soviet Union has consistently defended, and is defending, the cause of peace, and is pursuing a policy of collaboration with all countries desiring such collaboration. The Soviet Union threatens no one; it has not, and cannot have, any aggressive plans whatsoever. The peaceful policy of the Soviet Union is based on the fundamental principles which underlie the Soviet social structure and the interests of the Soviet people.

The efforts of the Soviet peoples are directed towards peaceful construction. The Soviet state is engaged in expanding civilian industry, in bringing into being the giant hydroelectric power stations and irrigation systems on the Volga, the Dnieper, and the Amur-

Darya, and in carrying out its plan to transform nature in order to secure abundant and stable harvests. The peaceful constructive labor of the Soviet people in the postwar years has led to a considerable rise in the population's standard of living.

As a result of rising wages, of the systematic reduction of prices, and of increased state expenditure on social and cultural objects, the total income of workers, employes, and peasants rose by 62 per cent in 1950, as compared with the prewar total for 1940. Obviously, the development of civilian construction on such a scale and the considerable rise in the population's standard of living would have been impossible if the Soviet government had pursued not a policy of peace and construction but a policy of competition in armaments and armed forces.

In contravention of the United Nations resolution concerning prohibition of war propaganda, hundreds of newspapers and journals in the United States are daily and openly calling for an attack on the Soviet Union. At the same time, no one can name a single USSR newspaper which called for an attack on the United States or any other country whatsoever. In the USSR a special law has been passed punishing as penal offenders any who might try to conduct war propaganda.

The Soviet Union bases its policy on the possibility of the peaceful coexistence of the two systems, socialism and capitalism, and steadfastly pursues the course of maintaining loyal and peaceful relations with all states which show a desire for economic cooperation, provided that the principals of reciprocity and observance of accepted obligations are respected.

With regard to relations between the Soviet Union and the United States, as long ago as 1932, in reply to the questions asked by the American journalist, Ralph V. Barnes, "Could not the Soviet and American peoples be convinced that an armed conflict between their two countries should never under any circumstances take place?" Stalin replied as follows:

"Nothing is easier than to convince the peoples of both countries of the harmfulness and criminality of mutual annihilation. Unfortunately, however, questions of peace and war are not always settled by the peoples. I have no doubt that the masses of the people of the United States did not want a war with the peoples of the USSR in 1918–19. That did not prevent the United States government, however, from attacking the USSR in 1918 (together with Japan,

England, and France) and continuing armed aggression against the USSR until 1919.

"As far as the USSR is concerned, it seems hardly necessary to supply further proof of the fact that both the peoples of the USSR and the government of the USSR are anxious that an armed conflict between their two countries should never under any circumstances arise."

The Soviet government has defended and continues to defend the program of strengthening peace and international security. That program includes the cooperation of the great powers, which has been expressed in the proposal for the conclusion of a pact to strengthen peace. It provides for the reduction of armaments, the absolute prohibition of atomic weapons, with the establishment of international control to implement that prohibition, and also the strict implementation of the Potsdam decision on the German problem, a peace settlement with Germany and Japan, and the expansion of commercial and economic ties between all countries.

It this program is not being carried out, it is only because it does not suit the forces of aggression in a number of countries, which are afraid that the carrying out of such a program would undermine their aggressive measures, would make an armaments race impossible, and would thus deprive them of an opportunity to obtain further billions in excess profits from war orders.

The Soviet Union took an active part in the establishment of the United Nations. The Soviet Union took this action in the belief that the strength of this international organization lies in the fact that it is based on the principle of the unanimity of the five great powers, on the inadmissibility of isolating any of those powers, and on the fact that its action will be effective only if the great powers respect that principle. Nevertheless, mainly through the fault of the United States, this principle is continually being violated, and three of the five great powers, the United States, the United Kingdom, and France, are systematically pursuing the policy of isolating the other two great powers, the USSR and the People's Republic of China.

In setting up the United Nations, the peoples of the world hoped that the organization would become a reliable instrument for the maintenance of international peace and security and would fulfill the obligation of saving "succeeding generations from the scourge of war'" which it assumed under the charter.

During the whole existence of the United Nations, the Soviet Union has been taking steps to strengthen that organization and has resisted any and every attempt made by certain states, especially the United States, to by-pass the Security Council, which was given the main responsibility for the maintenance of peace and security, and to turn this international organization into a tool of one or more states.

By the efforts of the ruling circles in the United States, however, the United Nations is being transformed more and more into an instrument of war, a means for unleashing a new world war; and at the same time it is ceasing to be a world-wide organization of nations endowed with equal rights. The United Nations adopted the illegal decision sanctioning, post factum, the American aggression in Korea and China. The United Nations branded as an "aggressor" the People's Republic of China, which is defending its own frontiers and endeavoring to secure the return of the island of Taiwan, which has been seized by the American forces. This is also borne out by the illegal decision to declare an embargo against China and by the fact that four hundred millions of Chinese people are still not represented in the United Nations.

The Soviet Union will continue its struggle to strengthen peace and avert a new world war. The peoples of the Soviet Union believe that this is possible to defend the cause of peace.

The Soviet peoples further believe that the most acute problem of the present day—the problem of the armed conflict in Korea—could also be settled.

This would require the readiness of the parties to enter on the path of a peaceful settlement of the Korean question. The Soviet peoples believe that as a first step discussions should be started between the belligerents for a cease-fire and an armistice providing for the mutual withdrawal of forces from the Thirty-eighth Parallel.

Can such a step be taken? I think it can, provided there is a sincere desire to put an end to the bloody fighting in Korea.

I think that, surely, is not too great a price to pay in order to achieve peace in Korea.

IV

AGREEMENT FOR THE REPATRIATION OF SICK AND INJURED CAPTURED PERSONNEL

The Senior Member of the United Nations Command Liaison Group and the Senior Member of the Korean People's Army and the Chinese People's Volunteers Liaison Group, in order to effect the repatriation of sick and injured captured personnel in accordance with the provisions of Article 109 of the 1949 Geneva Convention Relative to the Treatment of Prisoners of War, agree to the following:

1. Repatriation shall be accomplished at Panmunjom.

2. Repatriation shall commence at Panmunjom not later than ten (10) days after the signing of this agreement.

3. a. The Korean People's Army and the Chinese People's Volunteers shall deliver sick and injured captured personnel at the rate of approximately one hundred (100) per day until delivery of all sick and injured captured personnel to be repatriated by the Korean People's Army and the Chinese People's Volunteers is completed. The number of persons actually delivered each day shall be contingent upon the ability of the United Nations Command to receive them, but delivery shall in any case be completed prior to the termination date of this agreement.

b. The United Nations Command shall deliver sick and injured captured personnel at the rate of approximately five hundred (500) per day until delivery of all sick and injured captured personnel to be repatriated by the United Nations Command is completed. The number of persons actually delivered each day shall be contingent upon the ability of the Korean People's Army and the Chinese People's Volunteers to receive them, but delivery shall in any case be completed prior to the termination date of this agreement.

4. The United Nations Command shall deliver sick and injured captured personnel in groups of approximately twenty-five (25); the Korean People's Army and the Chinese People's Volunteers shall deliver sick and injured captured personnel in groups of approximately twenty-five (25). Each group shall be accompanied by rosters, prepared by nationality, to include:

    a. Name

    b. Rank

    c. Internment or military serial number

5. After each group of sick and injured captured personnel is delivered and received, a representative of the receiving side shall sign the roster of the captured personnel delivered as a receipt and shall return this to the delivering side.

6. In order to insure that the sick and injured captured personnel of both sides are given maximum protection during the full period of repatriation, both sides agree to guarantee immunity from all attacks to all rail and motor movements carrying sick and injured captured personnel to Kaesong and Munsan-ni, respectively, and thence through presently established immunity routes to Panmunjom, subject to the following conditions:

    a. Movement of motor convoys to Kaesong and Munsan-ni, respectively, shall be restricted to daylight hours, and each convoy shall consist of not less than five (5) vehicles in close formation; except that north of Panmunjom, because of actual conditions, the latter provision shall apply only to the route from Pyongyang to Kaesong.

    b. Each car in rail movements and each vehicle in motor convoys shall display clearly visible identification markings.

    c. Each side, prior to the initial movement, shall provide the Liaison Group of the other side with a detailed description of the markings utilized to identify motor convoys and rail movements. This shall include color, size and manner in which the markings will be displayed.

d. Each side, prior to the initial movement, shall provide the Liaison Group of the other side with the sites and markings of the bivouac areas and night stop-over locations for motor convoys.

e. Each side shall inform the Liaison Group of the other side, twenty-four (24) hours in advance of each movement, of the selected route, number of cars in rail movement or number of vehicles in motor movement, and the estimated time of arrival at Kaesong or Munsan-ni.

f. Each side shall notify the Liaison Group of the other side, by the most expeditious means of communications available, of the location of emergency stop-overs.

7. During the period while sick and injured captured personnel are being repatriated through the Panmunjom conference site area, the October 22, 1951 Agreement Between Liaison Officers, with the exception of the part therein provided for in Paragraph 8 of this Agreement, shall continue in effect. Liaison Groups of both sides and their parties shall have free access to, and free movement within, the Panmunjom conference site area. The composition of each Liaison Group and its party shall be as determined by the Senior Member thereof; however, in order to avoid congestion in the conference site area, including captured personnel under its control, shall not exceed three hundred (300) persons at any one time. Each side shall transfer repatriated personnel out of the Panmunjom conference site area as expeditiously as possible.

8. During the period while sick and injured captured personnel are being repatriated through the Panmunjom conference site area, the armed military police of each side, who undertake to maintain order within the conference site area, shall be increased from the maximum number of fifteen (15), as provided for in the October 22, 1951 Agreement Between Liaison Officers, to thirty (30).

9. Other administrative details shall be mutually arranged by officers designated by the Senior Member of the Liaison Group of each side.

10. This agreement is effective when signed and will terminate twenty (20) days after the commencement of repatriation of sick and injured captured personnel at Panmunjom.

Done at Panmunjom, Korea, this 11th day of April 1953, in the English, Korean and Chinese languages, all texts being equally authentic.

[signed]

LEE SANG CHO
Major General
Korean People's Army
Senior Member
Korean People's Army and
Chinese People's Volunteers
Liaison Group

[signed]

J. C. DANIEL
Rear Admiral
United States Navy
Senior Member
United Nations Command
Liaison Group

V

TEXT OF ARMISTICE AGREEMENT

Agreement between the Commander-in-Chief, United Nations Command, on the one hand, and the Supreme Commander of the Korean People's Army and the Commander of the Chinese People's Volunteers, on the other hand, concerning a military armistice in Korea.

Preamble

The undersigned, the Commander-in-Chief, United Nations Command, on the one hand, and the Supreme Commander of the Korean People's Army and the Commander of the Chinese People's Volunteers, on the other hand, in the interest of stopping the Korean conflict, with its great toll of suffering and bloodshed on both sides, and with the objective of establishing an armistice which will insure a complete cessation of hostilities and of all acts of armed force in Korea until a final peaceful settlement is achieved, do individually, collectively, and mutually agree to accept and to be bound and governed by the conditions and terms of armistice set forth in the following articles and paragraphs, which said conditions and terms are intended to be purely military in character and to pertain solely to the belligerents in Korea:

Article I

Military Demarcation Line and Demilitarized Zone

1. A military demarcation line shall be fixed and both sides shall withdraw two (2) kilometers from this line so as to establish

a demilitarized zone between the opposing forces. A demilitarized zone shall be established as a buffer zone to prevent the occurrence of incidents which might lead to a resumption of hostilities.

2. The military demarcation line is located as indicated on the attached map.[1]

3. This demilitarized zone is defined by a northern and a southern boundary as indicated on the attached map.

4. The military demarcation line shall be plainly marked as directed by the Military Armistice Commission hereinafter established. The Commanders of the opposing sides shall have suitable markers erected along the boundary between the demilitarized zone and their respective areas. The Military Armistice Commission shall supervise the erection of all markers placed along the military demarcation line and along the boundaries of the demilitarized zone.

5. The waters of the Han River Estuary shall be open to civil shipping of both sides wherever one bank is controlled by one side and the other bank is controlled by the other side. The Military Armistice Commission shall prescribe rules for the shipping in that part of the Han River Estuary indicated on the attached map. Civil shipping of each side shall have unrestricted access to the land under the military control of that side.

6. Neither side shall execute any hostile act within, from, or against the demilitarized zone.

7. No person, military or civilian, shall be permitted to cross the military demarcation line unless specifically authorized to do so by the Military Armistice Commission.

8. No person, military or civilan, in the demilitarized zone shall be permitted to enter the territory under the military control of either side unless specifically authorized to do so by the Commander into whose territory entry is sought.

9. No person, military or civilian, shall be permitted to enter the demilitarized zone except persons concerned with the conduct of civil administration and relief and persons specifically authorized to enter by the Military Armistice Commission.

10. Civil administration and relief in that part of the demilitarized zone which is south of the military demarcation line shall be

---

[1] See frontispiece. The original of this map is on file at the United Nations Library, New York. Four additional maps accompanied the Armistice Agreement.

the responsibility of the Commander-in-Chief, United Nations Command; and civil administraton and relief in that part of the demilitarized zone which is north of the military demarcation line shall be the joint responsibility of the Supreme Commander of the Korean People's Army and the Commander of the Chinese People's Volunteers. The number of persons, military or civilian, from each side who are permitted to enter the demilitarized zone for the conduct of civil administration and relief shall be as determined by the respective Commanders, but in no case shall the total number authorized by either side exceed one thousand (1,000) persons at any one time. The number of civil police and the arms to be carried by them shall be as prescribed by the Military Armistice Commission. Other personnel shall not carry arms unless specifically authorized to do so by the Military Armistice Commission.

11. Nothing contained in this article shall be construed to prevent the complete freedom of movement to, from, and within the demilitarized zone by the Military Armistice Commission, its assistants, its Joint Observer Teams with their assistants, the Neutral Nations Supervisory Commission hereinafter established, its assistants, its Neutral Nations Inspection Teams with their assistants, and of any other persons, materials, and equipment specifically authorized to enter the demilitarized zone by the Military Armistice Commission. Convenience of movement shall be permitted through the territory under the military control of either side over any route necessary to move between points within the demilitarized zone where such points are not connected by roads lying completely within the demilitarized zone.

Article II

Concrete Arrangements for Cease-Fire and Armistice

A. *General*

12. The Commanders of the opposing sides shall order and enforce a complete cessation of all hostilities in Korea by all armed forces under their control, including all units and personnel of the ground, naval, and air forces, effective twelve (12) hours after this armistice agreement is signed. (See paragraph 63 hereof for effective date and hour of the remaining provisions of this armistice agreement.)

13. In order to insure the stability of the military armistice so as to facilitate the attainment of a peaceful settlement through the holding by both sides of a political conference of a higher level, the Commanders of the opposing sides shall:

(a) Within seventy-two (72) hours after this armistice agreement becomes effective, withdraw all of their military forces, supplies, and equipment from the demilitarized zone except as otherwise provided herein. All demolitions, minefields, wire entanglements, and other hazards to the safe movement of personnel of the Military Armistice Commission or its Joint Observer Teams, known to exist within the demilitarized zone after the withdrawal of military forces therefrom, together with lanes known to be free of all such hazards, shall be reported to the MAC by the Commander of the side whose forces emplaced such hazards. Subsequently, additional safe lanes shall be cleared; and eventually, within forty-five (45) days after the termination of the seventy-two (72) hour period, all such hazards shall be removed from the demilitarized zone as directed by and under the supervision of the MAC. At the termination of the seventy-two (72) hour period, except for unarmed troops authorized a forty-five (45) day period to complete salvage operations under MAC supervision, such units of a police nature as may be specifically requested by the MAC and agreed to by the Commanders of the opposing sides, and personnel authorized under paragraphs 10 and 11 hereof, no personnel of either side shall be permitted to enter the demilitarized zone.

(b) Within ten (10) days after this armistice agreement becomes effective, withdraw all of their military forces, supplies, and equipment from the rear and the coastal islands and waters of Korea of the other side. If such military forces are not withdrawn within the stated time limit, and there is no mutually agreed and valid reason for the delay, the other side shall have the right to take any action which it deems necessary for the maintenance of security and order. The term "coastal islands," as used above, refers to those islands which, though occupied by one side at the time when this armistice agreement becomes effective, were controlled by the other side on 24 June 1950; provided, however, that all the islands lying to the north and west of the provincial boundary line between HWANGHAE-DO and KYONGGI-DO shall be under the military control of the Supreme Commander of the Korean People's Army and the Commander of the Chinese People's Volunteers, except the island groups of PAENGYONG-DO (37°58′N., 124°40′E.). TAECHONG-DO (37°50′N., 127°42′E.), SOCHONG-DO (37°46′N., 124°46′E.), YONPYONG-DO (37°38′N., 125°40′E.), and U-DO (37°36′N., 125° 58′E.) and which shall remain under the military control of the Commander-in-Chief, United Nations Command. All the islands on the west coast of Korea lying south of the above-mentioned boundary line shall remain under the military control of the Commander-in-Chief, United Nations Command.

(c) Cease the introduction into Korea of reinforcing military personnel; provided, however, that the rotation of units and personnel, the arrival in Korea of personnel on a temporary duty basis, and the return to Korea of personnel after short periods of leave or temporary duty outside of Korea shall be permitted within the scope prescribed below:

"Rotation" is defined as the replacement of units or personnel by other units or personnel who are commencing a tour of duty in Korea. Rotation personnel shall be introduced into and evacuated from Korea only through the ports of entry enumerated in paragraph 43 hereof. Rotation shall be conducted on a man-for-man basis; provided, however, that no more than thirty-five thousand (35,000) persons in the military service shall be admitted into Korea by either side in any calendar month under the rotation policy. No military personnel of either side shall be introduced into Korea if the introduction of such personnel will cause the aggregate of the military personnel of that side admitted into Korea since the effective date of this armistice agreement to exceed the cumulative total of the military personnel of that side who have departed from Korea since that date. Reports concerning arrivals in and departures from Korea of military personnel shall be made daily to the MAC and NNSC; such reports shall include places of arrival and departure and the number of persons arriving at or departing from each such place. The NNSC, through its Neutral Nations Inspection Teams, shall conduct supervision and inspection of the rotation of units and personnel authorized above, at the ports of entry enumerated in paragraph 43 hereof.

(d) Cease the introduction into Korea of reinforcing combat aircraft, armored vehicles, weapons, and ammunition; provided, however, that combat aircraft, armored vehicles, weapons, and ammunition which are destroyed, damaged, worn out, or used up during the period of the armistice may be replaced on the basis of piece-for-piece of the same effectiveness and the same type. Such combat aircra't, armored vehicles, weapons, and ammunition shall be introduced into Korea only through the ports of entry enumerated in paragraph 43 hereof. In order to justify the requirements for combat aircraft, armored vehicles, weapons, and ammunition to be introduced into Korea for replacement purposes, reports concerning every incoming shipment of these items shall be made to the MAC and the NNSC; such reports shall include statements regarding the disposition of the items being replaced. Items to be replaced which are removed from Korea shall be removed only through the ports of entry enumerated in paragraph 43 hereof. The NNSC, through its Neutral Nations Inspection Teams, shall conduct supervision and inspection of the replacement of combat aircraft, armored vehicles, weapons, and ammunition authorized above, at the ports of entry enumerated in paragraph 43 hereof.

(e) Insure that personnel of their respective commands who violate any of the provisions of this armistice agreement are adequately punished.

(f) In those cases where places of burial are a matter of record and graves are actually found to exist, permit graves registration personnel of the other side to enter, within a definite time limit after this armistice agreement becomes effective, the territory of Korea under their military control, for the purpose of proceeding to such graves to recover and evacuate the bodies of the deceased military personnel of that side, including deceased prisoners of war. The specific procedures and the time limit for the performance of the above task shall be determined by the Military Armistice Commission. The Commanders of the opposing sides shall furnish to the other side all available information pertaining to the places of burial of the deceased military personnel of the other side.

(g) Afford full protection and all possible assistance and cooperation to the Military Armistice Commission, its Joint Observer Teams, the Neutral Nations Supervisory Commission, and its Neutral Nations Inspection Teams, in the carrying out of their functions and responsibilities hereinafter assigned; and accord to the Neutral Nations Inspection Teams, full convenience of movement between the headquarters of the Neutral Nations Supervisory Commission and the ports of entry enumerated in paragraph 43 hereof over main lines of communication agreed upon by both sides, and between the headquarters of the Neutral Nations Supervisory Commission and the places where violations of this armistice agreement have been reported to have occurred. In order to prevent unnecessary delays, the use of alternate routes and means of transportation will be permitted whenever the main lines of communication are closed or impassable.

(h) Provide such logistic support, including communications and transportation facilities, as may be required by the Military Armistice Commission and the Neutral Nations Supervisory Commission, for such uses as the Commission may determine.

(i) Each construct, operate, and maintain a suitable airfield in their respective parts of the demilitarized zone in the vicinity of the headquarters of the Military Armistice Commission, for such uses as the Commission may determine.

(j) Insure that all members and other personnel of the Neutral Nations Supervisory Commission and of the Neutral Nations Repatriation Commission hereinafter established shall enjoy the freedom and facilities necessary for the proper exercise of their functions, including privileges, treatment, and immunities equivalent to those ordinarily enjoyed by accredited diplomatic personnel under international usage.

14. This armistice agreement shall apply to all opposing ground forces under the military control of either side, which ground forces shall respect the demilitarized zone and the area of Korea under the military control of the opposing side.

15. This armistice agreement shall apply to all opposing naval forces, which naval forces shall respect the water contiguous to the demilitarized zone and to the land area of Korea under the military control of the opposing side, and shall not engage in blockade of any kind of Korea.

16. This armistice agreement shall apply to all opposing air forces, which air forces shall respect the air space over the demilitarized zone and over the area of Korea under the military control of the opposing side, and over the waters contiguous to both.

17. Responsibility for compliance with and enforcement of the terms and provisions of this armistice agreement is that of the signatories hereto and their successors in command. The Commanders of the opposing sides shall establish within their respective commands all measures and procedures necessary to insure complete compliance

with all of the provisions hereof by all elements of their commands. They shall actively cooperate with one another and with the Military Armistice Commission and the Neutral Nations Supervisory Commission in requiring observance of both the letter and the spirit of all of the provisions of this armistice agreement.

18. The costs of the operations of the military armistice Commission and of the Neutral Nations Supervisory Commission and of their Teams shall be shared equally by the two opposing sides.

B. *Military Armistice Commission*

1. *Composition*

19. A Military Armistice Commission is hereby established.

20. The Military Armistice Commission shall be composed of ten (10) senior officers, five (5) of whom shall be appointed by the Commander-in-Chief, United Nations Command, and five (5) of whom shall be appointed jointly by the Supreme Commander of the Korean People's Army and the Commander of the Chinese People's Volunteers. Of the ten members, three (3) from each side shall be of general or flag rank. The two (2) remaining members on each side may be major generals, brigadier generals, colonels, or their equivalent.

21. Members of the Military Armistice Commission shall be permitted to use staff assistants as required.

22. The Military Armistice Commission shall be provided with the necessary administrative personnel to establish a Secretariat charged with assisting the Commission by performing record-keeping, secretarial, interpreting, and such other functions as the Commission may assign to it. Each side shall appoint to the Secretariat a Secretary and an Assistant Secretary and such clerical and specialized personnel as required by the Secretariat. Records shall be kept in English, Korean, and Chinese, all of which shall be equally authentic.

23. (a) The Military Armistice Commission shall be initially provided with and assisted by ten (10) Joint Observer Teams, which number may be reduced by agreement of the senior members of both sides on the Military Armistice Commission.

(b) Each Joint Observer Team shall be composed of not less than four (4) nor more than six (6) officers of field grade, half of whom shall be appointed by the Commander-in-Chief, United Nations Command, and half of whom shall be appointed jointly by the Supreme Commander of the Korean People's Army and the Commander of the Chinese People's Volunteers. Additional personnel such as drivers, clerks, and interpreters shall be furnished by each side as required for the functioning of the Joint Observer Teams.

2. *Functions and Authority*

24. The general mission of the Military Armistice Commission shall be to supervise the implementation of this armistice agreement and to settle through negotiations any violations of this armistice agreement.

25. The Military Armistice Commission shall:

(a) Locate its headquarters in the vicinity of PANMUNJOM (37°57′29″N. 126°40′00″E.). The Military Armistice Commission may relocate its headquarters at another point within the demilitarized zone by agreement of the senior members of both sides on the Commission.

(b) Operate as a joint organization without a chairman.

(c) Adopt such rules of procedure as it may, from time to time, deem necessary.

(d) Supervise the carrying out of the provisions of this armistice agreement pertaining to the demilitarized zone and to the Han River Estuary.

(e) Direct the operations of the Joint Observer Teams.

(f) Settle through negotiations any violations of this armistice agreement.

(g) Transmit immediately to the Commanders of the opposing sides all reports of investigations of violations of this armistice agreement and all other reports and records of proceedings received from the Neutral Nations Supervisory Commission.

(h) Give general supervision and direction to the activities of the Committee for Repatriation of Prisoners of War and the Committee for Assisting the Return of Displaced Civilians, hereinafter established.

(i) Act as an intermediary in transmitting communications between the Commanders of the opposing sides; provided, however, that the foregoing shall not be construed to preclude the Commanders of both sides from communicating with each other by any other means which they may desire to employ.

(j) Provide credentials and distinctive insignia for its staff and its Joint Observer Teams, and a distinctive marking for all vehicles, aircraft, and vessels, used in the performance of its mission.

26. The mission of the Joint Observer Teams shall be to assist the Military Armistice Commission in supervising the carrying out of the provisions of this armistice agreement pertaining to the demilitarized zone and to the Han River Estuary.

27. The Military Armistice Commission, or the senior member of either side thereof, is authorized to dispatch Joint Observer Teams to investigate violations of this armistice agreement reported to have occurred in the demilitarized zone or in the Han River Estuary; provided, however, that not more than one half of the Joint Observer Team which have not been dispatched by the Military Armistice Commission may be dispatched at any one time by the senior member of either side on the Commission.

28. The Military Armistice Commission, or the senior member of either side thereof, is authorized to request the Neutral Nations Supervisory Commission to conduct special observations and inspections at places outside the demilitarized zone where violations of this armistice agreement have been reported to have occured.

29. When the Military Armistice Commission determines that a violation of this armistice agreement has occurred, it shall immediately report such violation to the Commanders of the opposing sides.

30. When the Military Armistice Commission determines that a violation of this armistice agreement has been corrected to its satisfaction, it shall so report to the Commanders of the opposing sides.

3. *General*

31. The Military Armistice Commission shall meet daily. Recesses of not to exceed seven (7) days may be agreed upon by the senior members of both sides; provided, that such recesses may be

terminated on twenty-four (24) hour notice by the senior member of either side.

32. Copies of the record of the proceedings of all meetings of the Military Armistice Commission shall be forwarded to the Commanders of the opposing sides as soon as possible after each meeting.

33. The Joint Observer Teams shall make periodic reports to the Military Armistice Commission as required by the Commission and, in addition, shall make such special reports as may be deemed necessary by them, or as may be required by the Commission.

34. The Military Armistice Commission shall maintain duplicate files of the reports and records of proceedings required by this armistice agreement. The Commission is authorized to maintain duplicate files of such other reports, records, etc., as may be necessary in the conduct of its business. Upon eventual dissolution of the Commission, one set of the above files shall be turned over to each side.

35. The Military Armistice Commission may make recommendations to the Commanders of the opposing sides with respect to amendments or additions to this armistice agreement. Such recommended changes should generally be those designed to insure a more effective armistice.

C. *Neutral Nations Supervisory Commission*

1. *Composition*

36. A Neutral Nations Supervisory Commission is hereby established.

37. The Neutral Nations Supervisory Commission shall be composed of four (4) senior officers, two (2) of whom shall be appointed by neutral nations nominated by the Comander-in-Chief, United Nations Command, namely SWEDEN and SWITZERLAND, and two (2) of whom shall be appointed by neutral nations nominated jointly by the Supreme Commander of the Korean People's Army and the Commander of the Chinese People's Volunteers, namely, POLAND and CZECHOSLOVAKIA. The term "neutral nations" as herein used is defined as those nations whose combatant forces have not participated

in the hostilities in Korea. Members appointed to the Commission may be from the armed forces of the appointing nations. Each member shall designate an alternate member to attend those meetings which for any reason the principal member is unable to attend. Such alternate members shall be of the same nationality as their principals. The Neutral Nations Supervisory Commission may take action whenever the number of members present from the neutral nations nominated by one side is equal to the number of members present from the neutral nations nominated by the other side.

38. Members of the Neutral Nations Supervisory Commission shall be permitted to use staff assistants furnished by the neutral nations as required. These staff assistants may be appointed as alternate members of the Commission.

39. The neutral nations shall be requested to furnish the Neutral Nations Supervisory Commission with the necessary administrative personnel to establish a Secretariat charged with assisting the Commission by performing necessary record-keeping, secretarial, interpreting, and such other functions as the Commission may assign to it.

40. (a) The Neutral Nations Supervisory Commission shall be initially provided with, and assisted by, twenty (20) Neutral Nations Inspection Teams, which number may be reduced by agreement of the senior members of both sides on the Military Armistice Commission. The Neutral Nations Inspection Teams shall be responsible to, shall report to, and shall be subject to the direction of, the Neutral Nations Supervisory Commission only.

(b) Each Neutral Nations Inspection Team shall be composed of not less than four (4) officers, preferably of field grade, half of whom shall be from the neutral nations nominated by the Commander-in-Chief, United Nations Command, and half of whom shall be from the neutral nations nominated jointly by the Supreme Commander of the Korean People's Army and the Commander of the Chinese People's Volunteers. Members appointed to the Neutral Nations Inspection Teams may be from the armed forces of the appointed nations. In order to facilitate the functioning of the Teams, sub-teams composed of not less than two (2) members, one of whom shall be from a neutral nation nominated by the Commander-in-Chief, United Nations Command, and one of whom shall be from a neutral nation nominated jointly by the Supreme Commander of the Korean People's Army and the Commander of the Chinese People's Volunteers, may be formed as circumstances require. Additional personnel such as drivers, clerks, interpreters, and communications personnel, and such equipment as may be required by the Teams to perform their missions, shall be furnished by the Commander of each side, as required, in the demilitarized zone and in the territory under his military control. The Neutral Nations Supervisory Commission may provide itself and the Neutral Nations Inspection Teams with such of the above personnel and equipment of its own as it may desire; provided, however, that such personnel shall be personnel of the same neutral nations of which the Neutral Nations Supervisory Commission is composed.

2. *Functions and Authority*

41. The mission of the Neutral Nations Supervisory Commission shall be to carry out the functions of supervision, observation, inspection, and investigation, as stipulated in sub-paragraphs 13 (c) and 13 (d) and paragraph 28 hereof, and to report the results of such supervision, observation, inspection, and investigation to the Military Armistice Commission.

42. The Neutral Nations Supervisory Commission shall:

(a) Locate its headquarters in proximity to the headquarters of the Military Armistice Commission.

(b) Adopt such rules of procedure as it may, from time to time, deem necessary.

(c) Conduct, through its members and its Neutral Nations Inspection Teams, the supervision and inspection provided for in sub-paragraphs 13 (c) and 13 (d) of this armistice agreement at the ports of entry enumerated in paragraph 43 hereof, and the special observations and inspections provided for in paragraph 28, hereof at those places where violations of this armistice agreement have been reported to have occurred. The inspection of combat aircraft, armored vehicles, weapons, and ammunition by the Neutral Nations Inspection Teams shall be such as to enable them to properly insure that reinforcing combat aircraft, armored vehicles, weapons, and ammunition are not being introduced into Korea; but this shall not be construed as authorizing inspections or examinations of any

secret designs or characteristics of any combat aircraft, armored
vehicle, weapon, or ammunition.

(d) Direct and supervise the operations of the Neutral
Nations Inspection Teams.

(e) Station five (5) Neutral Nations Inspection Teams at
the ports of entry enumerated in paragraph 43 hereof located in
the territory under the military control of the Commander-in-Chief,
United Nation Command; and five (5) Neutral Nations Inspection
Teams at the ports of entry enumerated in paragraph 43 hereof
located in the territory under the military control of the Supreme
Commander of the Korean People's Army and the Commander of
the Chinese People's Volunteers; and establish initially ten (10)
mobile Neutral Nations Inspection Teams in reserve, stationed in
the general vicinity of the headquarters of the Neutral Nations
Supervisory Commission, which number may be reduced by agreement of the senior members of both sides on the Military Armistice
Commission. Not more than half of the mobile Neutral Nations
Inspection Teams shall be dispatched at any one time in accordance
with requests of the senior member of either side on the Military
Armistice Commission.

(f) Subject to the provisions of the preceding sub-paragraphs, conduct without delay investigations of reported violations
of this armistice agreement, including such investigations of reported
violations of this armistice agreement as may be requested by the
Military Armistice Commission or by the senior member of either
side of the Commission.

(g) Provide credentials and distinctive insignia for its staff
and its Neutral Nations Inspection Teams, and a distinctive marking
for all vehicles, aircraft, and vessels, used in the performance of its
mission.

43. Neutral Nations Inspection Teams shall be stationed at the
following ports of entry:

Territory under the military control of the United Nations Command

INCHON	(37°28′N, 126°38′E)
TAEGU	(35°52′N, 128°36′E)
PUSAN	(35°06′N, 129°02′E)
KANGNUNG	(37°45′N, 128°54′E)
KUNSAN	(35°59′N, 126°43′E)

Territory under the military control of the Korean People's Army and the Chinese People's Volunteers

SINUIJU .... (40°06′N, 124°24′E)
CHONGJIM .... (41°46′N, 129°49′E)
HUNGNAM .... (39°50′N, 127°37′E)
MANPO .... (41°09′N, 126°18′E)
SINANJU .... (39°36′N, 125°36′E)

These Neutral Nations Inspection Teams shall be accorded full convenience of movement within the areas and over the routes of communication set forth on the attached map.

3. *General*

44. The Neutral Nations Supervisory Commission shall meet daily. Recesses of not to exceed seven (7) days may be agreed upon by the members of the Neutral Nations Supervisory Commission; provided, that such recesses may be terminated on twenty-four (24) hour notice by any member.

45. Copies of the record of the proceedings of all meetings of the Neutral Nations Supervisory Commission shall be forwarded to the Military Armistice Commission as soon as possible after each meeting. Records shall be kept in English, Korean, and Chinese.

46. The Neutral Nations Inspection Teams shall make periodic reports concerning the results of their supervision, observations, inspections, and investigations to the Neutral Nations Supervisory Commission as required by the Commission and, in addition, shall make such special reports as may be deemed necessary by them, or as may be required by the Commission. Reports shall be submitted by one or more individual members thereof; provided, that the reports submitted by one or more individual members thereof shall be considered as informational only.

47. Copies of the reports made by the Neutral Nations Inspection Teams shall be forwarded to the Military Armistice Commission by the Neutral Nations Supervisory Commission without delay and in the language in which received. They shall not be delayed by the process of translation or evaluation. The Neutral Nations Supervisory Commission shall evaluate such reports at the

earliest practicable time and shall forward their findings to the Military Armistice Commission as a matter of priority. The Military Armistice Commission shall not take final action with regard to any such report until the evaluation thereof has been received from the Neutral Nations Supervisory Commission. Members of the Neutral Nations Supervisory Commission and of its Teams shall be subject to appearance before the Military Armistice Commission, at the request of the senior member of either side on the Military Armistice Commission, for clarification of any report submitted.

48. The Neutral Nations Supervisory Commission shall maintain duplicate files of the reports and records of proceedings required by this armistice agreement. The Commission is authorized to maintain duplicate files of such other reports, records, etc., as may be necessary in the conduct of its business. Upon eventual dissolution of the Commission, one set of the above files shall be turned over to each side.

49. The Neutral Nations Supervisory Commission may make recommendations to the Military Armistice Commission with respect to amendments or additions to this armistice agreement. Such recommended changes should generally be those designed to insure a more effective armistice.

50. The Neutral Nations Supervisory Commission, or any member thereof, shall be authorized to communicate with any member of the Military Armistice Commission.

Article III

Arrangements Relating to Prisoners of War

51. The release and repatriation of all prisoners of war held in the custody of each side at the time this armistice agreement becomes effective shall be effected in conformity with the following provisions agreed upon by both sides prior to the signing of this armistice agreement.

(a) Within sixty (60) days after this armistice agreement becomes effective each side shall, without offering any hindrance, directly repatriate and hand over in groups all those prisoners of war in its custody who insist on repatriation to the side to which they belonged at the time of capture. Repatriation shall be accomplished in accordance with the related provisions of this article. In order to expedite the repatriation process of such personnel, each side shall, prior to the signing of the armistice agreement, exchange the total numbers, by nationalities, of personnel to be directly repatriated. Each group of prisoners of war delivered to the other side shall be accompanied by rosters, prepared by nationality, to include name, rank (if any) and internment or military serial number.

(b) Each side shall release all those remaining prisoners of war, who are not directly repatriated, from its military control and from its custody and hand them over to the Neutral Nations Repatriation Comission for disposition in accordance with the provisions in the annex hereto: "Terms of Reference for Neutral Nations Repatriation Commission."

(c) So that there may be no misunderstanding owing to the equal use of three languages, the act of delivery of a prisoner of war by one side to the side shall, for the purposes of this armistice agreement, be called "repatriation" in English, "Song Hwan" in Korean, and "Ch'ien Fan" in Chinese, notwithstanding the nationality or place of residence of such prisoner of war.

52. Each side insures that it will not employ in acts of war in the Korean conflict any prisoner of war released and repatriated incident to the coming into effect of this armistice agreement.

53 All the sick and injured prisoners of war who insist upon repatriation shall be repatriated with priority. Insofar as possible, there shall be captured medical personnel repatriated concurrently with the sick and injured prisoners of war, so as to provide medical care and attendance en route.

54. The repatriation of all of the prisoners of war required by sub-paragraph 51 (a) hereof shall be completed within a time limit of sixty (60) days after this armistice agreement becomes effective. Within this time limit each side undertakes to complete the repatriation of the above-mentioned prisoners of war in its custody at the earliest practicable time.

55. PANMUNJOM is designated as the place where prisoners of war will be delivered and received by both sides. Additional place(s) of delivery and reception of prisoners of war in the demilitarized

zone may be designated, if necessary, by the Committee for Repatriation of Prisoners of War.

56. (a) A committee for repatriation of prisoners of war is hereby established. It shall be composed of six (6) officers of field grade, three (3) of whom shall be appointed by the Commander-in-Chief, United Nations Command, and three (3) of whom shall be appointed jointly by the Supreme Commander of the Korean People's Army and the Commander of the Chinese People's Volunteers. This committee shall, under the general supervision and direction of the Military Armistice Commission, be responsible for coordinating the specific plans of both sides for the repatriation of prisoners of war and for supervising the execution by both sides of all of the provisions of this armistice agreement relating to the repatriation of prisoners of war. It shall be the duty of this committee to coordinate the timing of the arrival of prisoners of war at the places of delivery and reception of prisoners of war from the prisoner of war camps of both sides; to make, when necessary such special arrangements as may be required with regard to the transportation and welfare of sick and injured prisoners of war; to coordinate the work of the Joint Red Cross teams, established in paragraph 57 hereof, in assisting in the repatriation of prisoners of war; to supervise the implementation of the arrangements for the actual repatriation of prisoners of war stipulated in paragraphs 53 and 54 hereof; to select, when necessary, additional places of delivery and reception of prisoners of war; to arrange for security at the places of delivery and reception of prisoners of war; and to carry out such other related functions as are required for the repatriation of prisoners of war.

(b) When unable to reach agreement on any matter relating to its responsibilities, the Committee for Repatriation of Prisoners of War shall immediately refer such matter to the Military Armistice Commission for decision. The Committee for Repatriation of Prisoners of War shall maintain its headquarters in proximity to the headquarters of the Military Armistice Commission.

(c) The Committee for Repatriation of Prisoners of War shall be dissolved by the Military Armistice Commission upon completion of the program of repatriation of prisoners of war.

57. (a) Immediately after this armistice agreement becomes effective, Joint Red Cross teams composed of representatives of the National Red Cross Societies of the countries contributing forces to

the United Nations Command on the one hand, and representatives of the Red Cross Society of the People's Republic of Korea and representatives of the Red Cross Society of the People's Republic of China on the other hand, shall be established. The joint Red Cross teams shall assist in the execution by both sides of those provision of this armistice agreement relating to the repatriation of all the prisoners of war specified in sub-paragraph 51 (a), hereof, who insist upon repatriation, by the performance of such humanitarian services as are necessary and desirable for the welfare of the prisoners of war. To accomplish this task, the Joint Red Cross teams shall provide assistance in the delivering and receiving of prisoners of war by both sides at the place(s) of delivery and reception of war, and shall visit the prisoner-of-war camps of both sides to comfort the prisoners of war and to bring in and distribute gift articles for the comfort and welfare of the prisoners of war. The Joint Red Cross teams may provide services to prisoners of war while en route from prisoners-of-war camps to the places of delivery and receptions of prisoners of war.

(b) The Joint Red Cross teams shall be organized as set forth below:

(1) One team shall be composed of twenty (20) members, namely thirty (30) representatives from the national Red Cross soeties of each side, to assist in the delivering and receiving of prisoners of war by both sides at the place(s) of delivery and reception of prisoners of war. The chairmanship of this team shall alternate daily between representatives from the Red Cross societies of the two sides. The work and services of this team shall be coordinated by the Committee for Repatriation of Prisoners of War.

(2) One team shall be composed of sixty (60) members, namely thirty (30) representatives from the national Red Cross societies of each side, to visit the prisoner-of-war camps under the administration of the Korean People's Army and the Chinese People's Volunteers. This team may provide services to prisoners of war while en route from the prisoner-of-war camps to the place(s) of delivery and reception of prisoners of war. A representative of a Red Cross society of a nation contributing forces to the United Nations Command shall serve as chairman of this team.

(3) One team shall be composed of sixty (60) members, namely, thirty (30) representatives from the national Red Cross societies of each side, to visit the prisoner-of-war camps under the

administration of the United Nations Command. This team may provide services to prisoners of war while en route from the prisoner-of-war camps to the place(s) of delivery and reception of prisoners of war. A representative of a Red Cross society of a nation contributing forces to the United Nations Command shall serve as chairman of this team.

(4) In order to facilitate the functioning of each Joint Red Cross team, sub-teams composed of not less than two (2) members from the team, with an equal number of representatives from each side, may be formed as circumstances require.

(5) Additional personnel such as drivers, clerks, and interpreters, and such equipment as may be required by the Joint Red Cross teams to perform their missions, shall be furnished by the Commander of each side to the team operating in the territory under his military control.

(6) Whenever jointly agreed upon by the representatives of both sides on any Joint Red Cross team, the size of such team may be increased or decreased, subject to confirmation by the Committee for Repatriation of Prisoners of War.

(c) The Commander of each side shall cooperate fully with the Joint Red Cross teams in the performance of their functions, and undertakes to insure the security of the personnel of the Joint Red Cross team in the area under his military control. The Commander of each side shall provide such logistic, administrative, and communications facilities as may be required by the team operating in the territory under his control.

(d) The Joint Red Cross teams shall be dissolved upon completion of the program of repatriation of all the prisoners of war specified in sub-paragraph 51 (a) hereof, who insist upon repatriation.

58. (a) The Commander of each side shall furnish to the Commander of the other side as soon as practicable, but not later than ten (10) days after this armistice agreement becomes effective, the following information concerning prisoners of war:

(1) Complete data pertaining to the prisoners of war who escaped since the effective data of the data last examined.

(2) Insofar as practicable, information regarding name, nationality, rank, and other identification data, date and cause of death,

and place of burial, of those prisoners of war who died while in his custody.

(b) If any prisoners of war escape or die after the effective date of the supplementary information specified above, the detaining side shall furnish to the other side, through the Committee for Repatriation of Prisoners of War, the date pertaining thereto in accordance with the provisions of sub-paragraph 58 (a) hereof. Such data shall be furnished at ten (10) day intervals until the completion of the program of delivery and reception of prisoners of war.

(c) Any escaped prisoner of war who returns to the custody of the detaining side after the completion of the program of delivery and reception of prisoners of war shall be delivered to the Military Armistice Commission for disposition.

59. (a) All civilians who, at the time this armistice agreement becomes effective, are in territory under the military control of the Commander in Chief, United Nations Command, and who, on 24 June 1950, resided north of the military demarcation line established in this armistice agreement shall, if they desire to return home, be permitted and assisted by the Commander-in-Chief, United Nations Command, to return to the area north of the military demarcation line; and all civilians who, at the time this armistice agreement becomes effective, are in territory under the military control of the Supreme Commander of the Korean People's Army and the Commander of the Chinese People's Volunteers, and who, on 24 June 1950, resided south of the military demarcation line established in this armistice agreement shall, if they desire to return home, be permitted and assisted by the Supreme Commander of the Korean People's Army and the Commander of the Chinese People's Volunteers to return to the area south of the military demarcation line. The Commander of each side shall be responsible for publicizing widely throughout territory under his military control the contents of the provisions of this sub-paragraph, and for calling upon the appropriate civil authorities to give necessary guidance and assistance to all such civilians who declare to return home.

(b) All civilians of foreign nationality who, at the time this armistice agreement becomes effective, are in territory under the military control of the Supreme Commander of the Korean People's Army and the Commander of the Chinese People's Volunteers shall, if they desire to proceed to territory under the military control of the Commander-in-Chief, United Nations Command, be permitted and assisted to do so; all civilians of foreign nationality who, at the time this armistice agreement becomes effective, are in territory under the military control of the Commander-in-Chief, United Nations Command shall, if they desire to proceed to territory under the military control of the Supreme Commander of the Korean People's Army and the Commander of the Supreme Commander of the Korean People's Army and the Commander of the Chinese People's Volunteers, be permitted and assisted to do so. The Commander of each side shall be responsible for publicizing widely throughout the territory under his military control the contents of the provisions of this sub-paragraph, and for calling upon the appropriate civil authorities to give necessary guidance and assistance to all such civilians of foreign nationality who desire to proceed to territory under the military control of the commander of the other side.

(c) Measures to assist in the return of civilians provided for in sub-paragraph 59 (a) hereof and the movement of civilians provided for in sub-paragraph 59 (b) hereof shall be commenced by both sides as soon as possible after this armistice agreement becomes effective.

(d) (1) A committee for assisting the return of displaced civilians is hereby established. It shall be composed of four (4) officers of field grade, two (2) of whom shall be appointed jointly by the Commander-in-Chief, United Nations Comand, and two (2) of whom shall be appointed jointly by the Supreme Commander of the Korean People's Army and the Commander of the Chinese People's Volunteers. This committee shall, under the general supervision and direction of the Military Armistice Commission, be responsible for coordinating the specific plans of both sides for assistance to the return of the above-mentioned civilians, and for supervising the execution by both sides of all the provisions of this armistice agreement relating to the return of the above-mentioned civilians. It shall be the duty of this committee to make necessary arrangements, including those of transportation, for expediting and coordinating the movement of the above-mentioned civilians; to select the crossing points through which the above-mentioned civilians will cross the military demarcation line; to arrange for security at the crossing points; and to carry out such other functions as are required to accomplish the return of the above-mentioned civilians.

(2) When unable to reach agreement on any matter relating to its responsibilities, the Committee for Assisting the Return of Displaced Civilians shall immediately refer such matter to the Military Armistice Commission for decision. The Committee for Assisting the Return of Displaced Civilians shall maintain its headquarters in proximity to the headquarters of the Military Armistice Commission.

(3) The Committee for Assisting the Return of Displaced Civilians shall be dissolved by the Military Armistice Commission upon fulfillment of its mission.

Article IV

Recommendations to the Governments Concerned on Both Sides

60. In order to insure the peaceful settlement of the Korean question, the military commanders of both sides hereby recommend to the governments of the countries concerned on both sides that, within three (3) months after the armistice agreement is signed and becomes effective, a political conference of a higher level of both sides be held by representatives appointed respectively to settle through negotiation the questions of the withdrawal of all foreign forces from Korea, the peaceful settlement of the Korean question, etc.

Article V

Miscellaneous

61. Amendments and additions to this armistice agreement must be mutually agreed to by the Commanders of the opposing sides.

62. The articles and paragraphs of this armistice agreement shall remain in effect until expressly superseded either by mutually acceptable amendments and additions or by provision in an appropriate agreement for a peaceful settlement at a political level between both sides.

63. All of the provisions of this armistice agreement, other than paragraph 12, shall become effective at 2200 hours on July 27, 1953.

Done at PANMUNJOM, Korea, at 1000 hours on the 27th day of July 1953, in English, Korean, and Chinese, all texts being equally authentic.

[signed]

KIM IL SUNG

Marshal, Democratic People's Republic of Korea, Supreme Commander, Korean People's Army.

[signed]

PENG TEH-HUAI

Commander, Chinese People's Volunteers.

[signed]

MARK W. CLARK

General, United States Army, Commander-in-Chief, United Nations Command.

[signed]

NAM IL

General, Korean People's Army, Senior Delegate, Delegation of the Korean People's Army and the Chinese People's Volunteers.

[signed]

WILLIAM K. HARRISON, JR.

Lieutenant General, United States Army, Senior Delegate, United Nations Command Delegation.

ANNEX

TERMS OF REFERENCE FOR NEUTRAL NATIONS REPATRIATION COMMISSION

(See Subparagraph 51b)

I. GENERAL

1. In order to ensure that all prisoners of war have the opportunity to exercise their right to be repatriated following an armistice, Sweden, Switzerland, Poland, Czechoslovakia and India shall each be requested by both sides to appoint a member to a Neutral Nations Repatriation Commission which shall be established to take custody in Korea of those prisoners of war who, while in the custody of the detaining powers, have not exercised their right to be repatriated. The Neutral Nations Repatriation Commission shall establish its headquarters within the Demilitarized Zone in the vicinity of Panmunjom, and shall station subordinate bodies of the same composition as the Neutral Nations Repatriation Commission at those locations at which the Repatriation Commission assumes custody of prisoners of war. Representatives of both sides shall be permitted to observe the operations of the Repatriation Commission and its subordinate bodies to include explanations and interviews.

2. Sufficient armed forces and any other operating personnel required to assist the Neutral Nations Repatriation Commission in carrying out its functions and responsibilities shall be provided exclusively by India, whose representatives shall be the umpire in accordance with the provisions of Article 132 of the Geneva Convention, and shall also be chairman and executive agent of the Neutral Nations Repatriation Commission. Representatives from each of the other four powers shall be allowed staff assistants in equal number not to exceed fifty (50) each. When any of the representatives of the neutral nations is absent for some reason, that representative shall designate an alternate representatives of his own nationality to exercise his functions and authority. The arms of all personnel provided for in this Paragraph shall be limited to military police type small arms.

3. No force or threat of force shall be used against the prisoners of war specified in Paragraph 1 above to prevent or effect their repatriation, and no violence to their persons or affront to their dignity or self-respect shall be permitted in any manner for any purpose whatsoever (but see Paragraph 7 below). This duty is enjoined on and entrusted to the Neutral Nations Repatriation Commission. This Commission shall ensure that prisoners of war shall at all times be treated humanely in accordance with the specific provisions of the Geneva Convention, and with the general spirit of that Convention.

II. CUSTODY OF PRISONERS OF WAR

4. All prisoners of war who have not exercised their right of repatriation following the effective date of the Armistice Agreement shall be released from the military control and from the custody of the detaining side as soon as practicable, and, in all cases, within sixty (60) days subsequent to the effective date of the Armistice Agreement to the Neutral Nations Repatriation Commission at locations in Korea to be designated by the detaining side.

5. At the time the Neutral Nations Repatriation Commission assumes control of the prisoner of war installations, the military forces of the detaining side shall be withdrawn therefrom, so that the locations specified in the preceding Paragraph shall be taken over completely by the armed forces of India.

6. Notwithstanding the provisions of Paragraph 5 above, the detaining side shall have the responsibility for maintaining and ensuring security and order in the areas around the locations where the prisoners of war are in custody and for preventing and restraining any armed forces (including irregular armed forces) in the area under its control from any acts of disturbance and intrusion against the locations where the prisoners of war are in custody.

7. Notwithstanding the provisions of Paragraph 3 above, nothing in this agreement shall be construed as derogation from the authority of the Neutral Nations Repatriation Commission to exercise its legitimate functions and responsibilities for the control of the prisoners of war under its temporary jurisdiction.

III. EXPLANATION

8. The Neutral Nations Repatriation Commission, after having received and taken into custody all those prisoners of war who have not exercised their right to be repatriated, shall immediately make arrangements so that within ninety (90) days after the Neutral Nations Repatriation Commission takes over the custody, the nations to which prisoners of war belong shall have freedom and facilities to send representatives to the locations where such prisoners of war are in custody to explain to all the prisoners of war depending upon these nations their rights and to inform them of any matters relating to their return to their homelands, particularly of their full freedom to their home to lead a peaceful life, under the following provisions:

(a) The number of such explaining representatives shall not exceed seven (7) per thousand prisoners of war held in custody by the Neutral Nations Repatriation Commission; and the minimum authorized shall not be less than a total of five (5):

(b) The hours during which the explaining representative shall have access to the prisoners shall be as determined by the Neutral Nations Repatriation Commission, and generally in accord with Article 53 of the Geneva Convention Relative to the Treatment of Prisoners of war;

(c) All explanations and interviews shall be conducted in the presence of a representative of each member nation of the Neutral Nations Repatriation Commission and a representative from the detaining side;

(d) Additional provisions governing the explanation work shall be prescribed by the Neutral Nations Repatriation Commission, and will be designed to employ the principles enumerated in Paragraph 3 above and in this Paragraph;

(e) The explaining representatives, while engaging in their work, shall be allowed to bring with them necessary facilities and personnel for wireless communications. The number of communications personnel shall be limited to one team per location at which explaining representatives are in residence, except in the event all prisoners of war are concentrated in one location, in which case two (2) teams shall be permitted. Each team shall consist of not more than six (6) communications personnel.

9. Prisoners of war in its custody shall have freedom and facilities to make representations and communications to the Neutral Nations Repatriation Commission and to representatives and subordinate bodies of the Neutral Nations Repatriation Commission and to inform them of their desires on any matter concerning the prisoners of war themselves, in accordance with arrangement made for the purpose by the Neutral Nations Repatriation Commission.

IV. DISPOSITION OF PRISONERS OF WAR

10. Any prisoner of war who, while in the custody of the Neutral Nations Repatriation Commission, decides to exercise the right of repatriation, shall make an application requesting repatriation to a body consisting of a representative of each member nation of the Neutral Nations Repatriation Commission. Once such an application is made, it shall be considered immediately by the Neutral Nations Repatriation Commission or one of its subordinate bodies so as to determine immediately by majority vote the validity of such application. Once such an application is made to and validated by the Commission or one of its subordinate bodies, the prisoner of war concerned shall immediately be transferred to and accommodated in the tents set up for those who are ready to be repatriated. Thereafter, he shall, while still in the custody of the Neutral Nations Repatriation Commission, be delivered forthwith to the prisoner of war exchange point at Panmunjom for repatriation under the procedure prescribed in the Armistice Agreement.

11. At the expiration of ninety (90) days after the transfer of custody of the prisoners of war to the Neutral Nations Repatriation Commission, access of representatives to captured personnel, as provided for in Paragraph 8 above, shall terminate, and the question of disposition of the prisoners of war who have not exercised their right to be repatriated shall be submitted to the Political Conference recommended to be convened in Paragraph 60, Draft Armistice Agreement, which shall endeavor to settle this question within thirty (30) days, during which period the Neutral Nations Repatriation Commission shall continue to retain custody of those prisoners of war. The Neutral Nations Repatriation Commission shall declare the relief from the prisoner of war status to civilian status of any prisoners of war who have not exercised their right to be repatriated

and for whom no other disposition has been agreed to by the Political Conference within one hundred and twenty (120) days after the Neutral Nations Repatriation Commission has assumed their custody. Thereafter, according to the application of each individual, those who choose to go to neutral nations shall be assisted by the Neutral Nations Repatriation Commission and the Red Cross Society of India. This operation shall be completed within thirty (30) days, and upon its completion, the Neutral Nations Repatriation Commission shall immediately cease its functions and declare its dissolution. After the dissolution of the Neutral Nations Repatriation Commission, whenever and wherever any of those above-mentioned civilians who have been relieved from the prisoner of war status desire to return to their fatherlands, the authorities of the localities where they are shall be responsible for assisting them in returning to their fatherlands.

V. RED CROSS VISITATION

12. Essential Red Cross service for prisoners of war in custody of the Neutral Nations Repatriation Commission shall be provided by India in accordance with regulations issued by the Neutral Nations Repatriation Commission.

VI. PRESS COVERAGE

13. The Neutral Nations Repatriation Commission shall insure freedom of the press and other news media in observing the entire operation as enumerated herein, in accordance with procedures to be established by the Neutral Nations Repatriation Commission.

VII. LOGISTICAL SUPPORT FOR PRISONERS OF WAR

14. Each side shall provide logistical support for the prisoners of war in the area under its military control, delivering required support to the Neutral Nations Repatriation Commission at an agreed delivery point in the vicinity of each prisoner of war installation.

15. The cost of repatriation prisoners of war to the exchange point at Panmunjom shall be borne by the detaining side and the

cost from the exchange point by the side on which said prisoners depend, in accordance with Article 118 of the Geneva Convention.

16. The Red Cross Society of India shall be responsible for providing such general service personnel in the prisoner of war installations as required by the Neutral Nations Repatriation Commission.

17. The Neutral Nations Repatriation Commission shall provide medical support for the prisoners of war as may be practicable. The detaining side shall provide medical support as practical upon the request of the Neutral Nations Repatriation Commission and specifically for those cases requiring extensive treatment or hospitalization. The Neutral Nations Repatriation Commission shall maintain custody of prisoners of war during such hospitalizations. The detaining side shall facilitate such custody. Upon completion of treatment, prisoners of war shall be returned to a prisoner of war installation as specified in Paragraph 4 above.

18. The Neutral Nations Repatriation Commission is entitled to obtain from both sides such legitimate assistance as it may require in carrying out its duties and tasks, but both sides shall not under any name and in any form interfere or exert influence.

VIII. LOGISTICAL SUPPORT FOR THE NEUTRAL NATIONS REPATRIATION COMMISSION

19. Each side shall be responsible for providing logistical support for the personnel of the Neutral Nations Repatriation Commission stationed in the area under its military control, and both sides shall contribute on an equal basis to such support within the Demilitarized Zone. The precise arrangements shall be subject to determination between the Neutral Nations Repatriation Commission and the detaining side in each case.

20. Each of the detaining sides shall be responsible for protecting the explaining representatives from the other side while in transit over lines of communication within its area, as set forth in Paragraph 23 for the Neutral Nations Repatriation Commission, to a place of residence and while in residence in the vicinity of but not within each of the locations where the prisoners of war are in

custody. The Neutral Nations Repatriation Commission shall be responsible for the security of such representatives within the actual limits of the locations where the prisoners of war are in custody.

21. Each of the detaining sides shall provide transportation, housing, communication, and other agreed logistical support to the explaining representatives of the other side while they are in the area under its military control. Such services shall be provided on a reimbursable basis.

IX. PUBLICATION

22. After the Armistice Agreement becomes effective, the terms of this agreement shall be made known to all prisoners of war who, while in the custody of the detaining side, have not exercised their right to be repatriated.

X. MOVEMENT

23. The movement of the personnel of the Neutral Nations Repatriation Commission and repatriated prisoners of war shall be over lines of communication as determined by the command(s) of the opposing side and the Neutral Nations Repatriation Commission. Movement of such personnel, except within locations as designated in Paragraph 4 above, shall be under the control of, and escorted by, personnel of the side in whose area the travel is being undertaken; however, such movement shall not be subject to any obstruction and coercion.

XI. PROCEDURAL MATTERS

24. The interpretation of this agreement shall rest with the Neutral Nations Repatriation Commission. The Neutral Nations Repatriation Commission, and/or any subordinate bodies to which functions are delegated or assigned by the Neutral Nations Repatriation Commission, shall operate on the basis of majority vote.

25. The Neutral Nations Repatriation Commission shall submit a weekly report to the opposing Commanders on the status of pris-

oners of war in its custody, indicating the numbers repatriated and remaining at the end of each week.

26. When this agreement has been acceded to by both sides and by the five powers named herein, it shall become effective upon the date the Armistice becomes effective.

Done at Panmunjom, Korea, at 1400 hours on the 8th day of June 1953, in English, Korean, and Chinese, all texts being equally authentic.

VI

SUPPLEMENTARY AGREEMENT ON
PRISONERS OF WAR, 27 JULY 1953

In order to meet the requirements of the disposition of the prisoners-of-war not for direct repatriation in accordance with the provisions of the Terms of Reference for Neutral Nations Repatriation Commission, the Supreme Commander of the Korean People's Army and the Commander of the Chinese People's Volunteers, on the one hand, and the Commander in Chief, United Nations Command, on the other hand, in pursuance of the provisions in Paragraph 61, Article 5, of the agreement concerning a military armistice in Korea, agree to conclude the following temporary agreement supplementary to the armistice agreement:

1. Under the provisions of Paragraphs 4 and 5, Article II, of the Terms of Reference for Neutral Nations Repatriation Commission, the United Nations Command has the right to designate the area between the military demarcation line and the eastern and southern boundaries of the demilitarized zone between the Imjin River on the south and the road leading south from Okum-Ni on the northeast (the main road leading southeast from Panmunjom not included), as the area within which the United Nations Command will turn over the prisoners-of-war, who are not directly repatriated and whom the United Nations Command has the responsibility for keeping under its custody, to the Neutral Nations Repatriation Commission and the armed forces of India for custody. The United Nations Command shall, prior to the signing of the armistice agreement, inform the side of the Korean People's Army

313

and the Chinese People's Volunteers of the approximate figures by nationality of such prisoners of war held in its custody.

2. If there are prisoners of war under their custody who request not to be directly repatriated, the Korean People's Army and the Chinese People's Volunteers have the right to designate the area in the vicinity of Panmunjom between the military demarcation line and the western and northern boundaries of the demilitarized zone, as the area within which such prisoners-of-war will be turned over to the Neutral Nations Repatriation Commission and the armed forces of India for custody. After knowing that there are prisoners of war under their custody who request not to be directly repatriated, the Korean People's Army and the Chinese People's Volunteers shall inform the United Nations Command side of the approximate figures by nationality of such prisoners of war.

3. In accordance with Paragraphs 8, 9 and 10, Article I, of the armistice agreement, the following paragraphs are hereby provided:

a. After the cease-fire comes into effect, unarmed personnel of each side shall be specifically authorized by the Military Armistice Commission to enter the above-mentioned area designated by their own side to perform the necessary construction operations. None of such personnel shall remain in the above-mentioned areas upon the completion of the construction operations.

b. A definite number of prisoners of war as decided upon by both sides, who are in the respective custody of both sides and who are not directly repatriated, shall be specifically authorized by the Military Armistice Commission to be escorted respectively by a certain number of armed forces of the detaining sides to the above-mentioned areas of custody designated respectively by both sides to be turned over to the Neutral Nations Repatriation Commission and the armed forces of India for custody. After the prisoners of war have been taken over, the armed forces of the detaining sides shall be withdrawn immediately from the areas of custody to the area under the control of their own side.

c. The personnel of the Neutral Nations Repatriation Commission and its subordinate bodies, the armed forces of India, the Red Cross Society of India, the explaining representatives and observation representatives of both sides, as well as the required material and equipment, for exercising the function provided for in the Terms of Reference for Neutral Nations Repatriation Commission shall be specifically authorized by the Military Armistice Commission to have the complete fredom of movement to, from, and within the above-mentioned areas designated respectively by both sides for the custody of prisoners of war.

4. The provisions of sub-paragraph 3C of this agreement shall not be construed as derogating from the privileges enjoyed by those personnel mentioned above under Paragraph 11, Article I, of the armistice agreement.

5. This agreement shall be abrogated upon the completion of the mission provided for in the Terms of Reference for Neutral Nations Repatriation Commission.

Done at Panmunjom, Korea, at 1000 hours on the 27th day of July 1953, in Korean, Chinese, and English, all texts being equally authentic.

INDEX

Acheson, US Sec. State Dean, 17-18, 22, 116, 173-74, 220

"advisors," USSR, with North, 10

Agenda of truce talks, established and accepted, 31-43, 231-32; subsequent discussion of accepted items:

Item One, 43, 224, 226, 231

Item Two, 40, 43, 46-86 *passim*; 104, 224-25, 231-33, 236-39; ratified, 86, 239; final agreement text (Article I), 281-83; *see also* demarcation line; demilitarized zone; "line of contact"; 38th Parallel

Item Three, 43, 89-103, 108-13, 145, 224-25, 227, 232, 239 ff.; final agreement text (Article II), 283-96; *see also* Armistice Commission; ceasefire; Neutral Nations Supervisory

Item Four, 43, 91, 104, 108-9, 115-200 *passim*, 224-25, 227, 232, 239 ff.; final agreement text (Article III), 296-303; *see also* prisoners of war; sick and wounded

Item Five, 43, 103-9, 227, 232, 246-47; final agreement text (Article IV), 303; *see also* Recommendations . . .

airfields, rehabilitation and restriction of, 93, 96-99, 102-3, 111-12, 240, 245

Alemán, Mexican Pres. Miguel, 172

amendment of Armistice Agreement (Article V), 303

American Red Cross, 249

amnesty for POW's declared in South, 168, 172-73

Armistice Agreement, Military, 27, 90, 92-93, 101-3, 105, 111-13, 133, 137, 140-41, 180, 184-86, 194, 197, 200-201, 217, 224-26, 256-57, 265; reference to signing or taking effect of, 1, 85, 91, 94, 100, 108, 120, 125-27, 130, 133, 140, 142, 164-65, 174, 186, 191, 198-99, 202-3, 206, 238-39, 270, 283-84, 296, 297, 300, 302-4, 306, 311-12; text of, 281-312; effects of, 204-6, 217

Armistice Commission, Military (MAC), 34, 40, 43, 90 ff., 100-102, 125, 201, 282-312 *passim* (*esp.* 288-91), 314-15

asylum, right of, 158-60n

Austin, Col. Edward, USA, 265

Australia, 153; forces of, with UNC, 12n; prisoners from, in North, 126, 241; repatriation of, 183

Austria, 158-59n; prisoners from, still in USSR, 117, 117-18n

bacteriological warfare, charges of, 152, 154, 155-57, 179

Barnes, Ralph V., 274

Belgium, 158-59n; forces with UNC, 12n

Borchert, Lt. Col. J. J., USA, 255

Bradley, Gen. Omar, 16, 70

brainwashing, 169n

Bulgaria, 273; prisoners from, still in USSR, 117-18n

Burke, Rear Adm. Arleigh Albert, USN, 30, 228, 230, 233, 239

Burma, 189, 266

Byrnes, US Sec. State James F., 76-77n

Cairo Conference (1943) declaration on Korea, 4-5

Canada, forces of, with UNC, 12n; prisoners from, in North, 126, 241; repatriation of, 183

cease-fire discussion (Agenda Item Two), 15, 18-19, 21-22, 27, 33-34, 38, 40, 42, 43, 46 ff. *passim*, 84, 86, 89-114 *passim*, 175n, 206, 225, 229, 231-32, 238, 276, 281, 283-96, 314

Chang Chun San, Col., [N]KPA, 26-27, 60-64, 71-72, 233